WELCOME

In the 1950s, the United States and the Soviet Union were in the deep chill of a Cold War when the Space Age dawned and changed everything, adding a fiercely fought competition between ideological adversaries to the threat of a potential all-out nuclear conflict. The Space Age would quickly grow into a race to demonstrate technological supremacy indicative of national virility in science and engineering. Whoever won, it would demonstrate to its citizens and to uncommitted nations the superiority of one system over the other.

When the Russians sent the world's first satellite into orbit in October 1957, NASA was formed by the US government as an agency dedicated to space research, exploration and to achieving supremacy for the United States in that field. Soon, it connected industry with academia, uniting governments' agencies that previously had been conducting their own independent research, providing the United States with a polarising force for this new age.

Over time, NASA achieved great things, putting men on the Moon, landers and roving vehicles on Mars and sending robots to every major world in the solar system. Through an international effort to harness the best in global talent, it attracted people from many countries and those in turn encouraged space-faring nations to join NASA in achieving more

ABOVE • Permanently manned since 2000, the International Space Station is the greatest achievement of the post-Apollo space age. (NASA)

than they could accomplish on their own. So today, we have the International Space Station and, for the future, the Artemis Accords in which more than 40 countries have already pledged to work together to explore the Moon and, eventually, Mars.

This book highlights great moments, brave deeds and outstanding accomplishments while digging deep to unravel some of the challenges and tragedies, which, over time have altered the way humans explore space. It covers the politics, the industry game-changers, the meddlers and the disruptors that characterise an agency gradually changing and itself forging change in the commercial world, which it encourages and sustains through new deals and more cost-effective arrangements.

Along the way, NASA has been embraced by other government agencies monitoring weather, environmental damage, climate effects and the price paid by Earth through expanding urbanisation and industrial growth. The story told here reflects an enabling agency working in synergy with partners and players across the United States and around the world, a template for success, trial and error and for challenging the status quo in fields as diverse as communications, agriculture, astronomy and systems engineering.

It is a story told many times before and it will continue to change as events unfold, but here we take a more nuanced look and discover an agency that has suffered tragic loss of humans in the exploration of space yet has returned to correct and restore the goals and aspirations which forged that challenge in the beginning. It is a 'warts and all' deep-dive, the narrative of a storied agency that is not quite like anything that has gone before, a template for humans who will not succumb to failure and who collectively can realise the dreams of past generations — in the exploration of space.

David Baker
November 2024

LEFT • Astronaut Tom Marshburn suited and ready. (NASA)

CONTENTS

COVER IMAGE • *American astronaut Joseph Tanner waves to the camera during a space walk as part of the STS-115 mission to the International Space Station, September 2006. (NASA)*

ISBN 978 1 83632 027 2
Editor: David Baker
Senior editor, specials: Roger Mortimer
Email: roger.mortimer@keypublishing.com
Cover Design: Steve Donovan
Design: SJmagic DESIGN SERVICES, India
Advertising Sales Manager: Sam Clark
Email sam.clark@keypublishing.com
Tel: 01780 755131
Advertising Production: Becky Antoniades
Email Rebecca.antoniades@keypublishing.com

SUBSCRIPTION/MAIL ORDER
Key Publishing Ltd, PO Box 300, Stamford,
Lincs, PE9 1NA
Tel: 01780 480404
Subscriptions email: subs@keypublishing.com
Mail Order email: orders@keypublishing.com
Website: www.keypublishing.com/shop

PUBLISHING
Group CEO and Publisher: Adrian Cox

Published by
Key Publishing Ltd, PO Box 100, Stamford,
Lincs, PE9 1XQ
Tel: 01780 755131
Website: www.keypublishing.com

PRINTING
Precision Colour Printing Ltd, Haldane,
Halesfield 1, Telford, Shropshire.
TF7 4QQ

DISTRIBUTION
Seymour Distribution Ltd, 2 Poultry
Avenue, London,
EC1A 9PU
Enquiries Line: 02074 294000.

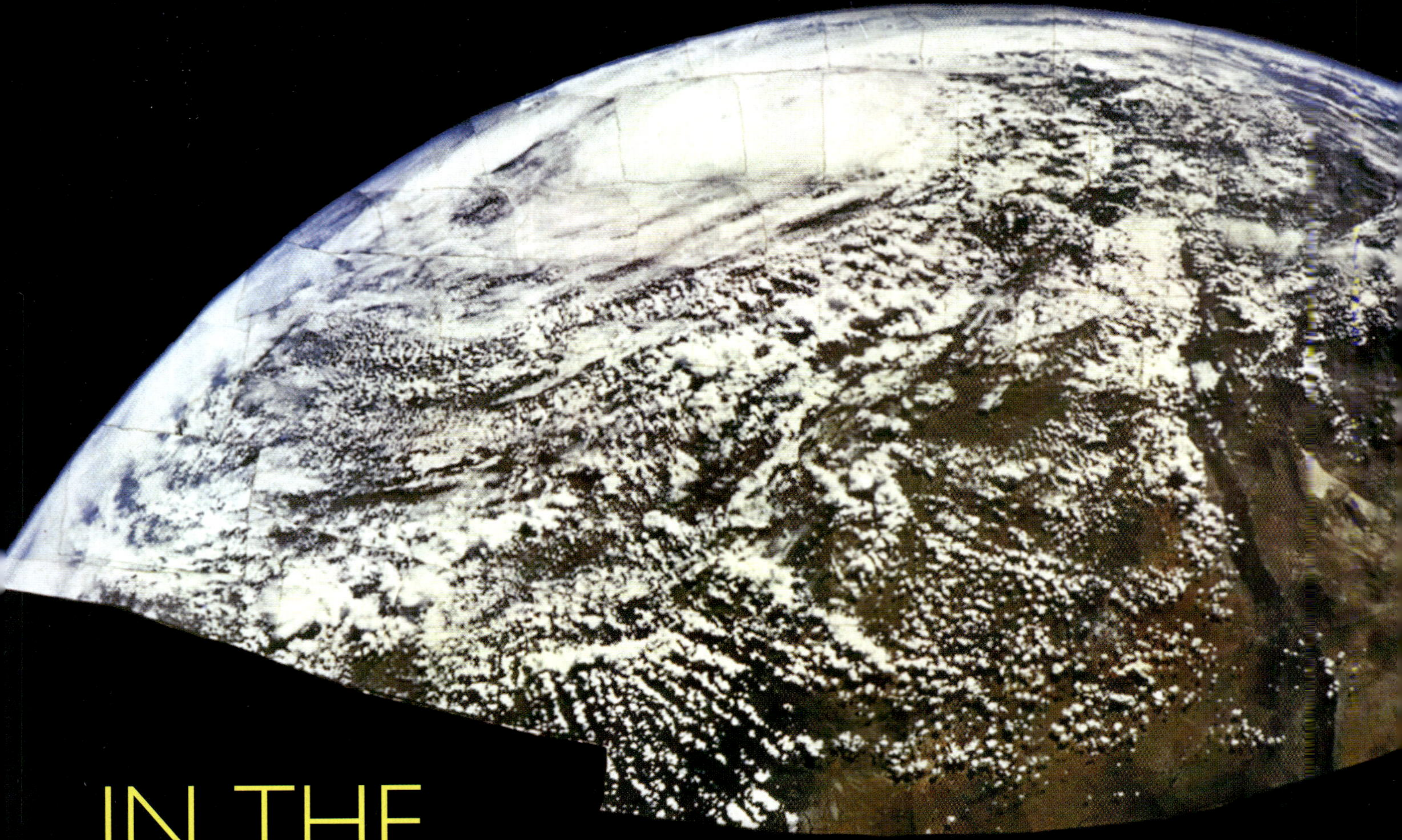

IN THE BEGINNING

Competition over who would control US space activities was fierce, but it took an uncompromising president to decide the outcome

ABOVE • Taken by an Aerobee sounding rocket on October 5, 1954, the first colour picture of Earth, beyond which NASA would take astronauts in the coming decade. (NACA)

When the Russians sent Sputnik 1, the world's first satellite, into space on October 4, 1957, it triggered a sequence of events that would result in the establishment of the world's first civilian space agency. It was now a matter of urgency to reassure concerned and alarmed Americans that a response was in hand and that national honour would soon be restored. Explorer I was launched from Cape Canaveral shortly before 10.48pm, local time, on January 31, 1958.

After Sputnik, everyone had an opinion about what was needed next to propel America into the new frontier. The US Army and the Air Force each assumed it would be their responsibility to mobilise men and materiel and drive forward with rockets, satellites, space stations, reusable ferry vehicles, bases on the Moon and Mars. The military wanted command and control of real estate, but the scientists had a view that differed in structure and purpose, seeing space as a place for research and exploration.

The National Academy of Sciences had a satellite research panel which, in November 1957, followed a call from the American Rocket Society for a new Astronautical Research and Development Agency. In January 1958, they combined their respective proposals with an ambitious timetable for manned flights starting in 1961, flights around the Moon in 1965 and a landing on the lunar surface in 1968 preceding a permanent Moon base from 1970. But none of this was influential in the numerous congressional hearings that ensued.

An initial reaction from Eisenhower was to establish the President's Science Advisory Committee (PSAC) led by James R Killian and it was from this that the idea of a

RIGHT • A model of Explorer 1, America's first artificial satellite launched on January 31, 1958. Seated facing the camera is Wernher von Braun with US General John Bruce Medaris to his right. (US Army)

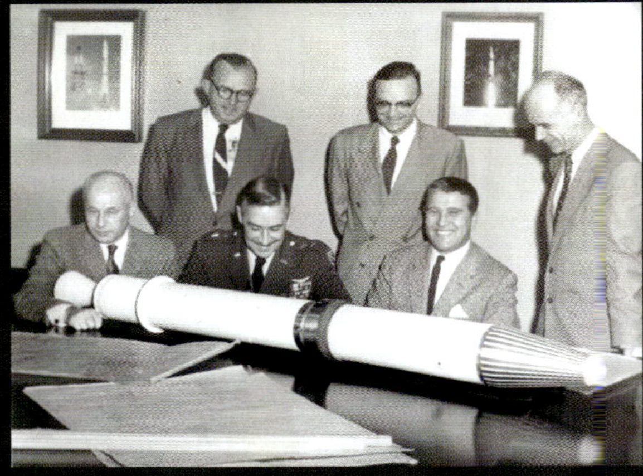

'civilian' space agency based on the National Advisory Committee for Aeronautics (NACA) emerged. Formed in 1915 to support the aeronautical industry with technical research and wind tunnel tests in a move to provide standards and reference data, the NACA was a relatively small organisation operated by the government. It played a major role in providing a set of aerofoil profiles applicable to a wide range of requirements for specific aircraft types and became the go-to source for information pertinent to overall aircraft design.

The architects of the plan to build a space agency out of the NACA, James McCormack and James B Fisk, pressed their case on the basis that if it did not get that job, it would quickly go out of business — so important the future for astronautics was believed to be. But the NACA was more like a corporation, with a board of directors that appointed a chairman who would then hire a director to run the agency and report progress to the board. The current chairman was James 'Jimmy' Doolittle; physicist Hugh L Dryden was its director.

When Eisenhower received the formal proposal to transform the NACA on March 5, 1958, it advised that since it judged there to be little military significance in space a civilian organisation should have management of all unclassified programmes and this was endorsed by Nelson Rockefeller, chairman of the Senate Committee on Government Organisation.

The NACA was already well prepared for any change that might be coming. It had formed a Special Committee on Space Technology as early as November 21, 1957, and on January 14, 1958, it issued 'A National Research Program for Space Technology', outlining how such a body should conduct an "energetic program" of research and development and work with "applied research and development groups" to provide "leadership in space technology".

It satisfied Eisenhower on two counts: it would retain civilian oversight and control of non-military space projects and it would sink the competition, sometimes confrontational, between the army and the air force for management of all US space projects.

The President put his own stamp on draft legislation when it went to Congress on April 2, 1958, citing the transformation of the NACA into the National Aeronautics and Space Administration. For its part, the NACA was timid over the prospect and although it was already deeply involved with research into high-speed flight, rocketry and probing space with suborbital sounding rockets, many of its staff were apprehensive about the awesome role to which it was bequeathed responsibility.

The single most influential factor in the National Aeronautics and Space Act signed into law was that the one individual responsible for managing space policy and resulting programmes reported directly to the President, thus locking in a political imperative which, had that not been the case, would have prevented later Presidents from authorising programmes as an executive decision rather than relying on a board vote. As it was, the National Aeronautics and Space Administration opened its doors for business on the first day of October 1958, the beginning of a monumental responsibility that would propel it to world fame under one of the most recognised acronyms in history — NASA.

THE DENVER POST

The Voice of the Rocky Mountain Empire

RUSS 'MOON' CIRCLING EARTH
560 Miles Up at 18,000 MPH

Rockefeller Says Crisis Hurts Arkansas Future

U. S. Scientists Attempting to Chart Course

More Join Rioting in Warsaw

Reds Say 'Moon Next' In Race Into Space

Hoffa Election May Spur Laws

Bright October Days in Store

Vital Facts On Satellite

THE WEATHER

IN TODAY'S POST

ABOVE LEFT • The National Advisory Committee for Aeronautics was founded in 1915 to advance the development of US aviation and to share with aircraft manufacturers, research and data obtained from wind tunnels and laboratories. (NASA)

ABOVE RIGHT • The badge for the newly formed NASA was designed by James Modarelli, formerly of the Lewis Research Center, in 1959 and was affectionately known thereafter as the 'meatball'. (NASA)

LEFT • When the Russians launched Sputnik 1 on October 4, 1957, the government held hearings and listened to ways in which it could improve co-ordination in space research and engineering. (Author archive)

NASA RISING

Nothing could have prepared NASA for what it was asked to do and few could have imagined the enormous tasks it would be authorised to perform

When it opened for business on October 1, 1958, NASA had a headquarters, several field offices and a lot of facilities, wind tunnels and test equipment. Badged as the NACA since 1915, it had grown according to the needs of an aeronautical industry hungry for data, information and test results on engines, aerofoils, ancillary equipment and test operations. Now, aeronautics would still be in the mix and it would continue forward with research into winged hypersonic flight through the North American X-15 rocket aircraft, but the majority of its activity would be for space research and development.

Where previously it had managed contracts from industry to conduct test flights, now it would write specifications for manned and unmanned spacecraft, source the manufacturing base from which they would be procured and operate them to fulfil national objectives. In some cases it would build its own satellites and spacecraft and it would need new facilities to do that. But in the main it would seek to have industry giants and some less well-known companies build the vehicles that would take humans into Earth orbit and on to the Moon.

When it began, NASA had little idea about how it would answer calls to make the US "pre-eminent in space" while fulfilling a mandate for openness, accountability and responsiveness to national objectives and to the public's appetite for success in all that it was asked to do. Along the way it would quickly learn how to handle the media, respond to public requests for information about its programmes and open its activity to scrutiny and investigation. Above all, it sought from the outset to acquire personnel skilled in sectors critical to its success and the satisfactory completion of its objectives.

At its head was administrator T Keith Glennan, with former NACA director Hugh Dryden his deputy. The existing resources of the NACA rebadged as NASA included the headquarters in Washington, DC, what became the Langley Research Center in Virginia handling aeronautics and research into manned flight, the Ames Research Center in California responsible for wind-tunnel research into propeller-driven aircraft and the Lewis Research Center in Ohio studying engines.

BELOW • Existing organisations would soon be swept into the new space agency, including the Jet Propulsion Laboratory near Santa Monica, California, where rocket research had been conducted in addition to tracking and radar networks. (NASA-JPL)

The first challenge discussed as NASA opened for business was manned space flight and it set to work integrating the Project Adam research from the Army and Project 7969 carried out by the air force. In its dash to bid for total control of the nation's space programme, in the first quarter of 1958, while legislation was being processed leading to the formation of NASA, Project 7969 merged into more extensive plans for the air force's human space programme and the Air Research and Development Command (ARDC) set up a Man-In-Space Task Force at the Ballistic Missile Division, with the ultimate objective of landing "a man on the Moon and returning him safely to Earth".

The Task Force came up with a four-phase plan. Phase one would comprise Man-In-Space-Soonest (MISS-1) involving a ballistic flight to the edge of space on a Redstone rocket followed by the first orbital flight on an Atlas; phase two was Man-In-Space-Sophisticated (MISS-2) involving a heavier spacecraft demonstrating manned flight up to 14 days; phase three (Lunar Reconnaissance) would place unmanned probes on the surface for evaluating conditions; phase four, Manned Lunar Landing and Return (MALLAR), would put chimpanzee test subjects on the Moon, followed by men. All these plans were presented to the US Air Force headquarters on May 2, 1958, in what some have claimed since was a thinly-veiled attempt to seize control of the nation's space programme.

At NASA's Langley Research Center, research scientist Maxime Faget and his small team in the Pilotless Aircraft Research Division (PARD) had designed the general configuration of a manned capsule that could support a single astronaut for at least a day in orbit. This capsule would be launched by an Atlas rocket with test shots adopting the army plan from Project Adam carrying a Mercury capsule on top of a Redstone rocket for a suborbital, ballistic shot straight up and down to prove it could support an astronaut.

Before NASA opened for business, on March 18, 1958, Faget and co-workers published a report with the title 'Preliminary Studies of Manned Satellites, Wingless Configuration, Non-Lifting', coinciding with a three-day conference at the Ames facility specifying the general characteristics required of the capsules which, it was agreed, would be contracted to an existing aircraft company. The programme was officially approved on October 7, 1958, but that would not be publicly declared before December 17.

The formal process for building the Mercury spacecraft had begun on October 20 when 40 companies received the requirements, of which 38 attended a conference at Langley on November 7. Bids from four companies were examined during the first week of 1959, which came down to a straight fight between McDonnell and Grumman. McDonnell had a

history of working with Langley on the overall configuration and many felt it was inevitable it would receive the contract, which it did on January 12. Grumman had a lot of defence work on and would have been stretched to accommodate Mercury as well, but the company retained a strong interest in space work and would have its day later.

McDonnell was challenged to produce a working spacecraft within the maximum payload capacity of the Atlas rocket, no more than 3,000lb (1,360kg), with a length of 10.8ft (3.3m) and a maximum diameter of 6ft (1.8m). The launch escape system, a solid rocket motor on top of a lattice support structure extending the overall length to 25.9ft (7.9m), would carry the spacecraft and its occupant in the event of a malfunctioning launch vehicle. It would be jettisoned 2min 10sec after lift-off when the two Atlas booster motors were jettisoned, after which the abort rockets could be fired to separate the spacecraft in the event of an emergency. An ejection seat would only have been effective at low altitude.

Propulsion incorporated thrusters to control roll, pitch and yaw, three tiny rockets for pushing the spacecraft away from the forward end of the Atlas rocket after it achieved orbit and three solid-propellant de-orbit motors for reducing the orbital speed to come back home. With the spacecraft base-end forward, these braking rockets would cause the spacecraft to slow and gradually descend, protected from burning up by a base heat shield and a shingle-covered forward section where the heat would not be as intense. Internally pressurised with pure oxygen at 5.5psi (38kPa), the astronaut wore a full pressure suit in case of a failure in that system or, in the event of a fire, to dump the cabin oxygen and use the suit supply to sustain life until descent to a safe splashdown.

Splashdown in the sea was the primary method of recovery, an extended bag connected to the base heat shield and deployed like an airbag during the descent cushioning the shock of hitting the water. Surface vessels would recover the pilot, who had the option of remaining inside the spacecraft or egressing to a life raft. McDonnell would build 20 Mercury capsules, most of which would be used for various tests, but five were never flown.

NASA recruited a team of astronauts to carry out these flights and, on April 9, 1959, the 'Mercury Seven' were announced to the world as the men selected for manned missions and including, from an initial group of 508 applicants, Malcolm Scott Carpenter, Leroy Gordon Cooper, John H Glenn, Virgil I Grissom, Walter M Schirra Jr, Alan B Shepard and Donald K Slayton. Detected to have a heart murmur, Slayton would never fly in a Mercury capsule, but after his medical condition was declared acceptable for space flight he commanded the first joint flight with a Russian Soyuz spacecraft in 1975.

Expansion and Growth

While preparations for manned space flight picked up pace, during 1959 NASA began acquiring organisations and facilities and planned construction of its first new research establishment: The Jet Propulsion Laboratory (JPL), a key player in the historic development of small solid-propellant rocket motors, was operated under agreement with the California Institute of Technology with inspirational leadership in the capable hands of New Zealand-born Dr William Pickering. Skilled in setting up radar and tracking facilities, the JPL was a key asset to NASA when it was formally transferred to the new agency on December 3, 1958.

BELOW • One of the first tasks for NASA was to prepare to put astronauts in space and in April 1959 it chose the first seven for the Mercury programme. Standing in front of Convair F-106B-25-CO Delta Dart used for training astronauts at Tyndall AFB, Florida, are (left to right): Malcolm Scott Carpenter, Gordon Cooper, John Glenn, Virgil Grissom, Walter Schirra, Alan Shepard and Deke Slayton. (NASA)

LEFT • Across the field stations operated by the NACA, signage was changed on October 1, 1958, when it was succeeded by NASA. (NASA)

A key success story for which JPL boasted great pride was its role in recruiting women into technical, mathematical and computer jobs on which the laboratory so heavily relied. To provide trajectories for sounding rockets developed at the JPL, Barbara Paulson had single-handedly pored through huge books containing the records of atmospheric densities for which the existing Friden mechanical calculators were inadequate as they could not handle logarithms. Many other women were brought in to the programme, displaying unique capabilities that few men were able to duplicate with quite the same fineness and accuracy.

Seeking a suitable location in which to build a laboratory for the development of satellites, on August 1, 1958, the acquisition of territory in Greenbelt, Maryland, was announced where the Goddard Space Flight Center (GSFC) would be built on land surplus to a research centre for the department of agriculture. Initially known as the Beltsville Space Center, it officially came into existence on January 15, 1959, renamed on May 1 in honour of Robert Goddard who had launched the world's first liquid propellant rocket on March 16, 1926.

For a period, Goddard had management of the Space Task Group (STG), which had been formed on November 5, 1958 at the Langley facility for managing NASA's manned space flight activity. Its personnel there were directly responsible to the Goddard facility until a completely new centre opened in Houston, Texas, several years later. When Canada cancelled the Avro Arrow air defence fighter and procured America's Bomarc air-defence missile instead, engineers at Avro-Canada were offered jobs with STG and several joined NASA's Mercury programme in 1959.

As NASA grew in size, acquiring personnel from the JPL to staff the Goddard Space Flight Center, pressure grew for German-American aerospace engineer Werner von Braun's Development Operations Division at the Army Ballistic Missile Agency in Huntsville, Alabama, to also join NASA. The army fought hard to retain the rocket team that had done so much for the early development of ballistic missiles and had placed the first American satellite in orbit. But the large Saturn booster programme led by von Braun had no part in the

BELOW • H Julian Allen conducted calculations to demonstrate how a blunt body entering the atmosphere would experience less heat conducted to the skin of the vehicle than it would with a pointed nose-first re-entry. (NASA)

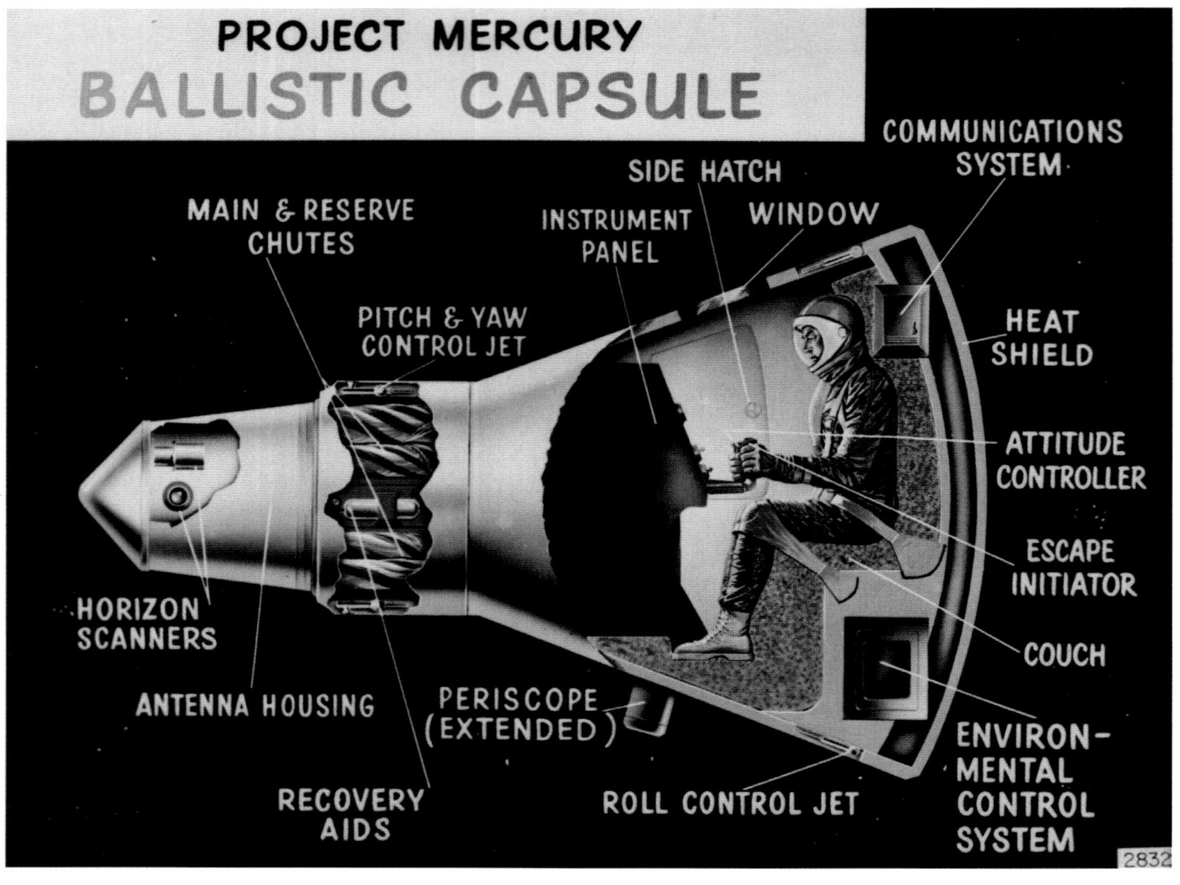

army's mandate and the entire team was moved across to NASA following approval by Eisenhower on October 21, 1959. It became an integral part of NASA on July 1, 1960 as the Marshall Space Flight Center, providing a major, heavy-lift launch vehicle for the nascent space programme.

Overall, NASA had significantly increased the resources available for a broad and ambitious space programme and the first year saw a wide range of programme plans formulated and discussed. It was clear that the agency could not do everything and priorities would have to take account of the budget it was allowed to deploy. As an arm of the government, its leadership would have to bid for funds like any other government office and the Bureau of the Budget had a lot of demands on the financial resources of the nation.

Resolving achievable objectives, there were four strands to the NASA programme: human space flight, initially reflected through the Mercury flights anticipated to begin in 1961; space science, which involved research satellites and data-gathering probes to measure and quantify the physics of space, the Sun and other objects in the Universe; space exploration, the physical probing of the Moon and the planets with spacecraft that would go into orbit about these worlds, land on the surface or roam about investigating their properties; and space applications, the use of satellites and orbiting platforms to study the atmosphere, provide weather forecasting and monitor the Earth's natural resources.

The JPL actively sought to play a lead role in the exploration of space through unmanned spacecraft sent first to the Moon and then to Venus and Mars, and it proposed various possibilities. With expertise in tracking and long-range communication, the JPL was well equipped to design and build planetary spacecraft and it set about the task for which it would become a household name. The Goddard Space Flight Center focused on space science and applications and recruited personnel from across the agency for those activities, also striking up relations with other government bodies and academic institutions.

The Marshall Space Flight Center had former German rocket scientists led by Wernher von Braun, now its director. Under his leadership, the facility would develop and test the giant Saturn rockets offering weight-lifting capacity unimagined only a few years before. The work at Huntsville attracted great political and public interest. The disparity between the power of the Russian rockets and that of the American equivalents had been a national embarrassment, at least at a popular level, and would become a campaign issue in 1960 as Americans went to the polls to elect a new president.

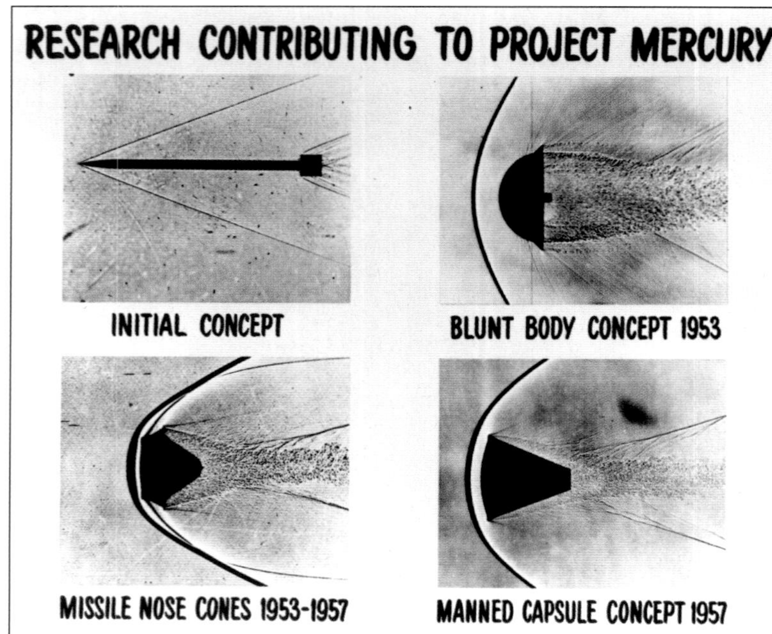

Seeing a productive opportunity to expand on existing capabilities, in the second half of 1960 NASA looked beyond the one-man Mercury programme to a more advanced spacecraft that could carry three men for several weeks, change its orbit as required and provide opportunities for Earth observation; circumlunar flight while providing the basic vehicle with the necessary capabilities for putting astronauts on the surface of the Moon. They called it Apollo and asked President Eisenhower for approval and funding.

Eisenhower saw the emerging space programme as a national commitment to science and the development of related technologies within the framework of a prudent economy into which these activities would have to fit. He was not convinced that there was any need to push strongly into manned space flight and preferred to wait until the results of the Mercury programme dictated the future path for astronauts in space. Others felt very differently and wanted to push ahead as far and as fast as possible. Nevertheless, in Eisenhower's final months in office, Apollo was put firmly back on the shelf.

To many Americans, Eisenhower was too fond of his golf to take seriously the challenges to American pre-eminence that most sought from their leadership, but this is not so. It had been under the Eisenhower administration that the government wrenched apathy from the Truman years (1945-1953), built a long-range missile programme, set up the highly classified Corona spy satellite programme and organised the establishment of the nation's civilian space agency. But the general public sought a more overt demonstration of a new decade full of promise and technological achievement.

To Go to the Moon

The men who recognised that was John F Kennedy who in 1960 ran for office against Eisenhower's candidate for successor, Richard M Nixon, on a platform of growth, expansion of military and space capabilities and won the election on November 8, albeit by just under 113,000 in a total of 68.3 million voting Americans. Inaugurated on January 20, 1961, JFK's initial activity was to look at government budgets and tweak the proposals made by his predecessor. NASA managers saw in this an opportunity to again push for Apollo funding, but got no further, while some additional money was provided for development of the Saturn rockets.

NASA continued with plans for an expanded manned flight programme and worked on the details for an Apollo spacecraft to follow Mercury, now expected to achieve the first ballistic Redstone flight within a few months. Information continued to flow from the CIA warning of imminent Soviet attempts to get a cosmonaut in orbit, but the pace at NASA was driven by the need for test and development and not money or personnel. Unmanned test shots were crucial to ensuing maximum safety and minimal risk – the consequences of failure with a man on board would be catastrophic.

Had urgency trumped caution, it is possible that NASA could have sent the first astronaut into space on a ballistic Redstone test flight launched on March 24, 1961, but minor technical issues with previous Mercury-Redstone flights, including one carrying chimpanzee Ham on a short ride in January, persuaded managers to add just one more unmanned test flight, which was a success. Had a man been on that flight an American would have been the first human in space, albeit not in orbit around the Earth.

That feat was achieved on April 12 by Russia's Yuri Gagarin in a Vostok spacecraft that made almost one complete revolution of the Earth before returning through the atmosphere where the cosmonaut ejected to a parachute

descent. To a president who had ridden to office promising Americans that they would not face an embarrassment like Sputnik again, it was shock made worse five days later when a CIA-backed coup against the Castro regime in Cuba backfired and became a fiasco on the beach at the Bay of Pigs.

There had been notice of Russia's intent when seven unmanned Vostok spacecraft were launched between May 15, 1960 and March 25, 1961, of which only three had been successful. The third mission had put dogs Strelka and Belka in space, the first animals safely retuned from orbit. Originally intending to launch a cosmonaut in December 1960, a catastrophic pad explosion with a very different programme killed 100 people and brought delays. Nevertheless, when he went to bed on the night of April 11, President Kennedy was told he would probably wake up to news of another Russian 'first' in space... and so it was.

As a prescient warning of the dangers involved, on March 23, 1961, Soviet cosmonaut Valentin Bondarenko died as a result of fire breaking out in a pure oxygen isolation chamber, an environment in which flames burn with great speed and intensity. Ironically, the Vostok spacecraft had a mixed gas, oxygen and nitrogen, Earth-like atmosphere, while US spacecraft used pure oxygen, which would itself claim the lives

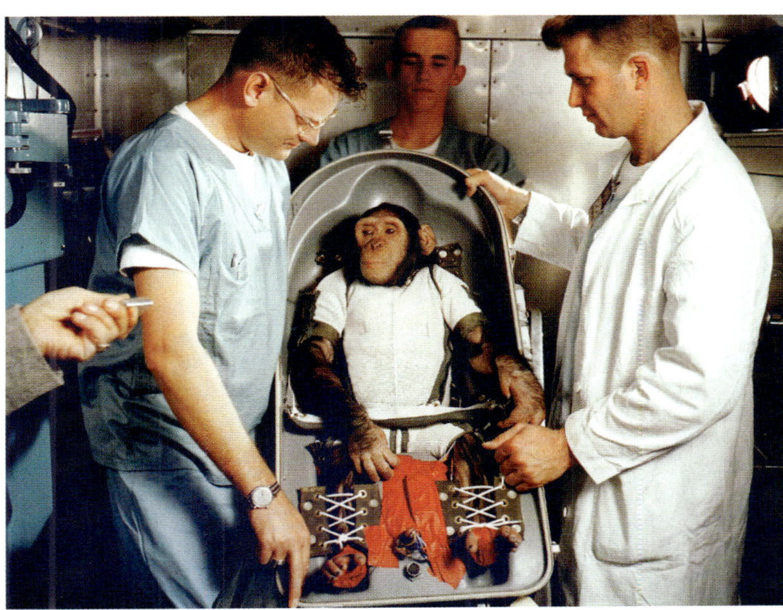

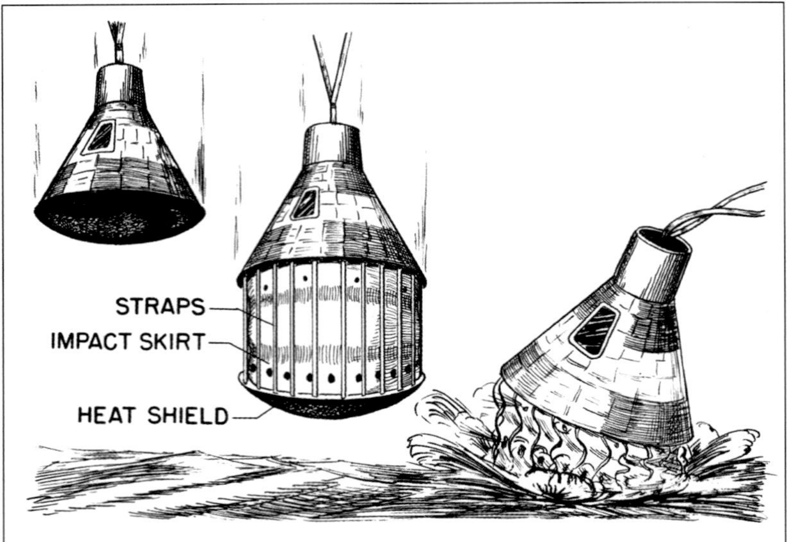

ABOVE • To cushion the impact of splashdown, after deploying the parachute the heat shield would be released to open an air-bag and soften the g-load. (McDonnell)

RIGHT • The trajectory of a typical Mercury flight showing g-levels of acceleration over the duration of a ballistic, straight-up/straight-down Redstone flight to space and back. Apollo flights would incur a maximum of less than 7g while Shuttle flight would be no higher than 3g. (NASA)

RIGHT • The design of the compact Mercury spacecraft had a few flaws, including the need to work inside the tiny vehicle after assembling the outer structure, preventing more than one or two technicians from working on the interior. (McDonnell)

of three astronauts less than six years later. Bondarenko's death led to rumours that cosmonauts were being killed in failed space missions and those myths continue to go the rounds today. There is no evidence from any source that these claims are true.

Kennedy's response to the flight of Gagarin and the Bay of Pigs fiasco was to seek advice from senior officials, from Vice-President Lyndon Johnson and from NASA chiefs. A presidential appointee, James E Webb became NASA administrator on February 14, replacing T Keith Glennan, with Hugh Dryden as his deputy. This would prove to be one of the most important leadership changes in NASA's history, Webb seen as a seasoned government official with an impressive record and a reputation for tough talking and resolute decisions. But the Gagarin flight was of such magnitude that policy to restore both political and public confidence, demonstrating to the world that America would respond to this, would rest with the President alone.

Initially, Kennedy was inclined to find a completely different way of achieving pre-eminence for the United States, and when discussing options with his science advisor, Jerome Wiesner, said: "If you had a scientific spectacular on this Earth that would be more useful or something that is just as dramatic as space, then we would do it," referring later to, for example, a universal programme of desalinating the oceans to provide fresh water for everyone. But Wiesner and others brought him back to a space-first solution, despite Kennedy never having previously been classed as a 'space cadet'!

Two days after the Gagarin flight, Kennedy held a meeting in the cabinet room with the top leadership and asked the simple question: "Is there any place we can catch them?" Dryden wanted an all-out race to the Moon, Webb and Wiesner were cautious about that and David Bell, director of the Budget Bureau, claimed that would cost $40billion, equivalent to $424bn in 2024. Closing the meeting without a conclusion, Kennedy turned to the group and declared: "When we know

more, can decide if it is worth it or not. If somebody can just tell me how to catch up. There is nothing more important."

The one man who could provide the answer was Lyndon Johnson, instrumental in setting up NASA and now named by Kennedy to chair the Space Council. By April 20, Kennedy had committed to finding a response to Gagarin and sent a memo to Johnson asking him to conduct an overall survey of the space programme and to answer fundamental questions: "Do we have a chance of beating the Soviets by putting a laboratory in space, or by a trip around the Moon or by a rocket to land on the Moon and back with a man?" He asked if there was any other space programme promising "dramatic results in which we could win?"

Overturning Eisenhower's policy of not using NASA as a political tool, Kennedy was now looking to achieve pre-eminence on the world stage for the United States, with the space programme as the means but not the objective. Johnson consulted with a range of experts and received support for a Moon landing as the most probable objective the Americans could achieve before the Russians.

On April 22, Webb told Johnson there was a good chance of beating the Russians to the Moon if there was an immediate start with maximum effort toward a landing in 1967. This made good sense to the intelligence community as that year would mark the 50th anniversary of the 1917 revolution that took the Bolsheviks to power, a suitable date it was thought when the Russians might aim to mark that event and show the world another communist 'first'. In fact, the United States was ahead of the Russians in talking up the national challenge of a Moon Race while in reality the Soviet government was far from endorsing such a commitment. But nobody knew that at the time.

Meanwhile, the Mercury programme was moving quickly toward its first manned flight. That event took place on May 5, 1961 when Alan Shepard completed a 15-minute suborbital flight and was recovered from the Atlantic Ocean after splashdown. It was not an orbital flight – that would not be achieved for a further nine months after a second suborbital launch carrying Virgil 'Gus' Grissom on July 21, 1961 – but it restored a measure of pride in America, according to polls and opinion ratings conducted by the administration. Had Shepard's flight not been a success, the later events might never have happened and Kennedy's neutral instincts could have shifted his focus away from the space programme.

On May 6, Secretary of Defense Robert McNamara met with his staff at the Pentagon and concluded that a manned Moon landing was the best chance of beating the Russians, a memorandum incorporating that and the endorsement of other leaders being delivered to Johnson at noon on Monday, May 8. He delivered it to the President that afternoon. In the following days, Kennedy spoke with Congressional leaders and briefed them on the position, receiving universal encouragement that there would be support for this decision in both the House and the Senate.

LEFT • Training for high g-loads and potential disorientation, astronauts used a Multiple-Axis Space Test Inertia Facility (MASTIF) inducing simultaneous spinning and tumbling motion brought to a stop with hand controllers on the seat arms. (NASA)

LEFT • July 25, 1961 and President Kennedy announces the national goal of landing men on the Moon before the end of the decade at a Joint Session of Congress. (NASA)

Before a joint session of Congress on Thursday May 25, 1961, in a speech labelled 'Urgent National Needs', Kennedy delivered a lengthy report during which he made the national declaration that set the objective: "Now it is time to take longer strides – time for a great new American enterprise – time for this nation to take a clearly leading role in space achievement, which in many ways may hold the key to our future on Earth... I believe that this nation should commit itself to achieving the goal, before this decade is out, of landing a man on the Moon and returning him safely to the Earth. No single space project in this period will be more impressive to mankind, or more important for the long-range exploration of space."

When assuming office, Kennedy had little knowledge or interest in space and the public record of his electoral pronouncements and transcripts of both public and private meetings reflect that. Countless times in meetings at the Oval Office he argued the case with officials, seeking a way to set a goal that in his mind would have greater worth and be more beneficial to Americans in general. To him, the national interest embraced the idea that America should be superior in power to any other nation and that meant the Soviet Union in particular. But that would work if America won the Moon Race and on May 25, 1961, nobody at NASA quite knew how to do that.

LEFT • A model of Russia's Vostok spacecraft in which Yuri Gagarin became the first human sent into space on April 12, 1961. (de Benutzer HPH)

A DYNAMIC CHALLENGE

Accelerating toward several Moon missions, NASA was on full throttle with unprecedented growth and new spacecraft

With only one suborbital hop to the edge of space behind it, NASA was suddenly tasked with sending men to the lunar surface within a little more than eight years. NASA-led studies had considered a wide range of modes in which it could be carried out and all assumed that the Apollo spacecraft would be the crew vehicle. These fell into four categories: Earth Orbit Rendezvous (EOR); Lunar Surface Rendezvous (LSR); Lunar Orbit Rendezvous (LOR); and Direct Ascent (DA). The first three modes would use multiple Saturn rockets while the fourth would require a massive rocket then known as Nova.

EOR would require as many as 15 Saturn I rockets to assemble the spacecraft in Earth orbit, multiple launches within a brief period with complex rendezvous and assembly in space. The LSR mode envisaged two Saturn rockets, one to transport to a lunar landing site propellant that would be transferred into the second spacecraft launched by another rocket for return to Earth.

The LOR mode promoted by Dr John Houbolt from the Langley Research Center required two separate spacecraft on a single Saturn V rocket sent directly to lunar orbit from where the Apollo spacecraft would remain while a smaller Lunar Excursion Module, later shortened to Lunar Module, would carry two men down to the surface. This had the advantage of not having to carry the weight of the mothership and its return propellant all the way down to the Moon and up again to get back home.

The fourth mode was Direct Ascent, a very large rocket much bigger than Saturn V, which would lift a single spacecraft straight to the surface for two astronauts to explore before returning to Earth. This had the advantage of simplicity and would not require more than one rocket or any complex orbital rendezvous manoeuvres. A big disadvantage was the amount of time needed to design and test such a large Nova-class rocket and the size of the facilities required to launch it.

Debate over the way to reach the Moon occupied much of early 1962, but whichever mode was selected, each would require considerable expansion of existing resources, money, personnel and test facilities. To the infrastructure inherited from the NACA had already been added the Jet Propulsion Laboratory and the Marshall Space Flight Center. Now there was a requirement for a dedicated facility for expanded manned flight operations, new rocket assembly and test facilities and a dedicated NASA complex

BELOW • Engines for the Saturn rockets, and later for the Shuttle then the SLS rocket, were test fired at the Mississippi Test Facility, later renamed the Stennis Space Center. (NASA)

at Cape Canaveral, where launch pads had previously been used in co-operation with the air force.

At NASA, thoughts of a spacecraft to follow Mercury had focused on the three-man Apollo, but in early 1961, McDonnell worked up a two-man Mercury Mk II to follow its one-man capsule. After Kennedy's Moon landing declaration, it was evident that NASA would need such an interim spacecraft to demonstrate manned flights lasting up to 14 days, the duration of a mission to the Moon and back, to practise space walking or EVA (extra-vehicular activity in NASA-speak) and rendezvous and docking with a target vehicle.

McDonnell received a contract to build ten fight-ready spacecraft in December 1961, when it was named Gemini after the stellar twins Castor and Pollux, the pressurised forward crew section having about as much room for the two astronauts as the front of a compact Volkswagen car. But it was better designed than Mercury, much having been learned from that one-man spacecraft, and would be launched by a Titan II, an intercontinental ballistic missile (ICBM) developed as stop-gap to the Atlas missile used to put Mercury spacecraft in orbit. For a rendezvous and docking target, NASA chose the Agena D rocket stage, which would be carried into orbit by the Atlas launch vehicle.

With the Saturn rockets clearly the key element in getting men to the Moon, after taking over the US Army's Development Operations Division and renaming it the Marshall Space Flight Center, additional facilities would be required for manufacturing and for firing complete stages in test rigs. The entire Saturn programme had been developed and managed by rocket scientist Wernher von Braun and his staff, and his charismatic style of popular and public engagement was accompanied by an astute sense of technical and engineering requirements for a given task.

The attitude and inter-departmental relationships among the German-led teams working under von Braun were a shift from the cultural norms of American aviation and space industry organisations. Most of the managers and department heads had worked for, or were influenced by their former employment by the German Army under Walter Dornberger, who had recruited von Braun to work on rocket development. They were at home under a strict disciplinary system where chains of authority were clearly defined and this matched the US Army for which they had worked for more than a decade until taken over by NASA.

It was a very German way of operating, which did not suit everyone, and at times NASA struggled to accommodate the different approach to work and how management styles were installed. The goal could only be achieved if the von Braun team delivered promised capabilities and the design and production of Saturn rockets was key to how that could be accomplished.

New Facilities

Located approximately 430 miles (692km) southwest of the Marshall Space Flight Center, manufacture of the big rocket stages would be undertaken at the Michoud Assembly Facility (MAF). Operated by NASA from December 18, 1961, it was a government plant near New Orleans, Louisiana, where Chrysler would assemble Saturn I and Saturn IB first stage elements. The second new facility subordinate to the Marshall Space Flight Center in support of the rocket programme was the Mississippi Test Facility (MTF) located on the Pearl River and about 40 miles (64km) northeast from the Michoud facility. Both were connected by a waterway, easing the transfer of rocket stages from where they were assembled to the site where they would be test fired.

Although the Moon landing mission mode had still to be determined, the Saturn V was clearly going to play a major part and a large site would be required to assemble the stages and launch it. Noise and public safety were key considerations as well as ease of access and good road

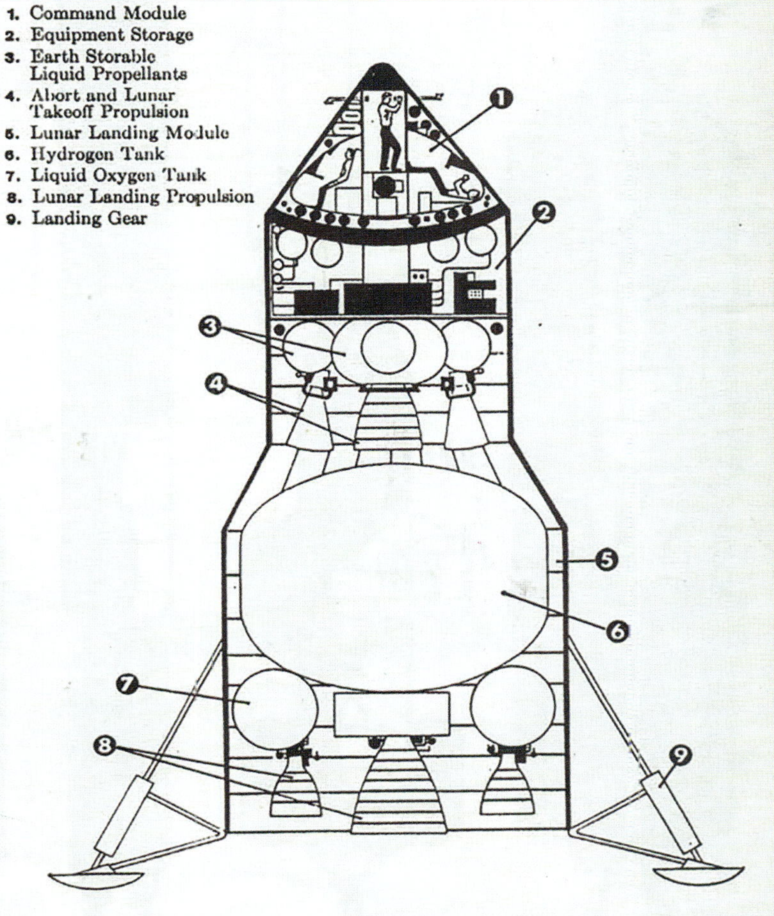

ABOVE • *This early depiction of the advantage in the Lunar Orbit Rendezvous mode was to reduce the size of the spacecraft needed to land on the Moon by Direct Ascent (left) to that with a Lunar Module, although in reality it was quite a bit larger when built. (NASA)*

and rail connections. Initially, the Launch Operations Center reporting to the Marshall facility was responsible for managing Saturn I test flights from air force launch pads at Cape Canaveral. A former German rocket scientist responsible for V2 test operations under von Braun, Kurt H Debus managed flights from the Cape.

Senior NASA executives adopted a division of tasks and responsibilities for individual centres and the selection of a launch complex owned and operated by the agency was key to that. This approach fostered a sense of pride in assignments, projects and programmes, each facility clearly identifiable as to function and purpose. That resulted in a sense of fulfilment, but also a degree of role-protection when other centres appeared to encroach on the assignments of another. As programmes grew in size and complexity, the spread of capabilities would necessarily spill across the defined roles of certain NASA field centres and that began to emerge with the decision over a suitable launch site for the giant Moon rocket, be it Saturn V or Nova.

The air force had no need of launch pads capable of supporting these mighty behemoths, focused as they were on testing much smaller ballistic missiles and launching military satellites and spacecraft into orbit. After a lengthy and extensive evaluation of a range of possible locations, NASA decided to build its own Moonport on land to the north of air force facilities at Cape Canaveral.

It would be known as the Launch Operations Center (LOC), independent of the Marshall Space Flight Center,

and from March 7, 1962, its director Kurt Debus would have a free hand over its design, construction and operation, reporting directly to D Brainerd Homes, then head of manned space flight, and administrator James Webb. Given his great experience in this field of activity, it was an appropriate appointment. The LOC was now the newest NASA field centre, but there was need for another – a facility to manage the entire gamut of manned space programmes under way and others planned for the future.

Traditionally, single-stage launchers were brought to the pad in a horizontal transporter and erected to a vertical position for launch. Multi-stage rockets were assembled vertically on the launch pad with upper stages and the spacecraft on top was added one at a time using lifting devices mounted on a gantry that doubled for checkout and for supplying fluids and propellants to fill the rockets. But for really big rockets that would not work.

The Saturn V was so large, 363ft (110.6m) tall and weighing 213tons empty, that this procedure was impractical. Moreover, with the amount of time required to assemble and check out the separate stages and spacecraft, a rocket exposed to the salty air of a beachside launch pad for several weeks in all kinds of weather could suffer badly and deteriorate. To solve the problem, NASA opted for assembly and initial checkout in a building so large that it would support the simultaneous preparation of four Saturn V rockets. Assembled in the vertical position on a mobile launch platform, it would be transported to the pad by a crawler-transporter that would lower it on to short pedestals from where it would be launched.

Perhaps the most famous of all NASA field centres and the home of human space flight was created by the need to establish a dedicated facility for managing and operating all manned missions. At the core of space flight operations would be a Mission Control where separate elements of the vehicle in space would be monitored by flight controllers and where the activities laid out in a previously assembled flight plan would be managed by a flight director, a concept developed at Cape Canaveral during Mercury flights.

To support all these requirements, the Manned Spacecraft Center was built in Houston, Texas, the

RIGHT • *President Kennedy chose James Webb (left) to lead NASA, with Wernher von Braun in charge of Saturn launch vehicle production and Kurt Debus managing the Launch Operations Center at Cape Canaveral. (NASA)*

decision to do so announced on September 19, 1961, with construction work starting the following April and officially opening for business in September 1963.

Management of future space flights would shift there from the Mercury Control Center at Cape Canaveral, beginning with the second manned Gemini mission launched on June 3, 1965. The Gemini programme involved two unmanned test flights in April 1964 and January 1965, followed by the first manned flight with astronauts Virgil 'Gus' Grissom and John Young two months later. By which date a lot had changed.

Moon Landers and New Recruits

The LOR mode had been selected in July 1962, nine companies showing interest in building the Lunar Module, a contract being awarded to Grumman on November 7, 1962, with work beginning immediately at the contractor's plant in Bethpage, New York. This was the last piece in the jigsaw of rocket motors, rocket stages, spacecraft and facilities.

The Mission Control method ensured that a range of information would be available to flight controllers and that a tiered chain of command would maintain strict lines of communication. Flight controllers would have separate consoles monitoring data from the spacecraft in areas such as environmental control, electrical power, propulsion, communications and other systems. Demands would increase when two spacecraft were being operated simultaneously at the distance of the Moon: Apollo in lunar orbit and the Lunar Module on the surface.

Several astronaut crews would be appointed for each mission, a prime crew with a back-up crew and later a support crew, each with three astronauts, to evaluate procedures in simulators and provide assistance. If a prime crew member fell ill before the flight, it was expected that the complete back-up crew would replace them, but that was not always adhered to. Crews were appointed up to a year before the planned flight and worked as a cohesive unit, the communications with Mission Control going through a fellow astronaut in Mission Control, a capsule communicator (CAPCOM) who would have worked in pre-flight preparations with both prime and back-up crews.

NASA selected crews on the basis of specific assignments and the urgent need to expand the pool available for flight began with the appointment of the second group in March 1962 when nine inductees joined the Mercury Seven, a further 14 being selected in October 1963. On joining NASA and after basic orientation and familiarisation with their role, astronauts were assigned specific programmes and particular specialities, frequently following their areas of expertise. Most were members of the armed services, but a number were civilian test pilots, many with previous military duty.

For Apollo flights, the overall mission was under the authority of the commander (CDR), who would usually occupy the left couch in the Command Module for launch and would also be at the controls of the Lunar Module after it separated and flew down to the surface. Seated in the centre couch at lift-off, the Command Module pilot (CMP) would have expertise in the Apollo spacecraft itself and would usually be responsible for 'flying' the vehicle and operating the navigation systems. He would remain aboard Apollo while the other two crew members flew the Lunar Module. In the right couch for launch, the Lunar Module pilot (LMP) would serve as the flight engineer, monitor systems and conduct that duty in the Lunar Module, feeding the CDR with computer information as he piloted the spacecraft.

ABOVE • Chosen as the interim between Mercury and Apollo, the Gemini spacecraft would rehearse all the essential techniques for getting to the Moon, including two-week missions, spacewalking and rendezvous and docking. (McDonnell)

FAR LEFT • The Saturn V that would send men to the Moon was 20 times more powerful than the Atlas rocket which put Mercury astronauts in orbit and the first stage was assembled at the Michoud Assembly Facility. (NASA)

LEFT • The two-man Gemini provided orbital manoeuvring and pioneered the use of fuel cells providing electrical power from hydrogen and oxygen. (NASA)

TIMES OF CHANGE

Kennedy comes close to cancelling Apollo while NASA is reorganised and a new management structure replaces old methods of working

As NASA's budget soared and funding flowed from government coffers, word went out across the agency that all projects had to have a contributory value to the Apollo objective. What had initially been a carefully prepared route-map for a diverse and broad-based space research programme was now hostage to the political use of NASA as a propaganda tool with which to flaunt American capabilities and techno-leadership. In an attempt to garner support, discussions were held with the national scientific organisations and eminent scientists declared sides in arguments for and against the prioritisation of Moon trips.

Aware of this, NASA embraced the scientific community as widely as it could in efforts to recruit support and sustain political approval. As a US government agency, NASA had to present its case every year to support the requested budget, which was passed to Congress by the White House. In the 1960s, the US financial year began on July 1 and late in the preceding year negotiations would begin, with NASA asking the White House for a required amount of money and the Bureau of the Budget tweaking that before it was submitted to Congress, the latter holding hearings in the months preceding the start of that year for testimony from officials about the requested money. It was critical to keep the politicians on side.

One problem with maintaining an equitable balance was the need to keep the engineers in charge of the programme. The emerging Manned Space Flight Center in Houston took hold of the manned programme and made it central to everything the agency was involved with. The challenge required it to be so, but there was emerging tension between that group and the scientists who wanted to use the Apollo programme as a means of investigating the Moon's surface and its geophysical characteristics. Impatient to get to that capability, they would take second place to the fraternity of engineers who demanded prior claim on critical decisions about landing sites and the safety of the crew.

There was a universal expectation that NASA would restrict the first and possibly the second lunar landing to engineering tests of the spacecraft systems and the ability of two astronauts to work outside their lander. Science would have to wait until those goals and objectives had been met. There was increasing awareness that a strategic plan for the long-term exploration of the Moon was lacking and that this could only be produced with the co-operation of the scientists involved.

Most NASA personnel were blissfully unaware that the majority of politicians saw this as a single event and not the beginning of a new age of space exploration. They had supported Kennedy when he framed the goal as a demonstration of national capabilities, not the beginning of an enduring commitment to lunar bases and research stations. The engineers at NASA were excited by the challenge of such a demanding goal and relished the task in their struggle to find ways to make it happen. For their part, geologists and geophysicists eagerly awaited results directly from the lunar surface and began to develop ideas about experiments to leave on the surface, which would continue to send data back to Earth long after the astronauts had returned home.

By early 1963, senior NASA officials were getting very concerned that there was insufficient progress with the pace of its manned flight programme and the time it was taking to conduct test operations and to get the interim Gemini missions under way. Development of the Saturn

rockets, so critical to the success of Apollo, was slow-paced despite maximum effort. Scientist Wernher Von Braun and his team employed the tried and tested methods they brought from Germany and which, applied to the new rocket projects with the US Army, had produced good results. But the requirements were now very different and if Americans were to get to the Moon by the end of the decade, NASA would have to adopt an alternative way of working. As it stood in early 1963, they would never make it on time.

A lot of the concern surrounded the protracted flight testing of the Saturn I, the evolved variant Saturn IB and the Saturn V. In February 1963, von Braun planned to fly 16 Saturn Is, the first of four without an upper stage successfully launched on a ballistic trajectory in October 1961. The fifth flight planned for August 1963 would have the S-IV upper stage as would the remaining launches, the 11th Saturn I planned for March 1965 carrying the first of four manned Apollo spacecraft. NASA expected to start Gemini manned flights in 1964, missions overlapping from 1965 with the initial manned Apollo test flights while Gemini rehearsed operational techniques such as two-week missions, spacewalking and rendezvous and docking.

The last two Saturn Is would have been retained as spares in case they were required for further manned Apollo missions on this launcher. But the expectation was that the Saturn IB, carrying the more powerful S-IVB second stage, would make the first of three unmanned flights in August 1965, followed by the first of six manned missions testing the Apollo spacecraft in Earth orbit from March 1966 to May 1967. Clearly, even the Saturn IB would be unable to lift a fully fuelled Apollo spacecraft, the considerably larger Saturn V would be required for that, but the Saturn I and IB launchers could support early test flights with partially fuelled tanks in the spacecraft.

In early 1963, the initial flight of the Saturn V was scheduled for March 1966, the first six launches planned as unmanned flights progressing from just the first stage and dummy upper stages, then the first two stages and a dummy third stage and finally four test flights with a full three-stage configuration. The first of nine manned flights with an Apollo spacecraft was scheduled for June 1967 with the last of 15 launches in October 1968. The last few flights were expected to achieve the lunar landing with a reserve for contingencies.

Very few expected a successful touchdown on the first attempt and NASA aimed to try a landing in the first half of 1968. None of this was realistic. A detailed report dated July 15, 1963 labelled its conclusions as an 'alternative plan for Apollo', which made difficult reading.

Changing of the Guard

The man behind plans and schedules for NASA manned programmes, engineer D Brainerd Holmes had been brought in during the 1961 build-up, but NASA boss Jim Webb never quite got the measure of his approach. He departed on September 1, 1963, for a job with an electronics contractor and was immediately replaced by George Mueller. The replacement announcement had been made on July 23 and in the interim Mueller brought in his project management skills with a promise from Webb that he could have total control to completely reorganise the Office of Manned Space Flight and to bring in high achievers from the missile field to transform the programme and "set it alight".

Mueller had a long history of experience with air force missile programmes and had a reputation for tough-talking and getting things done on time. Working with aeronautical engineer Robert Seamans and directly with Webb, Mueller knew that he needed greater managerial weight behind him and it was agreed he could recruit Maj Gen Samuel C Phillips on secondment from Gen Bernard Schriever to become programme controller. Joining NASA in December 1963, and aware that the large cost overruns and schedule delays would require a new group of senior managers to get under control, he successfully negotiated for 57 high-ranking air force officers to join him. To tighten his grip and transform the way the entire programme was run, a further 128 air force officers were loaned to NASA.

Mueller himself was responsible for a lot of the changes that threatened to overwhelm the agency during early 1964, but which greatly benefitted not only Apollo but NASA in general, the issuing of an Apollo Configuration Management Manual being adopted verbatim from a similar document that defined the way the Minuteman intercontinental ballistic missile programme had been brought to fruition in record time. Another and universally applied change was the introduction of a new schedule planning and project control tool known as Program Evaluation and Review Technique (PERT).

Introduced to manage schedule and cost accounting for major US industrial projects during the 1950s, it had worked wonders on the US Navy Polaris nuclear missile programme. PERT was a network-type model that began

BELOW • President Kennedy at the original Manned Spacecraft Center following the orbital flight of John Glenn in February 1962. (NASA)

ABOVE • Kennedy is briefed on the Saturn programme at Cape Canaveral Launch Operations Center, renamed the Kennedy Space Center after the President's assassination in November 1963. (White House)

BELOW • President Kennedy, on his third and last visit to the Kennedy Space Center, views the Saturn I which will equal Russia's launch capacity, November 16, 1963. (NASA)

with the end product, a spacecraft or a launch vehicle for instance. It then added pegs for the start and finish dates specified, adding all the incremental steps, processes and procedures required to maintain both ends of the programme. It defined the time and cost required for each step and integrated them into a chart displaying when each should start and how it related to the others. It was very different to how NASA had worked before.

One advantage with PERT was how it could estimate the longest time required to complete the most problematic tasks, and list those in descending order of concern. Thus, it placed the longest lead items at the top, having those cut a path through less problematic steps, predicting how tolerating a delay in completing simple stages could add resources to shorten the delay time of the most troubling step, bringing them all to completion at the same time.

The most clearly applied lesson from that was how the Saturn rockets could be brought to operational status quicker, more effectively, at lower cost and with less potential for delays. It was known as 'all-up systems' testing.

Von Braun had been used to launching lots of rockets in the development of the V2 and in the Redstone and Jupiter programmes he developed for the US Army. That conservative approach in which each element of the rocket or guided missile was tested separately resulted in lots of launches over an extended period of time and the approach had been brought across to NASA. But with the size of the Saturn rockets and urgency of getting them operational, the ponderous approach had driven delays

and cost overruns across all these programmes. In the emerging computer age of the 1960s, this was both outdated and wasteful; programmes such as PERT, which could be conducted manually or electronically, promising to speed the entire process of detailed design, fabrication, contractor management, assembly and test.

What Mueller and Phillips imposed with 'all-up systems' testing was to take all the stages of a new and untried launch vehicle and send them all up together on the first attempt, risking total failure but with great savings in time and money if it all went off as expected. Initially, von Braun vehemently opposed this, but quickly came round to the idea and the protracted launch test sequence for the Saturn IB and the Saturn V were rewritten so that from the very first flight of each type, they would each be stacked with all the upper stages they were designed to fly with.

To familiarise the new team with what they had found at the NASA centres, Phillips went on the road for Mueller and spent the majority of his time travelling between contractors, visiting the manufacturing plants and educating the personnel from the top down into the new way of doing things. What he found was shocking. Poor workmanship and appalling quality control standards had permeated the manned programmes, an attitude born of confident familiarity, not so much through a lack of responsibility or care, rather a total unawareness of the critical margin between success and disaster. If left uncorrected, it would not have been possible for NASA to have reached the Moon when it did.

"A Lot of Dough"

But there were other, deeper threats to the entire programme. At various times during 1963, unaware of the management crisis at NASA, Kennedy travelled to various space centres to take stock of the progress being made and give heart to the rapidly expanding workforce. The agency had yet to reach peak funding requirements but already the Apollo programme had grown to dominate all NASA activities and there were grumbling complaints from politicians called upon to provide the cash as to the worthwhile nature of the effort.

Changed in his world view by the Cuban Missile Crisis where NATO and the Warsaw Pact came close to thermonuclear war in October 1962, the clarity of purpose was no longer quite so clearly defined. Never the ardent space enthusiast, a pragmatist to the core, Kennedy nevertheless became enthralled with what he was shown at the Manned Spacecraft Centre and at Cape Canaveral, where the Launch Operations Centre was now a busy construction site assembling the then largest building by volume on Earth, within which four giant Saturn V rockets could be made ready for flight.

But the cost, the achievements already being accomplished and the vibrant energy Kennedy felt when he visited these places caused him to question the necessity for NASA to rush with such haste. Seeking further political value, Kennedy invited Webb to the White House to get his opinion on a possible offer to the Soviet Union to "go to the Moon together", seeing in this a way to reduce the risk of a military confrontation. While not supportive of the idea, Webb was amenable to further discussions. When quietly approached about the idea, Congressional leaders were mixed, but many were concerned at the rising cost of the space programme.

During the closing months of 1963, NASA was negotiating with the Bureau of the Budget the amount of money it could request for fiscal year 1965, effective from July 1, 1964. NASA was required to carry out the

programme policies assigned by the White House and the overriding budget allocation for the agency was for Apollo. The government had to balance the total amount of money it wanted to ask Congress to approve. Unlike other democracies, the US government has to get its money from the representatives and senators of all the States, and agencies must argue their case to justify that request.

When NASA opened for business in 1958, it had a budget inherited from the NACA of about $331million, but that grew rapidly and by 1962, the first full financial year after the Kennedy Moon decision, NASA already had a budget of $1,825m. In the following year that had doubled and in fiscal year 1964 Congress approved $5,099m for NASA, equivalent to 4.2% of federal expenditure or 0.75% of GDP. As Kennedy reviewed government expenditure and national priorities for fiscal year 1965, NASA was already seeking a considerable increase beyond that.

Mindful of the pressures now being exerted by many politicians about the amount of money pouring into the space programme, Kennedy had a meeting with Webb on September 18 that was recorded by equipment he had had installed in the Oval Office the previous year. Selectively activated by a concealed switch, it is not certain that he was aware this this conversation was being recorded, but the contents of the tape disclosed just how little regard the President had for the space programme that he had publicly supported and expanded.

With unprecedented frankness, Kennedy told Webb: "This looks like a hell of a lot of dough to go to the Moon when you can go — you can learn most of what you want scientifically through instruments and putting a man on the Moon really is a stunt and it isn't worth that many billions," reasserting his belief that "the heat's going to be on unless we can say this has got some military justification and not just prestige... Why should we spend that kind of dough to put a man on the Moon...we've got to wrap around in this country, a military use for what we're doing." He concluded: "If the Russians do some tremendous feat, then it would stimulate interest again, but right now space has lost a lot of its glamour."

On September 20, 1963, Kennedy addressed the United Nations and, in a carefully crafted speech that staggered many, declared that the United States and the Soviet Union should "go to the Moon (as) representatives of all our countries" rather than compete at such cost and use of resources. Sensing a willingness on the part of Premier Khrushchev to warm to the idea of a joint, co-operative venture untethered from targets and deadlines, Kennedy set his advisers to work drafting through the National Security Council a memorandum of understanding and beginning the transition toward disengaging Apollo from national objectives.

To many this was a shock, a betrayal of leadership and national responsibility. The trade and specialist magazine *Missiles and Rockets* framed the shift as the conversion of "one of the most exciting challenges ever accepted by a nation to an unimportant pawn in the Cold War so as to be sacrificed in the first gambit of appeasement". Internally at NASA, Webb tried to contain the shift and to consolidate support for the work under way, seeing in leaked reports of this broader intention a disturbingly disruptive message that was very bad for morale.

On September 24, Kennedy signed off National Security Action Memorandum 271 and set up a meeting with key officials for December 15, 1963, largely with the group that had helped make his decision in late April 1961 to go to the Moon. It would be on that date that the full implications of Kennedy's intentions would be discussed, with an expectation that Webb and his immediate staff would make recommendations on how to make a formal offer to the Soviet Union and begin the process of deconstructing Apollo as a national objective.

Kennedy made his third visit to Cape Canaveral on November 16 and saw first-hand the progress made with bringing the Saturn I to maturity, the fifth flight of this rocket now equipped with the S-IV upper stage for placing payloads in orbit from early 1964. As he got out of his white, open-top limousine and walked a few short steps to the massive rocket, security men concerned that he should not be walking underneath the stage now erect on its launch pad were waved away as he lingered in visible admiration of the steps now made to equal Russian rockets in lifting capacity.

Just 11 days later, Kennedy lay dead in a Dallas hospital, struck down by an assassin who would himself be shot and killed as he was being taken from a police station. Lyndon Johnson, architect of NASA and the man behind the Moon decision was now President and there would be no more talk of sharing this capability with the Russians. It was to be business as usual.

ABOVE LEFT AND ABOVE RIGHT • A new generation of leaders arrived at NASA in 1963 including George Mueller (left) and General Sam Phillips to manage the Apollo programme. (NASA)

LEFT • The first Saturn I carrying the orbital upper stage, which would bring the United States level with the Soviet Union in lift capacity. (NASA-KSC)

ORBITAL BALLET AND A SPACEWALKING ASTRONAUT

Russia takes a walk in space, but NASA seizes the lead and prepares for Moon landings with reshaped plans for rendezvous and docking

In the nation at large, there was a reaffirmation of commitment to Kennedy's goal and NASA felt a deeper sense of responsibility to that objective. In memory of the man who started the race to the Moon, NASA's Launch Operations Center was renamed the Kennedy Space Center (KSC), but a plan to name the region Cape Kennedy was rejected by local officials.

The two-man Gemini programme had taken longer than expected to mature and the first unmanned test launch on a Titan rocket (GT-1) had not taken place until April 8, 1964. As a test of the compatibility of the spacecraft with the launch vehicle and of some on-board systems, the spacecraft was intentionally destroyed in the atmosphere as its orbit decayed. The second unmanned flight, GT-2 was delayed by hurricanes Cleo and Dora, and then by technical issues, until January 19, 1965, achieving a maximum altitude of 106.7 miles (171.1km) and splashdown 2,127 miles (3,422.4km) from Cape Canaveral.

Meanwhile, the Russians had been busy preparing for their next space spectaculars in an attempt to beat the Americans at two significant milestones: the first multi-person crew sent into orbit and the first spacewalk from an orbiting capsule. The political pressure applied by the Soviet leadership on Russia's rocket teams was at a high level and, with publicised knowledge about America's upcoming Gemini and Apollo flights, it was urgent for them to eclipse the US with a modified version of their one-person spacecraft.

Between the flight of Yuri Gagarin on April 12, 1961, and the sixth and last flight of a manned Vostok spacecraft on June 19, 1963, the Russians did little more than accomplish what NASA had achieved with the Mercury spacecraft. Each carried a single occupant and neither could change its orbit in space. The longest Mercury flight had been the last, piloted by Gordon Cooper, launched on May 15, 1963 for just over one day, ten hours. The longest Vostok flight had remained in orbit for almost five days, but on the last flight they had orbited the first woman to go into space, Valentina Tereshkova.

Political pressure on Russia's rocket teams was at a high level and knowledge was publicised about America's upcoming Gemini and Apollo flights, focusing ways to eclipse the US with a modified version of Vostok named Voskhod. On October 12, 1964, Voskhod 1 carried Vladimir Komarov, Konstantin Feoktistov and Boris Yegorov into space on a flight lasting a little over 26 hours, but with three cosmonauts there was insufficient room for ejection seats or for the crew to wear space suits, which were, in any case, a back-up in the event the cabin was punctured.

The architect of the early Soviet space programme, Sergei Korolev, planned at least six manned Voskhod missions, but the leadership redirected development to a new spacecraft called Soyuz that would support circumlunar and lunar landing flights. The next flight after Voskhod 1 was allowed to continue and that would beat NASA to the propaganda value of being the first to conduct a spacewalk.

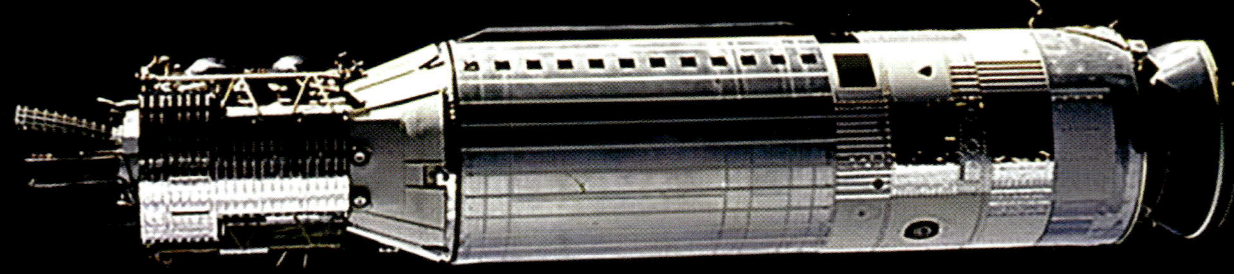

BELOW • *The Gemini 8 target vehicle to which Armstrong and Scott successfully conducted the first rendezvous and docking mission, March 1966. (NASA)*

Launched on March 18, 1965, Voskhod 2 carried a collapsed airlock in the form of a cylinder containing a bladder attached to a circular hatch on the outside of the spacecraft. A parallel hatch on Voskhod afforded access from the inside of the spacecraft when the airlock was inflated with oxygen to an elongated shape big enough to contain a man. When pressurised, cosmonaut Alexei Leonov opened the inner hatch and moved inside, closing it behind him. The airlock was depressurised and Leonov opened the hatch above his head and squeezed out, filmed for several minutes by a camera attached to the exterior of the spacecraft.

On trying to get back in, he discovered his suit had ballooned, requiring him to lower its pressure so that he could push himself back into the elongated, bag-like airlock. With the outer hatch closed, the airlock was re-pressurised and the inner hatch opened for Leonov to get back inside the spacecraft. During re-entry, the massive equipment module on the back of the spherical crew compartment, which contained the retro-rocket, failed to separate. Had it remained attached, both elements would have burned up in the atmosphere but as it descended it began to heat up and partially disconnected as flaming chunks fell away from the hurtling combination.

Held perilously on a single connecting line, it finally broke free and the crew compartment was able to descend on its own from an altitude of 62 miles (100km), just short of the height at which it would have been destroyed along with the cosmonauts. Landing 240 miles (386km) off target, the capsule came down in dense forest in the remote Upper Karma Upland in Russia.

With communication lost nobody knew if the crew was alive, their families nevertheless being told they were safe and resting. No one knew exactly where they were, but aircraft located their position, supplies were dropped and the following day a rescue party arrived on skis and built a small log cabin from felled trees, lighting a fire for warmth. The next day they set off on skis and eventually reached a clearing where air transport was available and a flight to Perm brought them respite from the ordeal.

Gemini Flies

For various reasons, the Russians did not launch another cosmonaut for two years before the first flight of Soyuz, but understanding what was going on in the Russian programme provided NASA with information from an increasingly capable array of intelligence-gathering air force spy satellites in Earth orbit. This gave NASA certain forewarning and an opportunity to shape the nature of their own mission plans and upstage the Russians, who were themselves trying to outwit the Americans.

Amateur enthusiasts in other countries were tracking Soviet satellites and frequently provided high-fidelity analysis and interpretation of what they were observing from radio signals and communications they were listening in to. Politicians were keen to know details too and Dr Charles Sheldon of the US Congressional Research Service began to compile open-source information as a reference base for this activity and incorporate reviews of non-US space activities in a series of published documents. While the intelligence community gathered information about Soviet space plans, NASA managers focused attention on manned Gemini missions.

Twenty-two months after the last Mercury flight, the first manned Gemini mission was launched on March 23, 1965 with astronauts Gus Grissom and John Young, just five days after the last Voskhod spacecraft went up, flying a three-orbit mission lasting four hours and 52 minutes. They used manoeuvring thrusters to change the orbit of their spacecraft, essential for

LEFT • Astronauts Gus Grissom (left) and John Young, the crew of the first manned Gemini flight launched in March 1965. (NASA)

LEFT • Ed White conducts America's first spacewalk on the second Gemini flight, June 3, 1965, and spends about 20 minutes outside the spacecraft. (NASA)

BELOW • Gemini 7 viewed by Gemini 6, the first rendezvous of two manned vehicles in space in December 1965. (NASA)

rendezvous missions; the first time a manned spacecraft had achieved that in space. Not until April 1967 would the Russians match this capability with their Soyuz spacecraft.

The crew had named their spacecraft *Molly Brown*, after the Broadway musical *The Unsinkable Molly Brown*, based on the *Titanic* survivor Margaret Brown, and a reference to Grissom's capsule — which sank after his ballistic flight in July 1961. After the flight, NASA issued new guidelines regarding naming future spacecraft, but this was the first in an unfolding sequence of mischievous gameplay between astronauts and the politically correct leadership in an agency increasingly exposed to public attention and scrutiny.

Single-minded and highly self-confident, astronauts of the Mercury-Gemini-Apollo era were largely irreverent, non-conformist and feisty individuals unlikely to bend to rules they judged unnecessary, frequently unpredictable and opinionated. The nature of the NASA astronaut would change over the coming decades to embrace a more establishment-savvy group less willing to challenge authority and to accept a more rigid code of behaviour, eventually succumbing to honed and politically correct demeanour.

The second manned flight (GT-4) was launched on June 3, 1965 and its task of putting an astronaut outside on a tether was moved up from GT-5 after that feat had been performed by Alexei Leonov on the Russian Voskhod 2 flight on March 18. Equipment essential for a spacewalk was still in development during the final few weeks prior to the flight, including a hand-held manoeuvring unit that expelled compressed oxygen from jets to operate like tiny thrusters and move the astronaut around while tethered to his spacecraft. Astronaut Ed White spent about 23 minutes outside Gemini 4, but a computer failure compromised splashdown, which was 50 miles (80km) short of the target, almost four days and two hours after launch.

The next objective for NASA was to extend the flight duration from four days to eight days and combine that with a test of the fuel cell technology vital for electrical production on the Apollo spacecraft. There was no other technology capable of producing the required amount of power for the weight offered by fuel cells. However, the fuel cells for Gemini were different from those being developed for Apollo, although the core principle was the same and it was necessary to get some flight time in for seeing just how well they performed.

Launched on August 21, 1965, Gemini 5 carried a radar evaluation pod in the back of the adapter section; this was released as planned so the crew could conduct tracking and rendezvous manoeuvres as though this was an active spacecraft. Shortly thereafter, pressure in the fuel cells threatened to cut short the flight, but after powering down, nursing the system and working with Mission Control to gradually bring the cells back up to an operating level, the mission proceeded. Gemini 5 returned to Earth just short of seven days 23 hours with the majority of mission tasks accomplished, proving that the hydrogen/oxygen fuel cells could provide electrical power as designed.

Gemini 6 was to be the first rendezvous and docking flight with the target vehicle's launch by an Atlas rocket on October 28, 1965, but the Agena engine exploded shortly after separating. The Gemini 6 crew members, Wally Schirra and Thomas Stafford, were in their spacecraft on the pad ready to launch in pursuit, but the mission was cancelled. Had Gemini 6 launched, Frank Borman and Jim Lovell would fly a 14-day endurance flight that December. Medical teams were keen to monitor physiological and psychological reactions to long-duration space flight and at this time a two-week stay in space was very long indeed!

But as a replacement Atlas-Agena D would not be ready before the flight of Gemini 7, NASA management decided on a bold initiative: launch Gemini 7 and then rapidly repair the pad and get Schirra and Stafford off on what would be designated Gemini 6A. There was always a little damage to every launch pad after each flight, but NASA knew from experience that it was doable – if everything worked as planned! Gemini 6A would use Gemini 7 as a passive target, but there was no way the two spacecraft could dock to each other. Nevertheless, it would be a very real demonstration of rendezvous techniques.

ABOVE • The nose of the Gemini spacecraft containing radar equipment used for orbital rendezvous. (NASA)

The crew for Gemini 7 flew in lightweight pressure garments with special helmets that could be unzipped, at which point they could remove their 'bone-dome' helmet and spend the rest of the flight in relative comfort. The spacecraft was far too small to allow them to completely remove their suits and medics were worried that a full pressure suit would be too bulky and uncomfortable to wear for two weeks.

Gemini 7 was launched on December 4, 1965, immediately followed by the pad clean-up crew scurrying to assess the damage and conduct repairs, ensuring that all the conduits, cables and electrical wires were repaired or replaced for the Gemini 6A flight. Ahead of the expected date, Schirra and Stafford were ready for a launch attempt on December 12, but 1.5 seconds after ignition the two powerful Titan II rocket motors shut down, computers detecting an anomaly somewhere in the rocket.

LEFT • A Gemini spacecraft and an Agena target vehicle are lined up on the ground for compatibility tests. (NASA)

ABOVE • *Armstrong and Scott after splashdown on the only emergency in-flight abort in the history of US manned space flight. (NASA)*

On the pad, a small fire from draining propellant broke out, but that was quickly dowsed before the gantry was raised back up and the crew extricated. Human error on two critical components had caused shutdown, but a second attempt three days later was a success as the Titan rocket put Gemini 6A into an initial elliptical orbit trailing Gemini 7 by 1,400 miles (2,253km), above and ahead of Gemini 6A. In that orbit it conducted several orbit changes using its thrusters and slowly

Table 1: Comparison of Mercury and Gemini Spacecraft

	Mercury	Gemini
Height	10.8ft (3.3m)	18.4ft (5.6m)
Width	6ft (1.8m)	10ft (3m)
Weight	2,900lb (1,35kg)	8,200lb (3,719kg)
First manned flight	1961	1965

closed on Gemini 7, raising its path and slowing down in the process.

Rendezvous was completed at five hours 56 minutes into the flight of Gemini 6A with the two spacecraft 120ft (36.5m) apart and stationary. The rendezvous had taken less fuel than expected so there was plenty left for manoeuvring around Gemini 7, powered-down and drifting, Schirra reporting that at times he got to within 12in (30cm) of Gemini 7. The two spacecraft remained together for five hours 19 minutes before Gemini 6A returned on December 15 after 25 hours 51 minutes, the first splashdown shown live on TV. Gemini 7 returned to Earth on December 18, completing a flight lasting almost two weeks in space.

Mix and Match in Space

Rendezvous and docking would be a part of remaining Gemini missions, with several different types to evaluate. Gemini 8 would fly the simplest and most forgiving profile, arriving at the Agena target on the fourth orbit, referred to as an M=4 rendezvous. Later Gemini missions would fly a third orbit rendezvous on Gemini 9-A (M=3) and a first orbit rendezvous (M=1) on Gemini 11, of the type astronauts coming up from the Moon would fly to get back to their Apollo mothership.

Gemini 8 began with the launch of its Agena D target vehicle on March 16, 1966, followed one hour 41 minutes later by the spacecraft carrying astronauts Neil Armstrong and Dave Scott. The rendezvous was the same type as that used by Gemini 6A in hunting down Gemini 7 and the first docking in space was achieved six hours 33 minutes after lift-off when the nose of the spacecraft was inserted into the docking cone on the Agena and secured with capture latches. Just 27 minutes later, the docked configuration began rotating in roll and yaw, the rates increasing.

To escape what they believed to be the erratic performance of the Agena, the astronauts separated from the stage, only to discover that the roll and yaw motions accelerated at an alarming rate. As the rates reached almost one revolution a second and with the crew on the point of blacking out, they isolated the main thrusters and switched to the small re-entry thrusters designed only to control the attitude of the crew compartment as it returned from orbit. Everything was back to normal 25 minutes after the drama began, largely a result of Armstrong's calm and effective management of the situation.

RIGHT • *Dubbed the 'angry alligator', the nose shroud remained stubbornly attached to the front end of the Augmented Target Docking Adapter. (NASA)*

With only 25% of re-entry propellant remaining, Gemini 8 had to make an emergency return on the seventh orbit for a splashdown in the Pacific Ocean 575 miles (925km) east of Okinawa, Japan. In a remarkable display of quick reaction, the return was almost perfect, splashdown occurring within eight miles (13km) of the planned spot just ten hours 41 minutes after launch. The incident prompted Robert Seamans to issue a management instruction on April 14 authorising the deputy administrator (himself) to undertake an independent investigation of any calamitous situation. It would be called into effect just ten months later.

NASA had already suffered astronaut fatalities, the first on October 31, 1964, when Theodore Freeman from the third group selected had crashed after a low-level bird strike on approach to Ellington Air Force Base near Houston. In training for their Gemini 9 mission and during bad weather, on February 28, 1966, Elliot See and Charles Bassett crashed into the building where their spacecraft was under construction at the McDonnell plant in St Louis, Missouri. Their places were taken by the back-up crew, Tom Stafford and Eugene Cernan.

During the first half of 1966, NASA was fighting for the money it needed to fulfil the national mandate to reach the Moon in that decade, a goal that had been endorsed by Congress and was now being asked to pay the bills for the task it had authorised. In the first quarter of 1966, hearings began on the fiscal year 1967 budget and would eventually award NASA $4.96billion. NASA's annual allowance had already fallen from a peak of $5.25bn in fiscal year 1965 to $5.17bn in 1966, significantly affecting plans for expanding planetary exploration and sustained manned spaceflight beyond the Apollo years.

For now, there were four more two-man missions and on May 17, 1966, the target vehicle for Gemini 9 was launched, but two minutes later the Atlas rocket failed and had to be destroyed as it turned turtle and headed back for Cape Canaveral! After the failure of the first Agena the previous October, NASA had ordered a standby replacement called the Augmented Target Docking Adapter (ATDA), which consisted of a standard Agena docking cone, a thruster control module for maintaining its attitude and orientation in space and a communications section, powered by a battery and weighing 1,748lb (793kg).

With the loss of the Gemini 9 Agena, the ATDA was brought out and launched on June 1 for the re-designated Gemini 9A mission. Delayed two days by a technical problem, Stafford and Cernan were finally launched, but after rendezvous with the ATDA they found the docking cone blocked by a protective cover that had failed to jettison. When the planned spacewalk ran into problems as Cernan struggled to attach a backpack for manoeuvring around, Gemini 9A returned to Earth after little more than three days in space.

Launched on July 18, September 26 and November 11, 1966, the last three Gemini flights focused on different types of rendezvous and docking operations with three different Agena vehicles. Astronauts found it difficult to conduct spacewalks in weightlessness due to the exertion required to maintain a fixed position at work stations and found tethers and body restraints the solution, leaving hands free to use tools and equipment. A record was established when the Agena docked to Gemini 11 boosted John Young and Michael Collins to a record height of 853 miles (1,372km).

FROM TRIUMPH TO TRAGEDY

Concern over poor workmanship is a portent of disaster before three astronauts lose their lives in a pad fire many said could have been prevented

ABOVE • The Apollo 1 crew (from left) of Gus Grissom, Ed White and Roger Chaffee posing for photographers in front of the LC-34 launch site where the Saturn IB was expected to carry them on the first manned Apollo flight. (NASA)

RIGHT • An evolution from the Saturn I, early flights in the Apollo programme would rely on the Saturn IB with an S-IVB upper stage, which would also be the third stage of the massive Saturn V. (NASA)

Mission analysts had been poring over Gemini data since the first unmanned test launch in April 1964, and the progress that had been made in that time was outstanding. In just 20 months, ten manned flights had been completed, albeit with a set of problems solved in flight or on the ground after splashdown. Confidence was riding high and optimism unequalled in both this and the upcoming Apollo programme.

Meanwhile, in the prestigious field of human space flight, nothing had been heard from the Russians since Alexei Leonov made the first spacewalk in history in March 1965. Many believed that if the Apollo programme progressed with the same success, American astronauts could be on the Moon by the end of 1968. Some concern was expressed over physical effects observed in the eight and 14-day missions, the astronauts showing loss of bone mass and an imbalance in blood cell counts, loss of muscle mass and increased water production within the human body tricked into conditions usually associated with ageing.

All of which worried physicians as to how those effects would pan out over several months in space; would they tail off, or get worse over time? This would not stop Moon landings, but could have an impact on post-Apollo programmes. Long-duration missions were being considered by NASA teams working on lunar bases and stations in orbit permanently manned with crews remaining in space for up to six months, plans that could be upset by physical limits to human survival. For the immediate future, those studies were noted by engineers while physicians awaited further results when longer flights became possible.

With the Gemini programme completed, demands on resources for crew training and mission planning at NASA's Manned Spacecraft Center in Houston could now concentrate on preparations for upcoming Apollo flights. Initially, those would be launched by the Saturn IB, a more powerful and upgraded variant of the Saturn I, which had flown ten flights between 1961 and 1965, the last six of which had carried an S-IV upper stage and placed itself and various payloads in orbit.

It had originally been planned to put astronauts in Block I Apollo spacecraft — early production vehicles that did not have docking equipment and which were unsuitable for deep-space operations — on the last four Saturn I rockets, but delays pushed those across to the Saturn IB, which had a greater payload capacity. Wernher von Braun's team had flown the first Saturn IB (AS-201) in a suborbital test of the Block I Apollo Command and Service Modules on February

26, 1966, followed by an orbital test of the rocket's S-IVB upper stage on July 5 (AS-203).

The S-IVB stage was also to be the third stage for Saturn V, which would push Apollo astronauts from Earth-orbit to a trans-lunar trajectory and this was an engineering test of critical propellant handling in space. Out of numerical sequence, the third Saturn IB (AS-202) was launched on August 25, 1966, another suborbital test of an unmanned Apollo spacecraft and clearing the rocket and Apollo for manned flights.

The schedule envisaged two manned Block I flights on Saturn IBs (AS-204 and AS-205) to check out the spacecraft, conduct tests and evaluate their performance and handling qualities. The first would be designated Apollo 1 and launch on February 21, 1967, initially assigned to veteran astronauts Gus Grissom and Ed White and rookie Donn Eisele on a flight lasting up to ten days in space, that crew selection having been announced in January 1966. When Eisele dislocated his shoulder during training he was replaced by Roger Chaffee, with Jim McDivitt, David Scott and rookie Russell Schweickart as the back-up crew.

On September 29, 1966, the crew for the second flight was announced, with Wally Schirra, Eisele and Walt Cunningham assigned to a repeat mission, but with very different tasks. Further analysis of assignments led to cancellation of AS-205 in December 1966 as a prudent move to reduce the number of missions overall and claw back some of the delays by eliminating unnecessary flights. AS-206 was scheduled as a test of the first Lunar Module (LM) in Earth orbit.

This would be followed by AS-207/AS-208 in August 1967, the launch of the second LM first quickly followed by the first of the Apollo Block II spacecraft, which would dock with it, two astronauts moving inside and flying it around

ABOVE • Production of the Saturn IB with its eight first-stage engines, the launch vehicle that enabled early Apollo flights and which would support the later Skylab programme. (NASA)

LEFT • Robert Gilruth managed the Manned Spacecraft Center responsible for flight operations development, planning and missions. (NASA)

before rejoining the third astronaut in Apollo for return to Earth. When the original AS-205 was cancelled, that dual mission was re-designated AS-205/AS-208, with McDivitt, Scott and Schweickart, the original back-up crew for the first manned Apollo flight, reassigned as its crew with Schirra, Eisele and Cunningham as their back-up.

Delays affected development of the Saturn V and the first unmanned test launch was not expected before November 1967. A second unmanned test would follow and it was now hoped that the third manned Apollo flight would be assigned to the third Saturn V launch, flying probably no earlier than mid-1968. But these schedules were prone to constant flux, with two launch vehicles and two different spacecraft all in various stages of preparation for flight. Whether it could all be brought together as desired would depend on a very special brand of engineer and manager.

A Breed Apart

A veteran of the NACA days since 1937, Robert Gilruth had maintained tireless support for satellites and spacecraft long before Sputnik changed everything and now ran the Manned Spacecraft Center with warmth, enthusiasm and a commanding grip on the needs of the facility and its people. It was the Kennedy Moon goal challenge that convinced Gilruth that Apollo would never be possible until an interim spacecraft had provided the means to test all the new processes and procedures required for that job. He would retire in 1972.

In Mission Control, Christopher Kraft developed and defined the way flights would be managed and controlled, his uncompromising and frequently brusque approach essential when working with astronauts displaying an abundance of ego and self-belief, men frequently resistant to orders and instructions. Kraft had joined the NACA in 1944 and was NASA's first flight director at Cape Canaveral, taking the lead in designing the Mission Operations Control Room and the several 'trenches', rows of consoles facing large wall displays keeping controllers aware of every part of a mission.

It was Kraft who produced a hardened generation of flight directors seared into the tough decisions they would have to make in both good and bad days, before moving to become director of Flight Crew Operations where he had a bigger role in the overall strategy of the manned programmes during the Apollo years and throughout the development of the Shuttle, until his retirement in 1982.

Key to Apollo hardware development, Joseph Shea was a systems engineer who joined NASA in 1961 as deputy director at the Office of Manned Space Flight under D Brainerd Holmes, who sent Shea off to the Langley facility to find out about the competing mission modes for lunar landings, quickly becoming an early convert to Lunar Orbit Rendezvous. By the end of 1963, Shea was manager of the Apollo Spacecraft Program Office, which put him in charge of design and assembly of both the Command and Service Modules and the Lunar Module.

Before taking up that position, Shea had formed a special review board to bring together the different operating modes of the separate NASA centres, each vying for autonomy and becoming self-protective in the process. In doing this he made enemies at a managerial level among disparate groups who recognised him as a brilliant engineer. But Shea was opposed to the independence sought by various facilities and at variance with von Braun's group who managed through consensual agreement rather than the centralised, top-down structure that HQ tried to impose.

Kraft's team at Houston were audibly averse to Shea's approach and found disagreement with his methods, frequently citing a chafing frustration over his management approach. There was good reason for Shea's abrasive frustration. With responsibility for ensuring good product delivery and quality control, Shea was shocked at what he found during visits to several companies with prime contracts on Apollo systems, claiming poor standards at North American Aviation building the Apollo spacecraft. While the contractors complained about the number of NASA-imposed changes to specifications and requirements, the situation had been smouldering for more than a year as the time approached for Apollo flights to begin.

Since the management changes in late 1963, NASA had been fighting inadequacies it found in several Apollo contractors. These had been reported through a variety of channels to middle managers and to some senior executives at the agency. One of those informants was Thomas Baron, a quality control inspector with North American Aviation at the Kennedy Space Center from September 1965 until

November 1966, when he took a leave of absence, before being dismissed on January 5, 1967.

There was some good reason for this as Baron had first reported to friends and colleagues his concerns over poor quality control before leaking information to the press. In 1966, Baron issued a 55-page report criticising the company for lack of proper work records, poor training and equipment, bad co-ordination between departments and a list of dangerous practices allegations. He concluded: "I am afraid the public had the wrong image in their minds when they think of project Apollo. They probably believe that everyone knows exactly what they are doing at all times. They probably also believe that the work out here at the launch complexes is done on a routine manner. They are wrong. I have been told by two managers that we are still in research and development stages even if we are going to send up a manned spacecraft. This, I firmly believe is the wrong approach to the project. Do they really know where all the parts and materials come from?"

Earlier, during a review conducted between November 22 and December 6, 1965, Lt Gen Sam Phillips had visited North American to see for himself the status of work on the S-I second stage for Saturn V and the Command and Service Modules for Apollo. Numerous concerns about lack of performance and poor quality in hardware arriving at the Cape had arrived at Phillips' desk earlier in the year, which prompted this inspection where he reportedly found serious deficiencies and a disorganised managerial structure.

In what has come to be known infamously as 'The Phillips Report', he cited a long list of inadequacies in costings, technical performance, scheduling, manufacturing standards and quality control, his covering letter to Lee Atwood, president of North American, dated December 19, 1965, asserting: "Even with due consideration of hopeful signs, I could not find a substantive basis for confidence in future performance."

The message was driven home in a second letter written the same day by his boss George Mueller when he reminded Atwood that: "In my letter of October 27, 1965, I conveyed to you the seriousness with which I viewed the state of affairs...at your Space and Information Systems Division. Phillips' report has not only corroborated my concern, but has convinced me beyond doubt that the situation at S&ID requires positive and substantive actions immediately in order to meet the national objectives of the Apollo Program...I can see no way of improving future performance, and meeting commitments...if we are to achieve the national objectives of Apollo, except to improve the management and technical competence of your Space and Information systems Division."

In just over two years, after saving the Kennedy goal from a managerial implosion through inadequate performance within the agency, the Apollo programme was again in crisis, this time one veiled from public scrutiny and even kept from NASA boss James Webb, who would only learn of Baron and the Phillips Report in hearings held after the tragic unravelling of those concerns brought NASA a catastrophe that would touch the lives of astronauts and almost all who were involved in the programme.

"Fire in the Spacecraft"

With the first manned Apollo flight scheduled for February 21, 1967, a series of countdown tests began on January 25, but communications were bad, the progress was slow and the back-up commander Wally Schirra suggested that Joseph Shea should accompany the crew in the spacecraft to see the problems for himself. That would have required extensive changes to the way the test was conducted and would not have contributed anything that could not be observed through the consoles or the audio links.

The culmination of this part of the simulated countdown was held on January 27, which was to end with an emergency egress. That required the crew to rapidly open the hatch and 'escape', as they would need to do, should they have to depart the spacecraft in a hurry. The Block I hatch was an unnecessarily complicated design incorporating three sections. It would take 90 seconds to get them open, believed

ABOVE • Designed by the crew, the Apollo 1 mission patch was professionally prepared by North American Aviation's Allen Stevens. (NASA)

LEFT • A photograph from the official report showing the poor quality workmanship that led to repeated problems encountered during checkout and rehearsals. (NASA)

ABOVE • *Senior NASA managers during Congressional hearings into the Apollo fire. From left: Robert Seamans, James Webb, George Mueller and Sam Phillips. (NASA)*

The test on February 27 was known as a 'plugs-out' event, in which the spacecraft itself would go on internal power in the way it would prior to launch. The first man in was Gus Grissom, who entered the spacecraft at 1pm local time, feet first to the centre couch before sliding across to the one on the left. Roger Chaffee was next, sliding across to the right couch followed by Ed White sliding on his back to the centre couch where they were strapped in securely as they would be for flight. Grissom sensed a bad odour coming into his oxygen supply, but a sample cleared the countdown to proceed.

The procedure to close and lock the hatches began at 2.45pm local time and the spacecraft was filled with pure oxygen and pressurised 2psi (14kPa) higher than local atmospheric pressure, so any leaks would flow out and not allow the mixed oxygen/nitrogen Florida atmosphere to leak in. For the next few hours the crew proceeded with checklists and communications that were scratchy and inaudible for a lot of the time. In one grumbling aside, Grissom asked how they were expected to get to the Moon when they were unable to talk to each other.

With intermittent and frequently inaudible sounds, the first indication of a problem was noted at 6.30.21pm when biomedical data from White indicated movement inside the spacecraft, followed by further activity until the first cries were heard from Grissom at 6.31.05: "Fire! We've got a fire in the cockpit!" Further cries. "Fire in the spacecraft" was heard, which had started down the left side of the spacecraft racing across flammable material, Velcro patches, netting and combustible material, as White tried desperately to open the inner hatch. All communication from the crew ended 15 seconds after the first report of a fire, dense carbon monoxide and noxious gases flooding into their suits and face area behind locked visors.

The fire went through three distinct phases, the first when it took hold and spread from left to right over

to be sufficient for emergencies. It was impossible to open in orbit unless the spacecraft was first depressurised to equal the outside vacuum; the pressure of the oxygen environment at 5.5psi (37.92kPa) would hold it firm as a 'plug', pressing outward against the recesses in the frame.

This was the only manned flight for which NASA intended to use the triple hatch. For subsequent Block II flights where a spacewalk could be performed if necessary, a new unified hatch integrating inner and middle hatches with 15 latches had already been adopted, hinged on one side and opened by the stroke of a ratchet in three seconds. In the event of a pad emergency, tests showed that all three astronauts could be out of the spacecraft within 30 seconds. But it was not fitted to Block I spacecraft.

RIGHT • *The official photograph of the Apollo 1 spacecraft as viewed through the crew entry hatch and after the removal of the bodies. (NASA)*

and across the top of the three couches, the second when the pressure built up rapidly to about 29psi (200kPa), twice atmospheric pressure, and the hull of the spacecraft split at bottom right at 6.31.19.5pm. Rushing to find a way out, drawing flames up and over the couches and down through the split between the Command Module and the Service Module, the fire exited with a roaring sound.

The third phase spread fire and dense smoke out around the spacecraft into the area surrounding it in an enclosure on top of the rocket known as the White Room. This eruption had the frightening potential of igniting the Launch Escape Rocket attached to the lattice tower above the Command Module fully fuelled with solid propellant and needing only an intense flame to ignite it, with the potential of taking Apollo and all technicians and pad crew in the White Room with it. Fortunately, the fire from the spacecraft damped itself out and hand-held extinguishers dealt with the secondary flames.

Autopsies revealed that the crew died of asphyxiation, also suffering burns that physicians testified would not have killed them. It had been so very quick due to the rate at which the fire had spread in the pure oxygen environment, a design feature that would bring questions about the wisdom of not having a mixed oxygen/nitrogen atmosphere. And questions would be asked about the 70lb (32g) of combustible material inside the pressurised crew compartment.

During Congressional hearings, Webb heard for the first time about the enduring concerns from which he had been shielded and Baron was brought to testify on April 21, 1967, but further investigation was denied. Six days after testifying, Baron, his wife and his step-daughter were killed when a train collided with their car.

Joseph Shea was deeply affected by the fire disaster and held himself personally responsible for events that contributed, suffering deep psychological anguish as a result of this, pressure imposed by the intensely personal association anyone working with or for NASA during this period felt for the programme and its objectives. Shea's psychiatrist wrote that in his view the man was "so intelligent" that he was trapped by his own brilliance.

Everyone was traumatised. Senior personnel from Houston would fly to meetings in Washington DC and, with time to think, break into fits of sobbing during their cross-country flight. Robert Seamans and Chris Kraft have each written extensively on the psychological breakdowns experienced by many people after the fire, Shea himself lapsing into incoherent ramblings during meetings, others resorting to barbiturates and alcohol.

On August 1, 1967, Shea left NASA and in 1990 became professor of aeronautics at MIT school of engineering. Forever changed and frequently lost in rambling thought and self-recrimination, he kept a picture on his wall given to him shortly before the fire by the Apollo 1 crew. Seated together, heads bowed and their hands folded as in prayer, it carried the inscription: "It isn't that we don't trust you Joe, but this time we've decided to go over your head." He never recovered from the effects of that message, sent in humour but with chilling poignancy.

MAN ON THE MOON

Resolved to recover quickly from the disastrous fire, NASA performs final tests and heads for the lunar surface

RIGHT • Apollo 4, the first Saturn V being readied for launch in November 1967 with the yellow inverted V-shaped blast deflector before being moved into position. (NASA)

Less than two months after the Apollo fire, on April 23, 1967, the Soviet cosmonaut Vladimir Komarov lost his life returning from orbit on Russia's first manned flight of a new spacecraft. Rushed into conducting manned flights before it was ready, like Apollo it suffered from hubris and haste. For the first time since the space programme began, so very different in their ideologies, the two competing countries shared grief and exchanged condolences.

The Apollo fire changed everything, not just within the Apollo programme but throughout NASA. The review board found scuffed wires, electrical conduits to systems boxes subsequently redundant to purpose were dead-ended rather than physically removed, running the risk of an arc. They found tools jammed between wire bundles and closeout panels pressed against electrical wiring, with an abundance of flammable materials.

Tragic as it was, the Apollo 1 fire increased safety by eliminating all combustible materials, even the flight plans carried on board now being flame-proof. Under rigorous tests, fires were tested under laboratory conditions and for pre-launch operations it was decided to fill the spacecraft with a mixed-gas atmosphere of nitrogen and oxygen, pure oxygen gradually replacing that on the way into orbit. During this phase the astronauts would be breathing pure oxygen in their suits.

On November 6, 1967, Robert Gilruth approved a revised launch schedule including the first test of the mighty Saturn V within the next few days, six flights in 1968 and five in 1969, the maximum pace in which spacecraft and Saturn vehicles could be prepared and assembled for launch. It helped that Apollo had a DX rating, which gave it exclusive access to materials and resources and that leveraged pressure against the unions where calls for a strike could bring the attention of the Justice Department. The most immediate challenge was to get the colossal Saturn V up and flying.

Construction of the Kennedy Space Center had been a multi-shift work commitment erecting the massive Vehicle Assembly Building (VAB) where the rocket and spacecraft would be assembled, the Crawler Transporter and the Mobile Launch Platforms that would carry the stack to Launch Complex pads A and B where it would be launched, all coming together simultaneously. The first visible spectacle of this massive rocket had been on May 25, 1966, when a full-size facilities checkout vehicle designated SA-500F was stacked in the VAB and moved out to the launch pad along the specially built crawlerway.

BELOW • The Earth rising above the limb of the Moon as viewed by the crew and photographed by Bill Anders on Christmas Eve, 1968. (NASA)

The stack was rolled to LC-39A on August 26, 1967. Interest in this launch was heightened by the sheer size of this rocket, weighing at launch more than a US Navy destroyer and predicted to produce a louder noise than any other event created by humans, apart from a nuclear explosion. More than a thousand media representatives from around the world gathered at Cape Canaveral with live TV covering the historic event.

At 7am local time, November 9, 1967, the five first-stage engines of the Saturn V ignited and the vehicle lifted off and cleared the launch tower, at which point control of the mission switched from the Launch Control Center to the Manned Spacecraft Center in Houston. It took 16 seconds for the sound waves to reach the area where invited visitors were located and the thunderous noise was greater than had been anticipated, noted *CBS* TV channel anchorman Walter Cronkite reporting the spectacle as the ceiling in his booth began to collapse and the windows threatened to cave in, production staff holding it all up with their hands.

Still attached to the Saturn V third stage, the Apollo spacecraft remained in low Earth orbit for two revolutions before the S-IVB was reignited for the first time to push the assembly to a maximum altitude of 10,700 miles (17,218km), after which the two separated leaving Apollo to fire its main engine to push the spacecraft further to a maximum altitude of 11,242 miles (18,092km). That engine fired again on the descending leg to push the speed of the spacecraft to 24,980mph (40,193km/h) by the time it re-entered the atmosphere, followed by splashdown only 9.9 miles (16km) from the target spot northwest of Midway Island in the Pacific Ocean, eight hours 37 minutes after launch.

The successful flight of Apollo 4 brought reassurance, elation and renewed confidence in the ability of the agency to get men to the Moon within two years. In comparison with the mood after the Apollo fire, employees at NASA and its contractors had cause for celebration. Numbering around 450 people, the launch control team at the Kennedy Space Center had done well, as had flight controllers in the Mission Operations Control Room in Houston. There would be need for a second unmanned Saturn V flight to satisfy some new engineering objectives, but the overriding question now concerned the Lunar Module, troublesome in its development and very late in delivering flight-rated hardware.

The first Lunar Module (LM-1), had been delivered to the Cape by air on June 23, 1967, but some deficiencies delayed the flight until January 22, 1968, launched by the Saturn IB (AS-204) repurposed from the Apollo fire, which had left it unscathed. Designed only to operate in the vacuum of space, LM-1 could not be used again and eventually the two stages burned up in the atmosphere. Although the flight had technical difficulties, overall it was a success, clearing the way for another LM, together with a manned Apollo spacecraft launched on a Saturn V, flown around in Earth orbit for final tests.

Mutiny in Orbit

NASA launched the second unmanned Saturn V on April 4, 1968, different from Apollo 4 in that it had an active emergency detection system. Essentially a repeat of that previous flight, Apollo 6 tested the Apollo spacecraft in other ways, but the mission came close to failure when two engines on the second stage shut down due to unexpected oscillations (known as the 'pogo' effect, after the jumping stick) in the rocket and two misconnected wires. The main objectives were achieved when the Apollo spacecraft itself reached the high altitude planned, after the third stage engine failed to fire.

ABOVE • The first Lunar Module was launched in January 1968 on the Saturn IB, repurposed after the Apollo fire that took the lives of Grissom, White and Chaffee. (NASA)

Apollo 6 was less than a total success and NASA admitted it was a partial failure, but lessons had been learned and the problems it encountered were fixable, giving the Saturn V clearance to carry astronauts on the next flight scheduled to take place after the first manned Apollo mission, launched on a smaller Saturn IB. Its veteran commander Wally Schirra had never really wanted a third spaceflight and the changes that resulted from a re-scheduling of his original Apollo flight into a repeat of Apollo 1 had annoyed him. But now it was different; after the fire it would be his crew who opened the door to the Moon, for if it were not a success it would upend succeeding missions and delay the landing attempt, which, as it was would be a close call on time.

It had been nearly two years since the last Gemini flight had carried US astronauts into space and when lift-off occurred on October 11, 1968, there was a sense of euphoria and expectation. But it failed to remain that way and will be remembered as the mission that saw the first in-space mutiny against increasingly ambitious flight control teams, which loaded extra tasks, adding flight plan details that had previously not been cleared with the crew. As the mission progressed, additional tests — conjured up by eager flight controllers trying new ways of operating systems — proved unworkable and ill-advised, bringing furious reactions from the crew.

It made matters worse that Schirra came down with a cold and chafed further at the imposition of TV schedules

LEFT • The Apollo 7 crew of Wally Schirra (centre), Donn Eisele (left) and Walter Cunningham. (NASA)

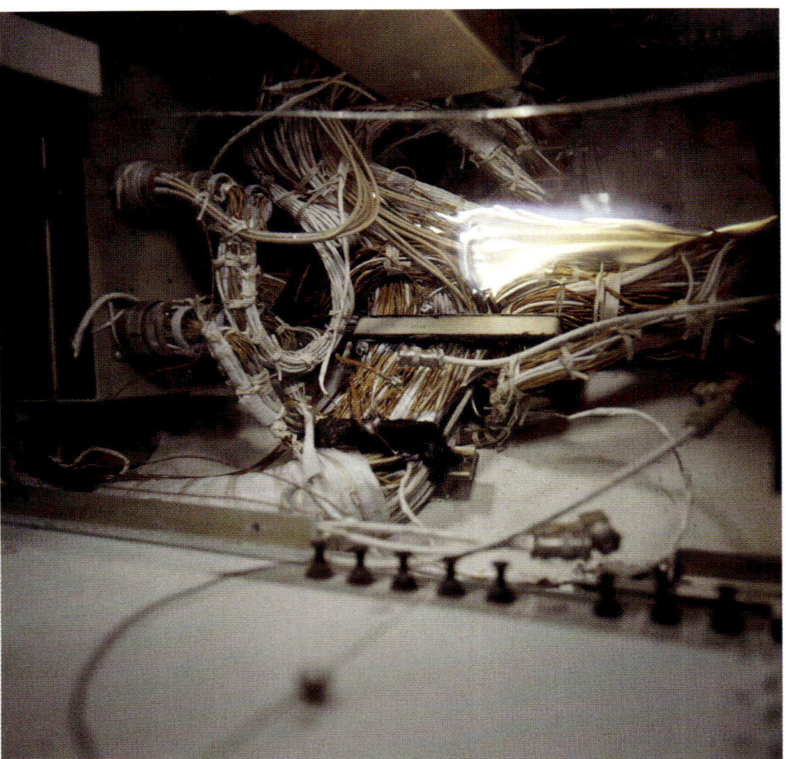

CIA indicating an intent to pre-empt the Americans with a major propaganda coup. Two months before the flight of Apollo 7, on August 9, 1968, Apollo programme manager George Low proposed an alternative strategy to Manned Spacecraft Center boss Bob Gilruth, flight director Chris Krafft and "Deke" Slayton, chief of flight crew operations, one which would put three astronauts around the Moon before Christmas.

Low's idea was to flip the mission objectives of the next two Saturn V/Apollo flights, fly the Apollo spacecraft on its own ahead of the combined flight of an Apollo/Lunar Module combination and send it to the Moon where it would remain in orbit for ten revolutions before returning home. The four men met with chief architect of the rocket programme Wernher von Braun, Kennedy Space Center director Kurt Debus and NASA Apollo Program director Sam Phillips to discuss the idea, receiving approval for what was by any measure an audacious idea with high risk.

It was a plan that would maintain momentum in the programme and, if successful, beat the Russians to the first manned circumlunar flight. When approached about the idea, NASA boss Jim Webb was reluctant and questioned whether the consequences of failure, so painfully experienced with the Apollo fire, were worth it for what he interpreted as a political objective. However, hearing virtually unanimous approval from his senior executives, he acquiesced to the majority view.

But it could only happen if the Apollo 7 mission were a success and approval would await the outcome of that mission, adding further tension to the Schirra crew when they successfully completed a full checkout on that mission. Asked if he wanted to fly the Moon mission as Apollo 8, McDivitt declined, citing the amount of time his team had already spent preparing for his own mission with the Apollo spacecraft and the Lunar Module. Slayton offered it to Frank Borman, James Lovell and William Anders, the crew

added to those already in the flight plan and burdening the crew amidst already complex scheduled activities, some of which included critical engine burns. It mattered not to Schirra that NASA wanted live prime-time TV broadcasts — one transmission was flatly turned down by the crew as being an imposition too far. With the increasingly complex mission envelopes, a discord with Mission Control was easy to build as tensions in space ran counter to elation from enthusiastic controllers on the ground.

When Apollo 7 splashed down after ten days, 20 hours and nine minutes, it brought relief to mission managers and senior NASA leadership... but in the Mission Operations Control Room it raised the spectre of recriminations. There had been one last revolt. Full of a head cold passed to fellow astronaut Donn Eisele, Schirra claimed commander's prerogative and, despite strict orders, refused to wear a helmet for re-entry, on the basis that with it on he could not clear his congested ear drums. Only over time did the full ramifications of these altercations emerge and never again would any member of this crew be selected for another flight.

Completing what NASA judged to be a "101% success", the flight of Apollo 7 was critical to the future of the Apollo programme and brought renewed optimism. The next sequence should have seen Apollo 8 fly LM-3 (LM-2 was overweight, assigned only if a second unmanned flight was deemed necessary) with James McDivitt, David Scott and "Rusty" Schweickart as the crew on the first manned Saturn V flight.

But LM-3 would not be ready before early 1969 and there were strong signs that the Russians were desperately trying to fly cosmonauts on a slingshot around the Moon and back before the end of 1968. For some time they had been testing a derivative of the Soyuz spacecraft in which Vladimir Komarov had been killed in April 1967, the government having already approved a circumlunar mission two months earlier to be conducted in June 1967.

During preparations for the first manned Apollo 7 flight, in mid-1968 this intelligence information was shared by the

originally assigned to fly their mission as a deep-space checkout of the two spacecraft, who accepted.

Christmas Around the Moon

The possibility that Russia might attempt a manned circumlunar flight ahead of NASA grew after Zond 5 was launched on September 14. A version of the Soyuz 7K-L1 adapted for a manned flight around the Moon, on this test flight the unmanned Zond carried biological samples to within 1,211 miles (1,950km) of the lunar surface before returning almost seven days later. It was followed by Zond 6 on November 10, again carrying biological samples but the cabin depressurised prior to re-entry and crashed when the parachutes failed. Still, the Russians hoped to send cosmonauts around the Moon in December, ahead of Apollo 8.

With more than 1,000 press reporters watching alongside several hundred invited guests, the first manned flight of the Saturn V began at 7.51am local time on December 21, 1968, a low Earth orbit being achieved almost 12 minutes after lift-off. After all relevant checks, at two hours 27 minutes Mission Control capsule communicator (or CapCom) Mike Collins gave the command to re-ignite the S-IVB third stage for Trans-Lunar Injection (TLI), which on Apollo 6 had failed to ignite. He spoke in a calm and controlled voice: "Apollo 8 you are go for TLI."

The third stage of the Saturn V fired for five minutes eight seconds, increasing speed from about 17,431mph (28,046km/h) to 24,225mph (38,978km/h), before the Apollo spacecraft pulled free. Quickly passing through the Van Allen belts, receiving radiation doses well within safe limits about an hour after leaving Earth orbit the crew were at such a distance that they became the first humans to see the whole Earth suspended like a blue marble against the blackness of space. Like all tourists, they took a picture.

On the way to the Moon, the crew used a small black-and-white TV camera to show life on Apollo and

ABOVE • A key purpose of Apollo 7 was the test of essential engineering elements, including the three fuel cells, the only way of producing a sustainable supply of electrical power. (NASA)

LEFT • Walt Cunningham using his special Fisher zero-gravity pens to make notes during the Apollo 7 mission. (NASA)

at selected places in the outbound leg, mid-course correction opportunities were built in, the first taking place 11 hours into the flight with a two-second burn of the main engine aiming precisely for an altitude of 74.8 miles (120.3km) above the lunar surface. A seminal moment came at 55 hours 40 minutes at a distance of 38,759 miles (62,377km) from the Moon when their speed had slowed to a mere 2,720mph (4,377km/h) and they left the gravitational influence of the Earth, now pulled ever faster by the Moon.

At 68 hours 59 minutes after lift-off, Apollo 8 slipped behind the Moon and for 33 minutes the crew were completely alone on the far side. The global audience was gripped, emotionally moved by the awe and magnitude of what had been accomplished. The crew would say that they first became aware of how close they were to the Moon when suddenly all the stars disappeared and they became aware of a massive object edging ever closer and filling every window.

As the spacecraft speeded up under the pull of lunar gravity, the crew prepared for Lunar Orbit Insertion (LOI), a burn of four minutes seven seconds, reducing speed from 5,720mph (9,203km/h) to a mere 3,721mph (5,987km/h). If it burned too long they would trim off too much speed and crash into the surface; too short and their course would place them on a long looping path from which they could never return home. However, it was perfect, placing the spacecraft in an elliptical path, circularised two orbits later at around 69 miles (111km) above the surface, each orbit taking about two hours.

It was the day before Christmas Eve and the crew took it in turns to read verses from the first chapter of the book of Genesis, beginning with Anders and ending with Borman who finished by saying, "...from the crew of Apollo 8, we close with goodnight, good luck, a merry Christmas and God bless all of you, all of you on the good Earth". This was heard by an estimated 800 million people around the world, many of whom fell silent, pausing in their own way to reflect on the momentous events they had witnessed.

Just 20 hours 11 minutes after slipping into lunar orbit, the crew of Apollo 8 fired the main engine again for three minutes 24 seconds on the far side of the Moon, increasing speed to 6,028mph (9,700km/h), with reassuring words for children everywhere: "Please be informed there is a Santa Claus!" They were coming home and on Earth it was Christmas Eve. Only one course correction was necessary before re-entry and splashdown in the Pacific Ocean on December 27 after a flight lasting six days three hours.

Earth Tests and a Moon Flight

Crew training for what would be Apollo 9 had begun just before the Apollo fire, with McDivitt, Scott and Schweickart committed to the first flight of both the Apollo spacecraft and the Lunar Module in addition to the only checkout of the Moonwalker's backpack before the scheduled Moon landing flight.

Launch occurred on February 28, 1969, several days later than planned as the crew recovered from head colds. Because two spacecraft would be operating in space at the same time, Apollo would be referred to as *Gumdrop*, due

to its blue coloured plastic shipment wrapping, while the Lunar Module was named *Spider* due to its gangly legs. The backpack Schweickart would test gave him the callsign 'Red Rover', alluding to his hair colour.

At launch, *Gumdrop* weighed 59,000lb (26,762kg) and *Spider* grossed 32,132lb (14,575kg), the heaviest load to date for a Saturn V flight. Within a few hours of reaching orbit, *Gumdrop* separated, turned around and docked with the top of *Spider*, remotely disconnecting it from its adapter on top of the S-IVB stage. For two days the crew checked out both vehicles, fired the main engine on *Gumdrop* several times and then fired *Spider's* descent engine for six minutes 12 seconds, which on a later mission would be used to land on the Moon.

six hours, McDivitt and Schweickart were on their own in *Spider*, moving up to 115 miles (185km) away before separating the two stages, firing the ascent engine and docking again with *Gumdrop*. After the ascent stage of *Spider* separated from *Gumdrop*, its engine was fired to depletion. The last three of eight main engine burns completed the flight prior to splashdown after ten days one hour, the mission receiving high marks for success and efficiency.

Launched on May 18, 1969, Apollo 10 was the final dress rehearsal for the Moon landing, following closely the procedures short of landing on the surface. The Apollo spacecraft was nicknamed *Charlie Brown* and the Lunar Module was known as *Snoopy*. After reaching lunar orbit, astronauts Thomas Stafford and Eugene Cernan undocked from *Charlie Brown*, leaving John Young in the Command Module for eight hours of activity demonstrating how the Lunar Module would begin the descent phase before climbing back up to dock with *Gumdrop*.

This second flight to the Moon completed 31 orbits and, in a flight lasting eight days three minutes, Apollo 10 had demonstrated the last elements in a complex web of events crucial to every Moon landing, operating the Lunar Module in the environment for which it was designed and providing the crew with navigational tasks and operating experience with the guidance equipment. But it required a few weeks of data analysis to grant approval for Apollo 11 to make a landing attempt.

ABOVE • The crew for the Apollo 9 Earth orbit test of both the Apollo spacecraft and the Lunar Module, consisting of (from left) Jim McDivitt, Dave Scott and Russell Schweickart. (NASA)

BELOW • The first astronauts to return from the vicinity of the Moon, Borman (left), Anders and Lovell express their excitement immediately after recovery to the deck of the carrier Essex. *(NASA)*

On the fourth day, Schweickart was to have conducted a spacewalk from *Spider* across to *Gumdrop*. Wearing the Personal Life Support Systems (PLSS) backpack, he would demonstrate how astronauts could move between vehicles if internal access between hatches was unusable. But Schweickart suffered from bouts of space-sickness and the full extravehicular activity (EVA) was amended so that he would merely stand on the platform outside the front hatch of *Spider* while Scott emerged from a depressurised *Gumdrop* to show that this process was feasible.

The fifth day was spent demonstrating that the Lunar Module could be flown manned and perform essential manoeuvres vital for a lunar landing. For more than

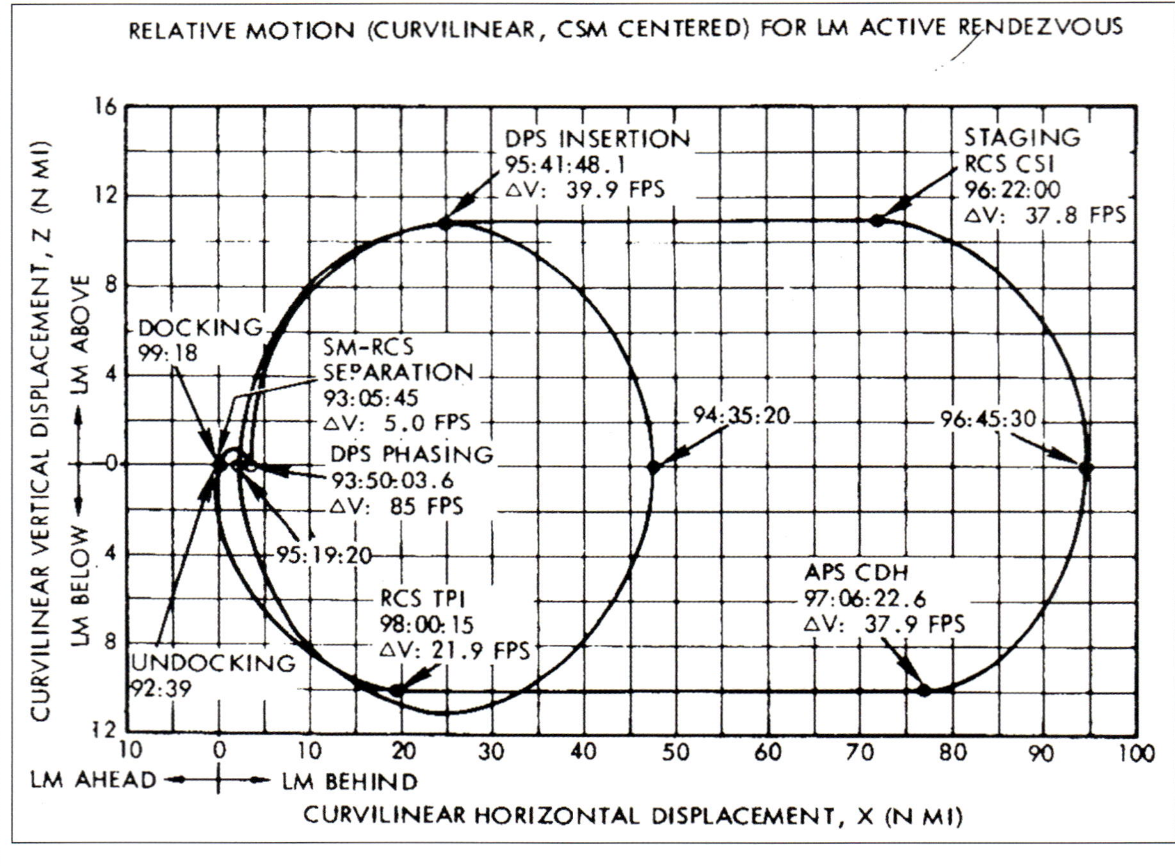

Preparation for the flight of Apollo 11 included public relations requirements with TV viewers around the world having access to live pictures in a way previous generations could never have imagined. A senior public affairs officer, Julian Scheer chose the callsign for the Apollo spacecraft from Jules Verne's mythical spaceship: *Columbia*; representing the national bird of America, the Lunar Module would be called *Eagle*. The emblem for the mission displayed an olive branch in an eagle's talons to represent the message of peace, and on a special plaque were the names of the astronauts with the words 'We Came in Peace for all Mankind'.

The hardware for Apollo 11 began arriving in early January 1969 and by the end of the following month it was at the Kennedy Space Center, with rollout to LC-39A on May 20. Initially, the crew for this flight comprised Neil Armstrong, Jim Lovell and Buzz Aldrin, but when Mike Collins had to have surgery bumping him from Apollo 8, Lovell had stood in and Collins was reassigned to Apollo 11. The final choice of crew members gave Armstrong great responsibility and the decision was made at the end of December 1968 in a discussion he had with Deke Slayton, who was in charge of crew selection.

Much had changed at NASA since Slayton had been selected as a Mercury astronaut ten years before and formalities over crew selection went right to the top, his recommendation being passed to senior management for approval. Mission commanders had the pick of candidates, but each prospective crew member had skill assignments and personality traits that figured in the decision, too. There was no certainty that Apollo 11 would achieve the first landing, but that possibility began to factor in to who was assigned for which slot.

Senior managers became involved with the choice of who would be the first man to walk on the lunar surface. In Gemini missions and on Apollo 9, the mission commander remained with his spacecraft and it had been assumed that the Lunar Module pilot would be the first man to walk on the surface. Hearing that the draft flight plan envisaged Armstrong going out first, Aldrin unsuccessfully lobbied other astronauts to support his case for being first, claiming that this would provide precedence for them, too.

There were some who questioned whether Aldrin was appropriate for that role. Armstrong was considered a natural choice, some said because he had been a civilian test pilot, while others would claim that it was because of the relative positions they occupied in the limited space of the Lunar Module that procedures for getting out favoured the mission commander first. Never one to play politics, Armstrong considered Aldrin a good team player, competent for his role on board as 'flight engineer'. Armstrong himself was the consummate engineer with an instinctive awareness of the capabilities and the limitations of machines.

If Aldrin were the scientist and Armstrong the engineer, Mike Collins was the ideal man to take charge of the Apollo spacecraft during the almost 34 hours he would be alone in *Columbia* while his crewmates went to the surface in *Eagle*. Deeply thoughtful and highly articulate, the slow-speaking Collins, precise with words and diction, could assimilate, assess, conclude and deploy decisions he would have to make alone.

After the flight, some would ask Collins whether he felt lonely, out of contact on the far side of the Moon for successive orbits, but he took apparent pride in asserting that "not since Adam has any human known such solitude", while clarifying that he had no such feeling on loneliness, only "awareness, anticipation, satisfaction, confidence, almost exultation".

"The Eagle Has Landed"

As launch day dawned, a million people were within sight and earshot of the event that would place the first humans on the surface of another world. It had brought the great and the good, the rich and the poor. Rev Hosea Williams led a host of the nation's poor from southern states converging on the Cape in wagons pulled by mules, asserting they wanted to get as "close as possible" to the launch and that they were "not against the space shot".

Spiritual successor to Martin Luther King, the Rev Ralph Abernathy led 25 more poor families to the Kennedy Space Center where NASA boss Tom Paine, successor to James Webb, met them and flung open the gate, inviting them in, declaring that "it will be a lot harder to solve the problems of hunger and poverty than it is to send men to the Moon", adding that if it were possible to solve those problems by cancelling the flight "we would not push that button".

Apollo 11 was launched on July 16, 1969, lift-off from LC-39A occurring at 9.32am local time. The three stages placed *Columbia* and *Eagle* in Earth orbit followed on the second revolution by a second burn of the S-IVB stage to send them on their way to the Moon. Preceded by the Apollo 10 pathfinder mission, all the steps were repeated with only minor changes and the two docked vehicles entered orbit with a burn of *Columbia*'s main engine just before 75 hours 50 minutes, followed by circularisation of that path two revolutions later.

A sleep session for all three crew preceded undocking of *Eagle* at 100 hours 12 minutes, just before they reappeared from the far side of the Moon. In Houston, it was 12.44pm on Sunday, July 20. To land, Armstrong and Aldrin would fire the descent engine for 30 seconds at 101 hours 36 minutes and drop down to within about 9.5 miles (15.2km) of the lunar surface, at which point they would be 425 miles (684km) up range of the planned touchdown spot. Had no further manoeuvre been performed, *Eagle* would have repeated this elliptical path, dropping down to that distance from the Moon on each successive path.

However, at 102 hours 33 minutes, with systems having checked out and moving now at a speed of 3,793mph (6,103km/h), *Eagle* began powered descent by firing the descent engine again. It would not be shut down before it reached the surface. For 12 minutes 35 seconds, standing in front of the spacecraft's left window, Armstrong piloted *Eagle* through various stages of descent, Aldrin alongside and only occasionally glancing through the window, his eyes glued to the instrument displays providing callouts to Armstrong.

Less than half way through the descent, radar data flooding into *Eagle's* computer caused a software overload and triggered 1201 and 1202 alarms simultaneously observed in Mission Control. One of the great achievements of the Apollo programme had been the development of guidance and navigation equipment and parallel evolution of advanced software and computer code. NASA had been an early beneficiary of introducing women as 'computers' with mathematical skills, a key player in Apollo being Margaret Hamilton, who worked at the MIT Instrumentation Laboratory designing and building the Apollo guidance computer, slightly different versions being used in both spacecraft.

Hamilton designed and developed many aspects of this equipment, the software they carried and the language they used. Her contribution was crucial to the entire lunar landing effort. As a result of this and recognising that the computer alarms were not terminal, the Mission Control guidance officer Steve Bales was assured by computer engineer Jack Garman that it was an overload problem, which has subsequently been attributed to computer error, or the fault of the crew in setting up an incorrect switch configuration.

Neither is true. A mismatch in the hardware configuration meant that the rendezvous radar was switched on in case it was needed for aborting the descent and firing the ascent engine to get back to *Columbia*. With the active landing radar feeding height and velocity information at the same time, a mismatch caused the software to issue an advisory in the form of a warning rather than shut down the system entirely, or as Margaret Hamilton recalled: "The result was that the computer was being asked to perform all of its normal functions for landing while receiving an extra load of spurious data which used up 15% of its time. The computer (or rather the software in it) was smart enough to recognise that it was being asked to perform more tasks than it should be performing.

"It then sent out an alarm, which meant to the astronaut, 'I'm overloaded with more tasks than I should be doing at this time and I'm going to keep only the more important tasks, ie, the ones needed for landing...' To blame the computer for the Apollo 11 problem is like blaming the person who spots a fire and calls the fire department."

The work that Hamilton and her colleagues had done over preceding years saved the mission and the crew continued with their descent. As he began to hover above the surface, slowly moving direction to avoid boulders and craters, Armstrong received callouts from Aldrin continuously feeding information on a balance between parameters controlled by *Eagle's* computerised guidance programme and manual inputs to avoid potential hazards on the surface visible through the windows.

A Giant Leap for Mankind

At 102 hours 45 minutes into the mission, at 3.18pm local time in Houston on Sunday July 20, *Eagle* touched down on the lunar surface, callouts from Mission Control indicating that they had less than 25 seconds of propellant remaining. Armstrong's first words from the surface specifically directed at Earth, "Houston, Tranquillity base here – the *Eagle* has landed", would be quoted, copied and parodied forever thereafter.

Following which came a stream of technical exchanges as flight controllers rapidly scanned their monitors to see whether *Eagle* could be given a "stay" command to remain on the surface or a "no stay" to leave immediately by firing the ascent stage and heading back into orbit. All looked good. They could stay. Only later would it become evident that there was more propellant in the descent tanks and that the low-level readout had been compromised by the sloshing liquids and tilting motion of the spacecraft as it manoeuvred around.

The plan had been for Armstrong and Aldrin to take a rest before conducting their exploration of the surface, but they had been awake for only nine hours and there had been an informal agreement between the crew and mission planners for an option to move that up and rest later. There was good reason for this. Nobody knew whether there would be a technical issue with *Eagle* requiring them to depart quickly and get back to *Columbia*.

With these considerations in mind, the crew prepared to get out of *Eagle*, the hatch being opened six hours 22 minutes after touchdown, or 9.40pm Houston time. In the UK and Europe, it was in the hour before dawn on Monday, July 21. Sixteen minutes later, standing at the bottom of the ladder, Armstrong stepped off the footpad on to the surface, declaring that it was "One small step for (a) man – one giant leap for mankind". Within 30 minutes he was joined on the surface by Aldrin before setting up a seismometer powered by solar arrays.

In a Moonwalk lasting two hours 32 minutes, Armstrong and Aldrin received a telephone call from President Nixon, set up the flag of the United States and collected 47.5lb (21.5kg) of samples. After climbing back inside *Eagle*, the crew had an eight-hour rest period and lifted off the surface 21 hours 37 minutes after landing,

docking with *Columbia* just over three hours later where they joined Collins and transferred samples. Splashdown in the Pacific concluded a flight lasting little more than eight days three hours with the crew returned to Houston and a period in quarantine – just in case they brought Moon bugs back to Earth!

LEFT • With the front hatch left partially open ("making sure not to lock it on my way out!") Buzz Aldrin begins his slow descent down the ladder to the surface of the Moon, July 20, 1969. (NASA)

BELOW • The Apollo 11 crew get a ticker-tape drive during a celebratory parade in New York on August 13, 1969. (NASA)

FIGHTING TO
SURVIVE

As Moon missions compete with funding cutbacks, Nixon seeks to axe NASA while plans develop for a new way of sending humans into space

ABOVE • NASA set its sights on big space stations and a fleet of reusable shuttlecraft to ferry cargo and crew back and forth to a permanently manned research facility. (NASA)

n the aftermath of success, NASA management was acutely aware of the dilemma facing them as dark clouds gathered over the space budget. Beginning July 1, 1967, the fiscal year 1968 budget had granted NASA $4.58billion, falling to $3.99bn for 1969, down 24% since 1965. But most of the previous years' money had gone on building up facilities and one-off development costs of the Saturn rockets and the spacecraft they would carry. Mission costs would be a fraction of the spent investment, or non-recurring costs as accountants call them.

Because of the declining budget there would be no money for more Saturn rockets, Apollo spacecraft or Lunar Modules beyond those already built or funded, although there was sufficient hardware for a further nine missions to the lunar surface. Before Apollo 11, NASA had scheduled a flight every two months and had not that flight landed as it did, two more opportunities were available before the end of the year – Apollo 12 in September 1969 and Apollo 13 two months after that. With success came an opportunity to relax the pace and NASA rescheduled Apollo 12 to fly that November.

Scientists benefitted from a slow-down, so as to digest the results from one mission into site planning and surveys for subsequent flights. Engineers sought intervals to allow better preparation and changes recommended from lessons learned on previous missions. At the Marshall Space Flight Center and the Kennedy Space Center, managers wanted to process and launch no fewer than two or three Saturn rockets a year to keep engineers and technicians current on procedures, to maintain familiarity with legacy equipment and to preserve skill levels at the various NASA facilities.

In January 1969, Richard Nixon was sworn in as US President and change was inevitable with a new occupant in the White House and the Republican Party in government for the first time since 1961. Everything altered. The original imperatives that had driven the expansion and diversification of NASA missions under Kennedy and Johnson had evaporated with the successful flight of Apollo 11 and while NASA scientists and engineers set about planning how best to use the remaining rockets and spacecraft for several more landings, a redirection of effort was inevitable. But not immediately.

While the Apollo 11 crew embarked on a world tour visiting 29 cities across 24 countries in 38 days, in the United States euphoria briefly overtook objectivity and in September 1969 Vice-President Spiro Agnew threw his weight behind an ambitious plan to seize the initiative and voice support for permanent bases on the Moon, the manned exploration of Mars and the assembly in Earth orbit of massive space stations where up to 100 people would carry out scientific research.

Just two weeks after taking office, on February 4, 1969, President Nixon had asked his science advisor Lee A DuBridge to prepare a report on the future of the space programme and, as chair of the Space Council, Vice-President Agnew was tasked with heading a Space Task Group (STG), not to be confused with that set up in 1958, to consult with NASA and other organisations and come up with a plan for the future. What it would recommend was the culmination of plans and proposals that began to emerge not long after the Apollo Moon goal had been launched by President Kennedy in 1961.

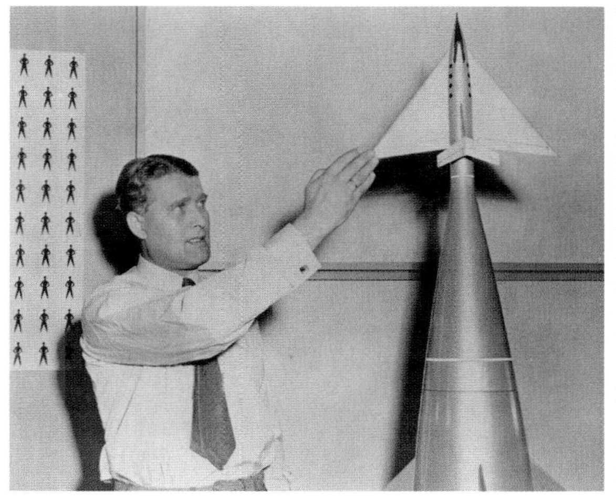

To a Future on the Moon and Mars

Believing that it was going to follow the first landing with a succession of missions to explore different sites across the surface, by 1964 NASA had some of its people working a series of advanced concepts for establishing camps and bases on the Moon. A variety of ideas were incorporated, and some contractor studies were completed for a range of items of equipment, including mobility devices from wheeled roving vehicles transporting astronauts, geological equipment, and samples between sites, to enclosed vehicles capable of travelling great distances.

Under a contract with NASA, Grumman worked up several optional configurations of the Lunar Module for unmanned cargo-carrying capacity by replacing the pressurised Ascent Stage and its crew compartment with logistics modules, cranes, and various packages in addition to wheeled vehicles and mobility devices that the Descent Stage would carry to the surface. Astronauts would go down in a standard Lunar Module and the unmanned

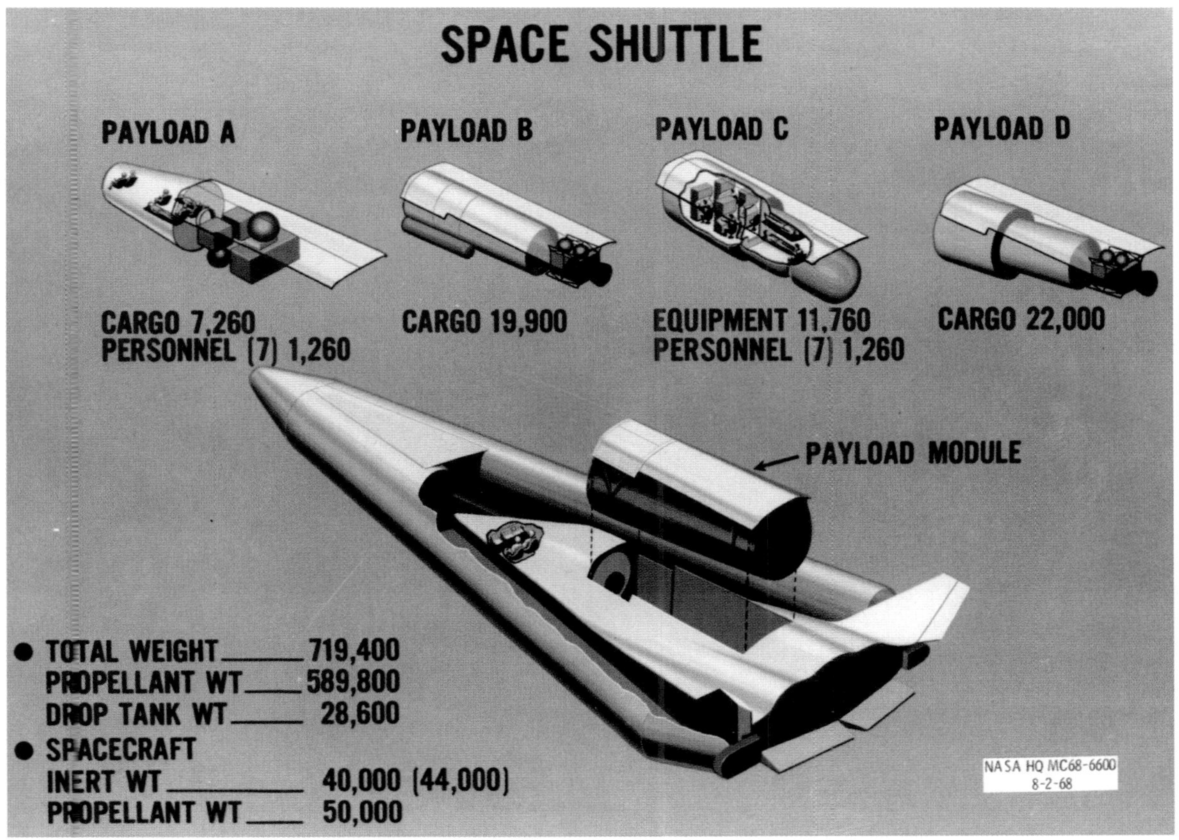

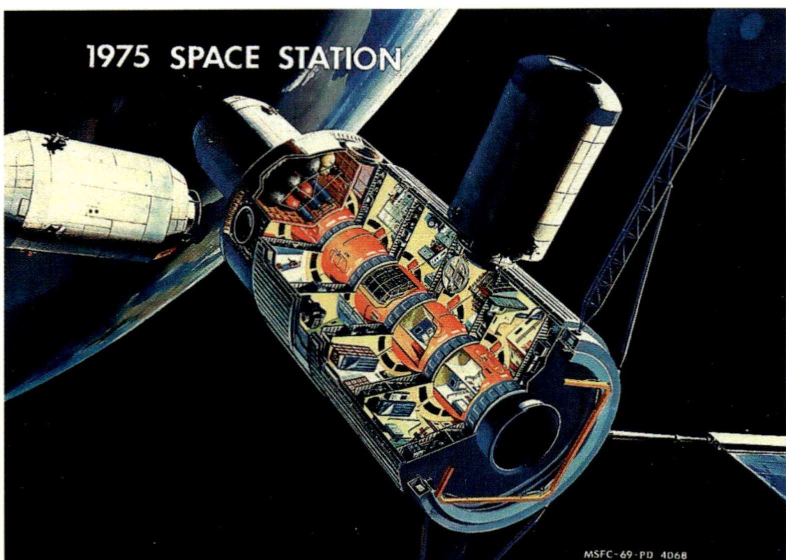

ABOVE • From the use of existing hardware for an early space station, a further development would be establishing a 50-person facility by 1975. (NASA)

BELOW • Post-Apollo plans would begin with the use of redundant Saturn launch vehicle upper stages for conversion into habitable workshops. (NASA)

NASA had been conducting research into lifting-bodies, vehicles capable of flight back from space to a controlled descent and landing on a conventional runway. The notion of such a possibility was the very opposite of expendable rocketry to date. But the expense of throwing away complex and costly vehicles after a single use was unlikely to ever drive opportunities for an expanding space programme — no single country could afford all the ambitious plans of scientists and engineers.

At a meeting of the British Interplanetary Society in the UK during 1968, NASA's George Mueller announced that the agency was looking to develop a reusable vehicle, an outgrowth of lifting-bodies that could be flown many times, dramatically cutting launch costs, and eliminating the need for long production runs of rockets and spacecraft. This would become known as the Space Shuttle, envisaged as a vehicle that could be used to lift satellites into space, carry laboratory modules to orbit, support deep-space operations and significantly lower the cost.

Steered by sustainability and reusability, maximum use would be made of existing technology developed widely for space programmes, with new forms of propulsion such as a nuclear shuttle, in effect a rocket stage powered by a nuclear reactor heating liquid hydrogen fuel. Conventional rockets are powered by a fuel and an oxidiser brought together in a combustion chamber where the resulting gases expand and are vented through a nozzle, that action producing a reaction to move the rocket in the opposite direction.

A nuclear rocket would dispense with the heavy oxidiser and employ a nuclear reactor to heat the fuel, dramatically lowering the weight of the rocket stage and producing a much more efficient system for reaching the Moon, Mars or anywhere else in the solar system. Such a rocket could never be used from the surface of the Earth because there would be some radiation leaked to the atmosphere from the reactor, but in the vacuum of space where a nuclear stage could be parked for use when needed, shuttles could bring up hydrogen fuel when required for a particular mission.

cargo-carriers could provide supplies to maintain manned surface operations for several weeks.

These plans assumed continuous production of Saturn rockets and spacecraft, about which there was a declining probability as the decade progressed. Nevertheless, plans extended to the conversion of spent Saturn rocket stages in orbit to a habitable configuration, space 'workshops' in which astronauts could fit them out for semi-permanent habitation and conduct scientific research with equipment and plug-in modules brought up on subsequent flights. Through this innovative reimagining of existing hardware, prime consideration was given to sustainability and reusability and these factors would come to dominate what eventually became known as the post-Apollo programme.

By the time Gemini flights were under way in 1965 and 1966, there was already little hope of any long-term use of Apollo equipment, the lack of any further manufacturing contracts restricting what could be achieved. For some time,

Because it would move back and forth carrying loads between Earth orbit and the Moon or Mars it became known as the Nuclear Shuttle, a similar name to that also proposed for moving payloads to different orbits around Earth which had been sent there by the Space Shuttle. This was called the Space Tug. With these three elements, a full set of reusable vehicles could support all the needs and requirements of a future space programme in which space stations, bases on the Moon and expeditions to Mars could operate with the minimum number of rockets and spacecraft.

But there was one flaw in this. Invigorated by their own euphoria over the success of the existing programme, proponents of such an ambitious plan assumed universal public and political support for space exploration, but that was a myth driven by their intense need to believe it. Statistical evidence from polls taken during the 1960s showed that for only a very brief period was the majority of Americans in support of the Apollo Moon goal, a slightly larger number supporting a watered-down space programme emphasising greater benefits for humankind on Earth, close to a majority believing it cost too much and had little benefit for them or their children.

Paradoxically, what the Apollo programme did do was to mobilise lobby groups and popular campaigns highlighting the need for regulation on the damaging effects of technological expansion and the unconstrained exploitation of natural resources. Of broader significance, driving these actions was the effect pictures of the whole Earth brought back by astronauts had on the environmental movement at a time when increasing concern over the future of the planet was beginning to gather strong support from many groups and organisations.

It inspired numerous books, including Barbara Ward's *Only One Earth*, which remains influential to this day, and which prompted a later US President, Jimmy Carter, to make a global resource inventory one of the cornerstones of his tenure in office from 1977 to 1981. This had great influence on the path NASA itself would take as it looked to the future and these movements would play no small part in reshaping political pressure, moving NASA toward a very different route, replacing the human exploration of space with a broad base of planetary, Earth science and environmental research.

Long before that day, NASA was concerned about the loss of skilled workers and the dilution of assets for supporting a strong space programme. By 1969, when the Space Task Group sent its finding to the White House, the total government and contractor workforce of 420,000 people in 1965 had withered away to 190,000 workers, in line with the continuous decline in budgets. Internally and at the very highest level, NASA was in crisis and desperately in need of major support to rescue it from oblivion. At a very

senior level, a handful of NASA executives knew there was a threat from the White House itself.

An Axe Held High

The report of the Space Task Group was presented to President Nixon on September 15, 1969, almost two months after the launch of Apollo 11, incorporating NASA's own plan to replace expendable rockets and spacecraft with the Space Shuttle, the Space Tug, and the Nuclear Shuttle as key elements in a programme of space stations, large space bases in Earth orbit, research facilities on the Moon and expeditions to Mars. It recommended three programme options to develop the hardware and deliver the programme objectives at various levels of government funding.

The most costly, Option I incorporated all NASA's proposed plans for stations and bases and headlined manned missions to Mars in the early 1980s, by which date the NASA budget would have doubled to pay for those capabilities. Option II deferred a Mars mission to 1986, holding NASA's budget at its current level before increasing to develop the Shuttle and a permanently manned space station while preserving other science and planetary missions with unmanned spacecraft. Option III was the same as Option II but deferring indefinitely any plan for a Mars landing, essentially eliminating everything for manned flight activity except an Earth-orbit programme for research serviced by the Shuttle and a station.

Agnew and the senior NASA leadership held a press conference on September 17 and were enthusiastic in supporting a high level of manned space activity, the space station and a Shuttle being the minimum core for

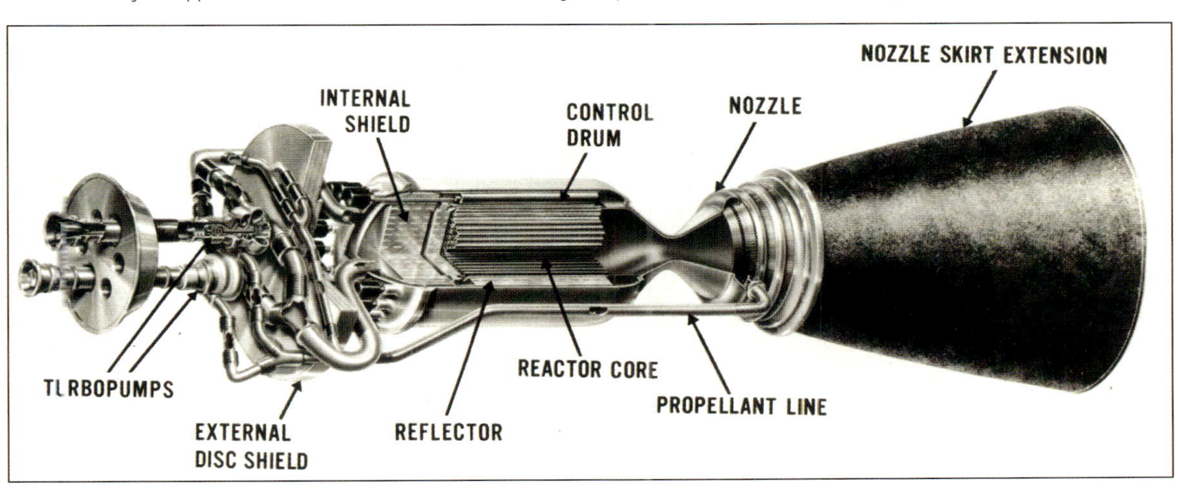

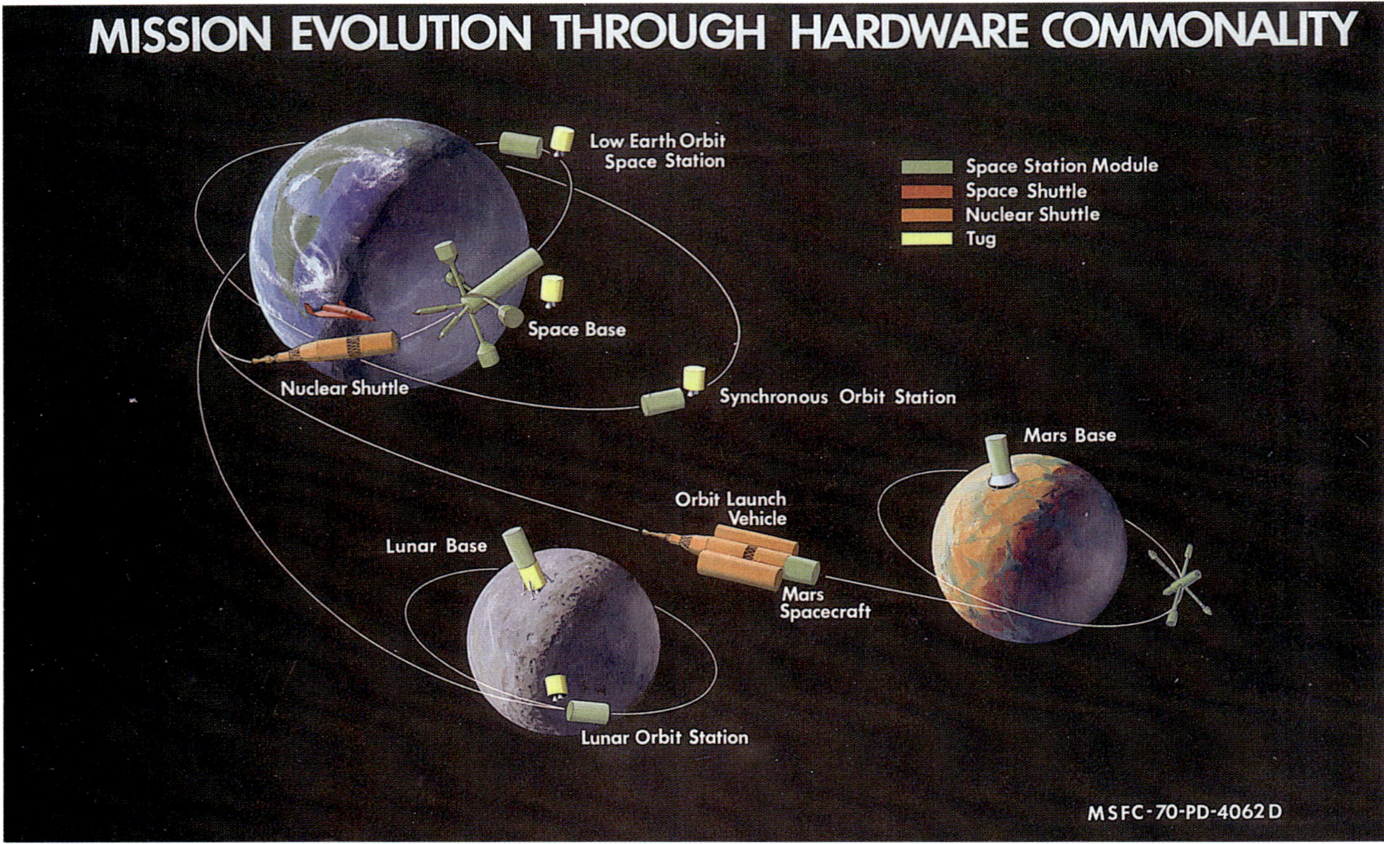

ABOVE • Integrating shuttlecraft, space stations, nuclear propulsion and space tugs would comprise what NASA called its Integrated Space Program, proposed in late 1969. (NASA)

a post-Apollo programme. Opposed to further political objectives for NASA and the implications of that for long-term government expenditures and yet to be convinced of the need for manned flight at all, Nixon failed to endorse any of these recommendations. But there was a further sting in the tail.

At the time, the only funded manned space flight programmes were Apollo and what NASA called the Apollo Applications Program (AAP). This was a legacy from the original repurposing of Moon-landing spacecraft for setting up bases on the lunar surface and for establishing permanently manned space stations in Earth orbit. Orbiting research facilities had been an original ambition of NASA immediately after it opened for business, inherited from what has forever been associated with Wernher von Braun as the 'von Braun paradigm'.

When it was formed, much of NASA's original planning revolved around space stations in orbit, reconnaissance flights around the Moon, expeditions to the surface and bases to follow. That would be a prelude — and would acquire the technology — to start the human exploration of Mars, a planet that was believed to support some form of life. All that

changed when Kennedy declared the Moon goal as NASA's top priority and turned the original sequence on its head. But NASA always wanted an Earth-orbiting space station and as part of the Apollo Applications Program, adapting existing equipment for expanded roles, it laid down the ambitious plan for both Moon bases and space stations.

Known originally as Apollo-X, then the Apollo Extension System, the AAP had a wide-ranging mandate to use existing hardware and that included the potential use of rocket stages in orbit. Having expended their propellant getting there, they could be pressurised with a breathable atmosphere and fitted out with living quarters and work space — laboratories where meaningful scientific research could be conducted. Apollo spacecraft could ferry teams of astronauts up and down and it would all use existing hardware built for the Moon landings.

This was the simplest way to get a cheap space station, using a two-stage Saturn IB in which the S-IVB second stage would put itself in orbit, although the uplift of equipment necessary to fit it out for habitation would partly offset the savings in using a less expensive rocket. This was known as a 'wet' concept in which the S-IVB was launched fully fuelled with propellants. A second option would take a standard S-IVB stage and adapt it into a habitable workshop on the ground for launch on a two-stage Saturn V, a 'dry' workshop.

The AAP workshop concept was renamed Skylab and the logical decision to use the 'dry' concept required one of the remaining Saturn Vs to be reassigned from a potential Moon mission, reducing the number of visits to the lunar surface. Skylab would be a transitional stage using existing hardware repurposed for a sustainable presence in space to learn how to live and work in a spacious facility for long periods. NASA envisaged launching three crews, one for 28 days and two lasting 56 days. To a fully configured space station, Skylab served the same function as Gemini to Apollo, providing training for more advanced purposes.

RIGHT • Other variants of the Lunar Module would have provided taxi services bringing down mobility vehicles and base support materials. (Grumman Corporation)

The decision to use a Saturn V for Skylab was announced on January 4, 1970, but eight months later two of the remaining Moon landings were cancelled when, after initial discussions with the White House, NASA was informed that the administration was not prepared to provide money for those missions. In early 1971, Nixon considered cancelling two more lunar landing flights but relented under pressure, about which more in the next chapter.

There were clear indications that Nixon wanted to repurpose NASA into an organisation focused on general science-based issues, including a major national effort to desalinate seawater, a surprising throwback to President Kennedy's desire for that as an alternative to the Moon race. Presidential advisor John Ehrlichman pressed Nixon to "take it out of their budget...cancel the rest of the Moon programme and save a lot on the Skylab and Mars". He continued: "We're not going to do any more Moon landings, we're going to take all that money...and we're going to put it on desalting possibilities."

Nixon liked that idea, asked for candidate names to rebadge NASA and even worried over the NASA leadership and whether it was up for a role change, asking the air force missile czar Gen Bernard Schriever if he would take on the job, which he refused. All these plans and aspirations came to nothing, but Nixon disliked the focal emphasis on space exploration.

As he said to his Congressional aide on March 24, 1971: "I don't give a damn about space. I'm not one of those space cadets!" Nixon could not understand the need for direct access to the Moon where scientific research could be conducted, asking the rhetorical question: "Why in the hell would they have to go up there and take a look around again...we have got to get off (of) those damn Moon shots!"

Paradoxically, but perhaps not unexpectedly, Nixon had use for the space programme as a political expedient, believing that if the United States were not the global leader in space technology "a great deal of national virtue" would be lost. Surprisingly, he supported manned flights to Mars, when that could be afforded, but only for its political value and sought to manipulate other aerospace assets for political prestige, lambasting Congress for cancelling plans for a supersonic transport aircraft to challenge Concorde on global markets.

While NASA held its breath and waited for a decision, Nixon held discussions with government advisors and related agencies, clearly exhibiting concern for how his actions would read in the polls. This was something Kennedy had never considered before making decisions, believing he had a mandate for change and that public opinion came secondary to that, as witnessed by his persuasively crafted support from Congress when the majority of Americans were indifferent to the Moon goal.

But NASA had an ace card. Nixon liked jobs programmes, and it was on that basis that its future would be decided while NASA was itself in a critical state of management realignment. James Webb had retired before the flight of Apollo 8 around the Moon, succeeded by Thomas O Paine, and Sam Phillips returned to head up the Space and Missile Systems Command in September 1969, his job steering the Moon commitment to conclusion done. Other senior managers would follow and many of the air force cadre brought in by Phillips had now gone too.

In the period 1969-1971, NASA was firefighting crises of identity and survival, struggling hard to reconfigure its manned space flight programme, arguing against further cuts from Congress threatening to decimate its planetary research and other science programmes, and tasked with justifying its existence. Meanwhile, there was a diminishing number of Moon missions to fly even as the workforce declined and hopes flagged.

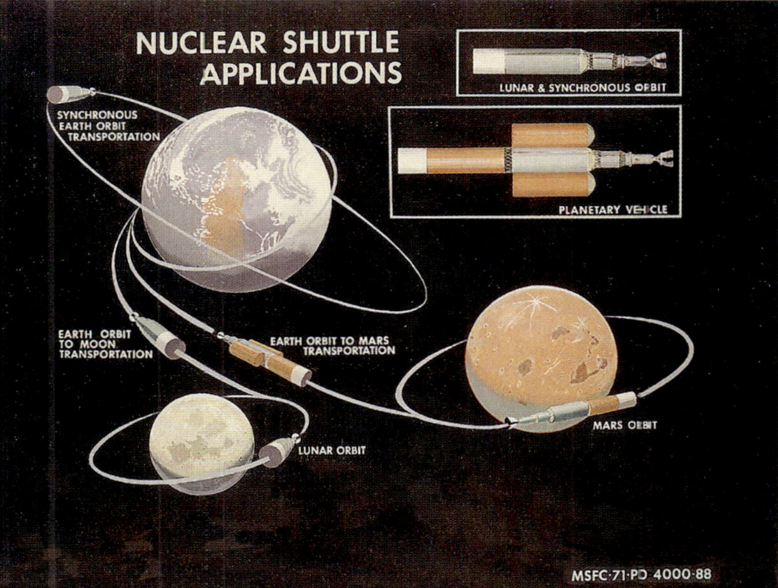

LEFT • In sustaining lunar exploration, NASA considered the use of a rocket-powered Lunar Flying Vehicle, here being tested at Hopi Buttes on the Colorado Plateau. (Aerospace Corporation)

LEFT • Utilising Apollo-generation hardware, variants of the Grumman Lunar Module would have provided cargo delivery to support other LMs bringing crew down from lunar orbit (Grumman Corporation)

BELOW • Applications for the nuclear shuttle would support expeditions to the Moon and Mars. (NASA)

APOLLO ON THE ROPES

A return to the Moon and a broken TV camera before NASA rescues astronauts from near disaster

When NASA sent Apollo 11 to the Moon in July 1969 it was in reality an engineering flight to verify Saturn V, the Apollo spacecraft and the Lunar Module. Tested too was the Manned Space Flight Network (MSFN) for global tracking, telemetry and voice communications together with ground stations and support assets such as the Apollo Range Instrumentation Aircraft (ARIA). ARIA were eight EC-135N aircraft each carrying a steerable antenna dish inside a 'droop-snoot' nose for collecting telemetry data and other communication equipment for data gathering and voice relay while the spacecraft were still orbiting the Earth.

That initial landing achieved the political goal set by Kennedy, satisfied critics and detractors who doubted that it could be done, and set the benchmark for a series of increasingly capable missions to follow. Scientists wanted to get to different parts of the Moon and bring back rocks and soil samples, the Moonwalkers becoming geologists, true explorers in carrying out standard surveys at selected sites. The engineers still had more to learn about the best way to use the spacecraft they had and technologists would develop better equipment including a Lunar Roving Vehicle (LRV) for moving greater distances across the surface.

Improved mobility was key to getting the most out of each visit, enabling astronauts to move quickly from one 'station' to another around any given landing site. As noted earlier, many studies had been conducted for different types of vehicle in support of the Apollo Applications Program, but when that was reduced to just the Skylab space station, NASA acted quickly to put as much of that equipment on to remaining Moon missions.

On July 11, 1969, it asked industry for proposals to build the Lunar Roving Vehicle, Boeing receiving a contract on October 28 to manage the programme for the Marshall Space Flight Center. It would build four LRVs that were allocated to later flights, Apollo missions having been given letter designations for incremental steps in reaching the Moon — the initial landing being mission G, the most conservative use of the spacecraft involved so as to minimise risk and learn about how each system performed.

The H missions maximised the design of the Lunar Module and extended the capabilities of the Apollo spacecraft within the design parameters of the original requirement, allowing for two spacewalks on the surface and a longer stay-time while deploying a more advanced set of scientific instruments. There was a proposed I mission, which would have flown Apollo spacecraft in polar orbit about the Moon, allowing full photography of the total surface area but dispensing with a landing. This was never pursued.

The advanced J missions used modified spacecraft and Lunar Modules (LM) that could remain on the surface for three days, supporting three periods of exploration using the LRV for moving far from the touchdown site. The lunar-orbiting Apollo spacecraft would carry a battery of remote-sensing instruments operating throughout a lengthy period around the Moon. In addition, the weight-carrying capacity of the LM was increased allowing more samples to be brought back than on the G or H missions.

After Apollo 11 returned to Earth at the end of July 1969, NASA expected to mount four H missions and five J missions with a tentative list of sites for each, utilising

improved navigation and landing techniques to put the LM down in rougher regions of greater scientific interest. Over time, as missions were deleted due to a lack of political and financial support, site selection became a balance between priorities and the science community became increasingly important for deciding where to go.

Initially, the flight schedule envisaged a Moon mission every four to six months beginning with Apollo 12, followed by the remaining H-series missions (Apollos 13, 14 and 15) in March, July and November 1970. The J missions (Apollos 16, 17, 18 and 19) utilising what Grumman called the Extended Lunar Module (ELM) in April and September 1971 and February and July 1972. Late in 1969, the last Saturn V was set aside for launching the Skylab space station in late 1972. This phasing would satisfy the operational training of crew members, the stacking and checkout of the flight hardware and would give scientists time to feed in to successive flights the information gathered on preceding expeditions.

The scientific study of the Moon by spacecraft had been a key pillar in NASA's programme of lunar and planetary exploration since its inception and as the first landing drew near, plans were made for a place where samples could be preserved in a sterile environment and studied by scientists from around the world. The establishment of a Lunar Science Institute at the Manned Spacecraft Center had been announced by President Johnson in March 1968, with the intention that Moonrocks would be loaned to research bodies throughout the country and across the globe.

Science was to play an increasing role in Apollo missions, with a growing awareness that this programme had the means to provide opportunities impossible to address without humans on the surface. Astronauts received lessons in geology and visited key places where surface conditions reflected a lunarscape in surface texture and where they

could receive tutorials from recognised experts helping them understand the roles they would be called upon to perform. Crew members assigned to remain in the Apollo spacecraft during lengthy periods in lunar orbit would play a vital role in observing the surface from above and providing information relevant to future missions.

While a lot of the engineering questions had been answered by Apollo 11, guidance specialists recognised that it had landed 4.3 miles (7km) from the planned site due to inconsistencies in the precise gravitational effect of the Moon on orbiting spacecraft and on uncertainties about navigating from a low lunar orbit down to the surface. On future missions there was a need to carry out precise landmark measurements to compare the exact position of the LM with predicted values obtained through the computer receiving data from the downward-facing radar and from inputs made by the crew.

For those reasons, NASA chose to send Apollo 12 to a site further west around the equatorial region of the Moon to the landing site of a robot spacecraft called Surveyor 3, which had touched down on April 20, 1967, carrying a TV camera and a surface sampler scoop for measuring the bearing strength of the soil and digging small trenches. As the first of the H missions, Apollo 12 was to land as close as

possible to the Surveyor spacecraft so that the crew could photograph it and retrieve a few structural items easily removed and returned to Earth.

While Apollo 11 had set down a seismometer powered by solar cells for recording Moonquakes and sending that data to Earth, all subsequent missions would carry a package of science instruments powered by a small thermonuclear generator using plutonium-238 dioxide as fuel to produce heat converted to electrical energy by thermocouples. Known as the Apollo Lunar Surface Experiments Package (ALSEP), these instruments would be carried in two cases on the outside of the LM.

To deploy an ALSEP package, an astronaut would retrieve the radioactive fuel from a special graphite cask and insert it into the power package, the instruments being unpacked and laid out in a precise configuration for securing a wide range of information about lunar surface properties. This information would be transmitted by a central data station about the size of a small table-top refrigerator to which cables from all the instruments were connected. Each different and with separates sets of equipment, ALSEP packages would be deployed on every flight beginning with Apollo 12.

it could access landing sites that could not be reached on a free-return path. But it used the Apollo main engine to change to a non-free-return path only after the LM had been extracted from the top of the S-IVB stage. If the main Apollo motor could not be used after that the LM's descent engine was available as a back-up, which was why it had been tried out in that mode during the Apollo 9 mission in Earth orbit.

The crew in Apollo 11's Lunar Module had remained on the surface for less than 22 hours supporting one Moonwalk of under three hours, while Apollo 12, the first of the H-series full-capability missions, would stay for more than 31 hours and conduct two excursions outside, each lasting almost four hours. With a full ALSEP science package and colour TV camera to be deployed on the surface for viewers to watch all the action, NASA hoped this mission would sustain the global attention captured by Apollo 11.

Carrying Pete Conrad, Dick Gordon and Al Bean, Apollo 12 was launched on November 14, 1969, into rain-filled skies and heavy cumulonimbus clouds, conditions that required a waiver for flight. Just 36 seconds after lift-off, a lightning strike caused by the ascending stack created a static electrical discharge that ripped all three fuel cells

Science on the Moon

Because it had no Lunar Module with a secondary propulsion system for use in the event of an emergency, Apollo 8 had been flown under some risk that the crew might be stranded around the Moon from which there was no possibility of rescue. Once inserted into lunar orbit, the main rocket motor on the Apollo spacecraft had to work to get the crew back home. On Apollos 10 and 11 the LM descent stage engine was available as a back-up, at least until the descent stage was discarded after going down toward the lunar surface. The trajectory chosen for those missions was a 'free-return' type because, had Apollo's main engine not been used for some reason, it would have looped around the Moon and put the spacecraft back toward Earth within the manoeuvring capabilities of the small attitude-control thrusters doubling as course correction motors. This was known as a 'free-return' trajectory because the main engine could fail to fire without compromising the lives of the crew. But Apollo 12 and subsequent flights would transfer to a non-free-return flight path.

This was necessary to change the angle of the trajectory with respect to the position of the Earth and Moon, so that

RIGHT • *Bean removes the radioisotope fuel core that he would insert into the finned power module seen here in the foreground. The hand-tool carrier is to the left of picture. (NASA)*

BELOW • *The routes taken by the Apollo 12 crew on the second Moonwalk for sample gathering and a visit to Surveyor 3. (NASA)*

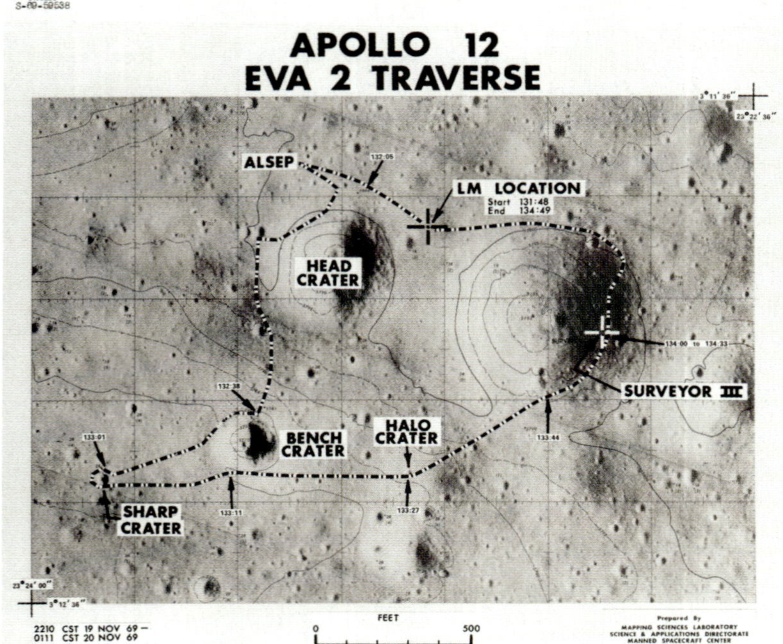

off line, switching power to Command Module batteries that had insufficient power for all functions. Less than 16 seconds later, another lightning strike took out the spacecraft's attitude indicator display, which told the crew the orientation of the spacecraft. Suddenly in the spacecraft all the caution and warning lights lit up with a glowing red colour and the crew had no idea what was going on.

Encountering conditions into which no Saturn V had been launched before, with winds aloft at 175mph (281km/h), Apollo 12 was controlled by the rocket's own computer and instruments while Mission Control assessed the situation, relaying instructions to the crew to throw certain switch positions, reconnect the fuel cells and get everything back on line. It caught controllers out, unfamiliar with precisely this condition, and had it not been for a recollection from flight controller John Aaron of a similar problem that had come up in a simulator test, it could have resulted in a different situation.

It had been close. Had the Saturn Vs own instrument unit been struck and thrown offline it would have triggered an abort, firing the Launch Escape System and catapulting the Command Module and its crew away from the ascending rocket uncontrollably running amok until intentionally destroyed. Quietly, and without informing the crew, some engineers feared that the explosive bolts triggering parachute deployment in the final minutes of the flight may have been damaged, in which case the Command Module would have hurtled to destruction with the loss of the crew. That possibility would haunt flight controllers until splashdown.

Events proceeded on the now familiar pattern until the main Apollo rocket motor was fired for the first time on this flight for nine seconds at 30 hours 52 minutes, changing the speed of the docked vehicles by 42mph (67.5km/h), sufficient to shift the flight path to a non-free-return trajectory, but setting it up to get to the desired landing point. Apollo 12 entered lunar orbit 83 hours 31 minutes after lift-off and, after a crew rest period, the Lunar Module (*Intrepid*) separated from the Apollo spacecraft (*Yankee Clipper*) 24 hours 23 minutes later. The descent engine fired to place *Intrepid* in an elliptical path carrying it down to a low point of seven miles (11km) from where it began its descent to the lunar surface.

Intrepid landed at 110 hours 32 minutes after a descent burn of 11 minutes 58 seconds, touching down a mere 590ft (180m) from the Surveyor 3 spacecraft, which rested on the flanks of an adjacent crater. This was as close as flight controllers wanted it to be so that surface dust thrown out by the LM's rocket motor would not cover the exterior of Surveyor 3. Nevertheless, a blast of surface particles removed more dust from Surveyor 3 than had accumulated since it landed! Short of stature, on stepping off the final rung of the ladder, Pete Conrad offered a parody of Armstrong's first comments: "Whoopee! Man, that may have been a small one for Neil, but that's a long one for me."

The first visit outside *Intrepid* consisted of laying out the ALSEP experiments, but when Al Bean began to set up the colour TV on a pole he inadvertently pointed it at the Sun and burned out the vidicon tube. That was the end of live broadcasts from the surface. After a sleep session aboard the LM, the second Moonwalk had the crew circling around the edge of the adjacent crater to the opposite side to visit Surveyor 3. Conducting their first geologic sample-collecting expedition, Conrad and Bean applied what they had learned over many hours of training in which geologists taught Earth-based techniques with specially adapted tools such as rakes, core tubes and scoops using standard sampling procedures for different places called 'stations'.

When they approached the Surveyor spacecraft, they found its white colour had been bleached ochre by the Sun and a thin layer of dust had been partially swept away by the blast from their rocket motor on touchdown, albeit some distance away. Snapping off the TV camera with a cutting tool, they removed pieces of tubing and stowed them for return to *Intrepid* and back to Earth.

Less than four hours after getting back inside from the second Moonwalk, Conrad and Bean lit up the ascent engine and left the Moon, docking with *Yankee Clipper* just over three hours after that. In technical and scientific terms, the mission had been a great success, demonstrating pin-point landing, retrieval of pieces from Surveyor 3, laying out the array of science instruments that would continue to transmit data to Earth for almost eight years, and gathering up 73.75lb (33.45kg) of samples including cores from 15in (40cm) below the surface. With waning interest and believing that the programme had served its purpose, the general public saw it as superfluous and voiced those opinions in the press.

The crew of Apollo 12 returned to Earth on November 24, 1969, to splashdown in the South Pacific Ocean after a flight lasting ten days four hours 36 minutes. For NASA, there was uncertainty. Public attention was polarised around worsening crises in the war in Vietnam and adjacent countries such as Cambodia and Laos. The Nixon administration swept to office on the promise of ending the conflict that many believed had been escalated by mismanaged policies in the Johnson years, blaming US Secretary of Defense Robert McNamara.

The belief in US technological supremacy over the Soviet Union had been reinforced by the failure of the Russians to put cosmonauts on the Moon and a last-ditch attempt to retrieve samples from the Moon and get them back to Earth before the Americans using the unmanned Lunar 15 failed when it crashed on the day Armstrong and Aldrin were walking on the surface. It had been the second Soviet attempt in little more than four weeks.

A Crippled Spacecraft

Detailed analysis of the performance of both the Saturn V and the Apollo spacecraft during the lightning strike on Apollo 12 prompted a complete re-examination of launch weather rules and changes were made to prevent such an occurrence happening in the future. But there were discussions as well about the level of information that should be shared with the crew. Every mission was a learning curve and there were several instances where the crew were not informed, before or during flight, of situations that were close to being life-critical.

As an example of this, the Apollo 11 crew had not been told that data analysis from previous Saturn V launches indicated that if one of the five first-stage rocket motors shut down within seconds of lift-off, stress on the structure would have caused a total break-up of the stack before the launch escape system could be triggered. When asked about that several decades after his flight, Buzz Aldrin was visibly surprised. But there were uncertainties in the level of training given to Moonwalkers.

BELOW • Setting up the ALSEP instruments — one of the most scientifically rewarding achievements of the Apollo programme, but the least discussed through the news media. (NASA)

RIGHT • With Intrepid on the edge of the crater in which it had landed almost three years previously, Surveyor 3 visits to retrieve the camera and other items for return to Earth. (NASA)

In pre-flight rehearsals for Apollo 12, the crew had been told that the TV camera could face directly into the Sun for up to 15 seconds and not burn out and they had practised using a wooden mock-up without seeing the flight hardware until they unpacked it on the Moon. In setting it up, the lens had traversed the Sun's disc for no more than two seconds. In that one incorrect brief, Apollo 12 lost an audience that would otherwise have watched events live with far greater picture quality than had been possible with Apollo 11. For ever after, the crew were blamed for an error not of their making and NASA had a PR disaster.

The next flight was targeted for a region known as Fra Mauro. Apollos 11 and 12 had been to relatively flat places, great expanses of dried basaltic lava that had flooded out across vast stretches of the surface billions of years ago, filling relatively low-lying areas much as seas do on Earth. The original crust dating back to the origin of the Moon existed in areas scientists termed 'highland' regions, the brighter regions as viewed from Earth yet rougher and more pock-marked with craters and fractured rifts. These areas held keys to unlocking the secrets of the Moon's origin and its evolution over time. To get there required skilled piloting and precise targeting.

As the NASA budget failed to support the post-Apollo programme presented by the Space Task Group only a few months earlier, on March 1, 1970, disillusioned by the retraction from deep-space exploration, Werhner von Braun moved from his position as director of the Marshall Space Flight Center to headquarters to become Deputy Associate Administrator for Planning, his place taken by Dr Eberhard Rees, another German from the old days at Peenemünde.

Astronauts Jim Lovell, Bill Anders and Fred Haise began training in January 1969 as the back-up crew for Apollo 11 and that made them prime crew for the Apollo 13 flight, but when Anders left to join the National Aeronautics and Space Council, Ken Mattingly replaced him. Just days before the planned launch date, Mattingly was exposed to rubella (German measles), which might not manifest itself until he was well on the way to the Moon, so he was replaced by Jack Swigert.

The registered press corps for Apollo 13 was a quarter of the contingent that flocked to gawp at Apollo 11, with only one-tenth as many spectators turning up at Cape Canaveral, most from the local area flying in to landing strips or arriving on small boats. But NASA wanted to recoup lost support and had 11,500 distinguished guests brought in, of which 4,500 had passes to the VIP stands alongside the Vehicle Assembly Building, a greater number than for Apollo 11. Special descriptive brochures were prepared and the political caucus was specifically encouraged to have the experience of a lifetime.

When lift-off of Apollo 13 occurred at 2.13pm on April 11, 1970, it didn't disappoint, but the second stage centre engine shut down two minutes early due to a violent increase in the pogo effect and vibrations approaching 50 cycles per second. This was a phenomenon that had afflicted Apollo 4, but with a greater amplitude than experienced on any other Saturn V, to such an extent that post-flight analysis

RIGHT • The crew of Apollo 13 were (left to right) Jim Lovell, Jack Swigert and Fred Haise, aiming for the third lunar landing. (NASA)

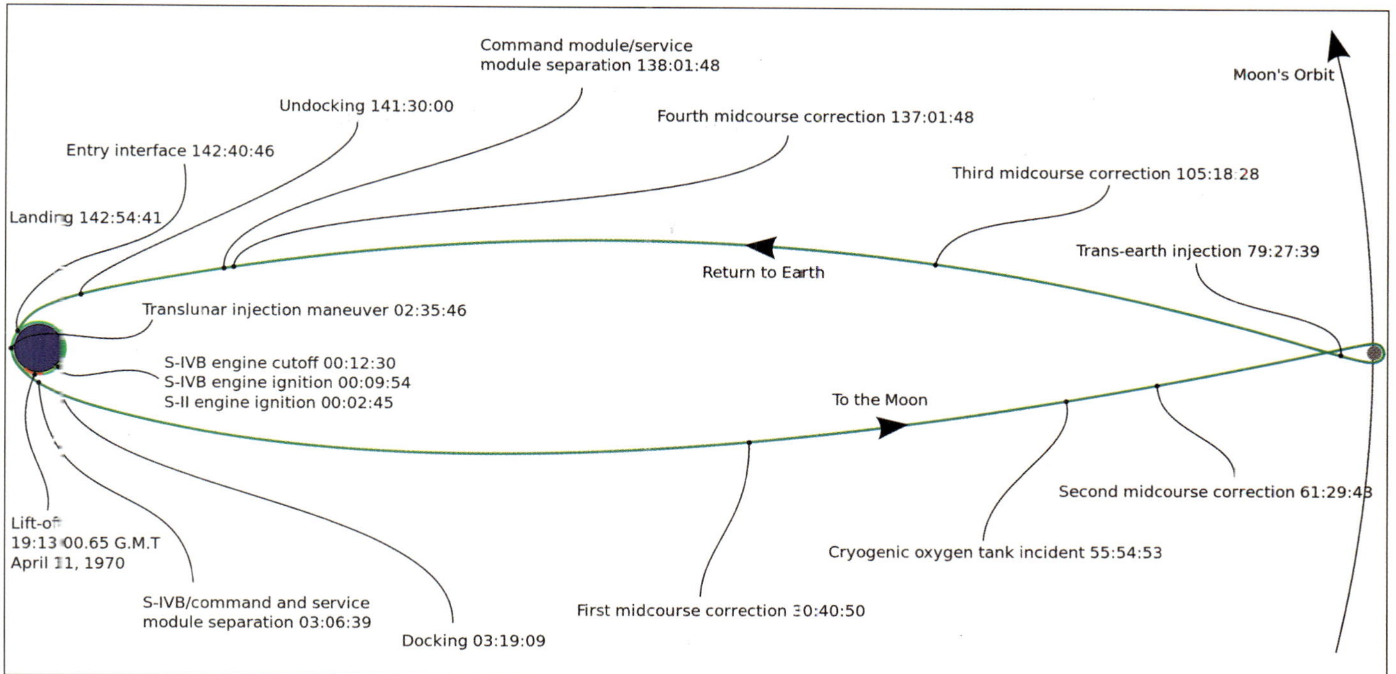

indicated that one more oscillation cycle would have destroyed the vehicle. However, the outer four engines were unaffected, operating longer and consuming propellant unused by the retired engine.

After departing from an initial orbit around the Earth and setting course for the Moon, the LM (*Aquarius*) was checked out and, at an elapsed time of 30 hours 40 minutes, the main rocket engine on the Apollo spacecraft (*Odyssey*) was fired to put the trajectory on to a non-free-return path ready for slipping in to lunar orbit at the appropriate inclination. With most of the trans-lunar journey over, at a distance from Earth of approximately 210,000 miles (330,000km), the crew were getting ready for a sleep period shortly after a telecast showing activity on board the spacecraft.

Without warning, after activating the fan in one of the two liquid oxygen tanks, the crew heard a loud bang along with a slight rocking motion and thrusters firing to stabilise the attitude. Almost immediately, the crew saw particles streaming past the windows and the instruments showed the No 2 tank empty and the No 1 tank bleeding down. The two oxygen tanks were all that kept the crew breathing, as well as supplying the oxygen to meet hydrogen over a catalyst for power, a system that had been reliably supplying electrical energy for both Gemini and Apollo spacecraft since August 1965. Aboard Apollo 13, two of the fuel cells were not operating and the third was fluctuating.

In Houston it was just after 9.00pm, April 13, and Mission Control had few options. With the one remaining oxygen tank leaking, the single remaining fuel cell would quickly fail and there was no other electrical supply other than entry batteries in the Command Module, which would normally be switched on shortly before re-entry at the end of the mission and clearly those were reserved for that use. These batteries were used initially, but then recharged for re-entry from the power supply in *Aquarius*.

The Lunar Module had full oxygen tanks together with electrical power, but only from batteries designed to support operations for two men in 41 hours of independent operations free of *Odyssey*, including a planned 33 hours 27 minutes on the surface. It would take at least 87 hours for the three astronauts to get back to Earth. Moreover, the filters to remove exhaled carbon dioxide were different in the two spacecraft, those from *Odyssey* would not fit in *Aquarius*. Eventually, a makeshift adaptor had to be put together to keep the scrubbers working.

The most immediate need was to buy time, power down the Apollo spacecraft and set up *Aquarius*, with life-sustaining oxygen flowing up the short tunnel between the two spacecraft, and transfer computer and navigation instructions to the Lunar Module so that it became the command centre for rescue operations. For the immediate future, *Aquarius* could serve as a lifeboat, but both docked vehicles were hurtling away from Earth on a trajectory that would, without a further engine burn, swing them around the Moon but not toward Earth.

Odyssey was dead, so the main rocket motor could not be used, but there was a back-up. Just five hours 34 minutes after the catastrophic event, the descent engine on *Aquarius* was fired for 34 seconds to get the flight path back on a free-return trajectory. A further burn lasting four minutes 23 seconds made just two hours after passing across the far side of the Moon speeded up the return journey, from which point — 79 hours 27 minutes after lift-off — it was a matter

RIGHT • *Jack Swigert works on a modified carbon dioxide cleaner box from Apollo spacecraft* Odyssey *modified to work in* Aquarius. *(NASA)*

of survival for the next 44 hours on diminishing quantities of water, battery power and luck.

Coming Home

Events associated with getting Apollo 13 back home are well documented and familiar to many. Less well known is the reaction at NASA and among the political leadership in Washington DC to what they perceived to be a disaster unfolding live on radio channels around the world. General interest in the space programme had waned and live coverage of the launch had been spasmodic with not a single US channel carrying it because they deemed it to have little public interest. Now it was on every US station, with foreign broadcasters handing over some channels to continuous coverage.

Minutes after events began to unfold, just after 10pm in Washington DC, NASA called the White House situation room and told them what was happening, the national security advisor Henry Kissinger being told about an hour later. Nixon had retired to bed, but Kissinger called chief of staff Bob Haldeman and suggested he wake the President; he refused to do that believing it to be merely a "technical problem". As events worsened, around 4am the following morning Haldeman decided to rouse Nixon and impart the news while instructing the President's press secretary Ron Ziegler to tell journalists that Nixon had been up all night and had taken "personal charge of the crisis".

Under some pressure and clearly anxious and uneasy about what to do, White House staffers advised that Nixon

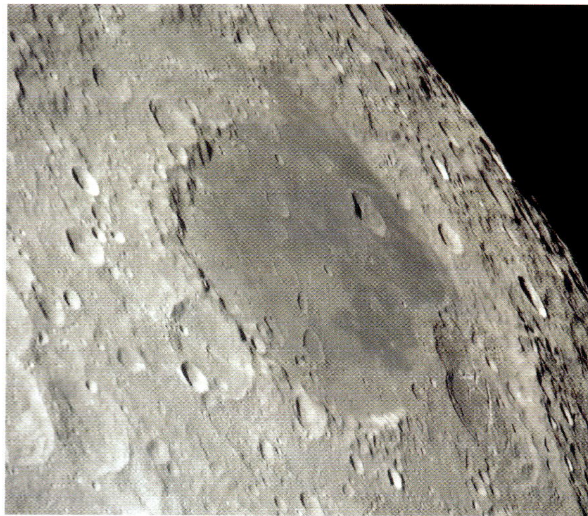

RIGHT • *Despite their fight to eke out consumables and stay alive, the crew managed to take this picture of Mare Moscoviense, an area of particular interest on the far side. (NASA)*

fly to Houston and rally support for the rescue effort, but Frank Borman claimed that would be a distraction, while at the same time dealing with the Vice-President's staff, who wanted Agnew to fly to Houston himself and "take charge of the rescue effort". On hearing this, Bob Gilruth tasked Borman with standing up as a firewall between these political interventions, telling him: "Agnew's presence in Houston would be about as welcome as a Martian invasion."

Over the next three days, Nixon became obsessed with the unfolding drama, hopping around with uncertainty and anticipation, unable to fully comprehend the technical details and totally awestruck by the stoicism of the human spirit in the survivability of the crew and the steadfast resolve of Mission Control to get them back alive. Less than two years earlier he had rehearsed a speech prepared in case Armstrong and Aldrin were stranded on the Moon, now he scanned copy prepared by his staff in the event Apollo 13 never made it back safely.

Powered down to the minimum, aboard Apollo 13 temperatures stabilised at 38°F (3°C), about the same as a domestic refrigerator, with condensation building up on internal surfaces. Lovell and Haise were able to wear their lunar suit boots, but Swigert did not have those as he would not walk on the Moon. Usually jettisoned overboard, urine had to be stored on board. Much depended on using the Lunar Module for guidance and navigation in conjunction with Mission Control to align the trajectory and conduct two small course corrections on the way back.

There were uncertainties regarding the state of the heat shield, located close to the trouble which had erupted with the burst oxygen tank, and procedures for separating *Aquarius* from *Odyssey* were very different from those on any other flight. The Service Module was jettisoned less than five hours before re-entry, the crew observing for the first time that one side had been blown away, the Lunar Module being released little more than an hour before the command module reached the atmosphere, flying a shallower trajectory than usual.

When the crew did return to Earth on April 17 at the end of a flight lasting five days 22 hours 54 minutes, it was

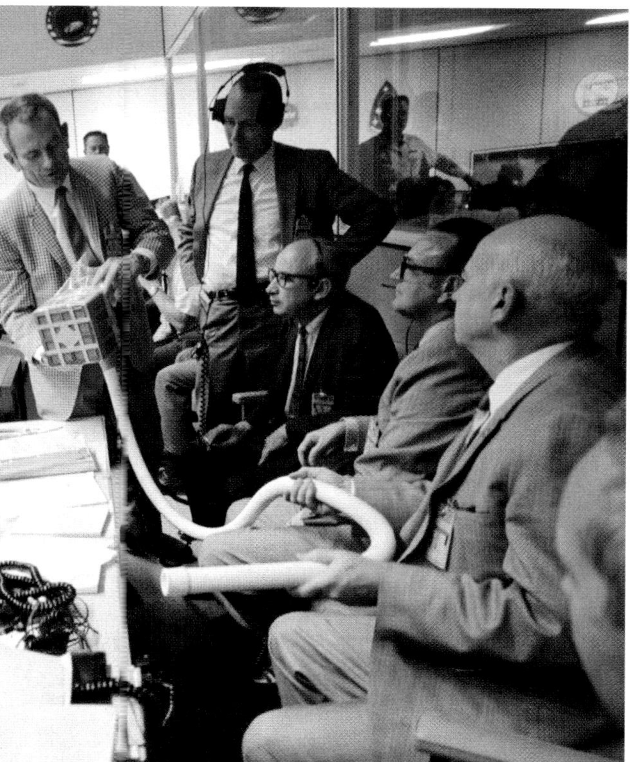

the spacecraft. Consequently, partial melting during successive cycles had occurred in the interior of that tank before the flight to a critical point where a fan shorted when switched on by the crew shortly before the explosion. There had been problems filling and emptying the tank during tests, but those had been bypassed when the tank was successfully filled for the mission.

Every tank on all Apollo missions had that exposure to an electrical fault and had it occurred on Apollo 8 the result would have been disastrous because there was no Lunar Module on that mission to serve as a lifeboat. Changes would be made and they would bring a delay to flight resumption; a third oxygen tank would be added, more water provided and additional battery power given to the spacecraft. But it had been a close call.

late morning at the White House with a NASA squawk box set up in the office of an aide. Nixon was on a continuous information loop and Kissinger was watching with him alongside astronauts Collins and Anders, ordering cigars all round to mimic the tradition in Mission Control for celebration of a successful landing followed by a succession of meetings with Congressional leaders to celebrate. When Nixon met with the crew he told them that "this mission was a successful mission...We realise that greatness comes not simply in triumph, but in adversity".

It is easy to see in Nixon's response to the successful splashdown of Apollo 13 an admiration for what NASA's manned space flight programme had achieved. In reality, it was more a relief that he would not have to face the nation and explain a catastrophe. Nixon hated bad news, was nervous regarding public perception, of his presidency and of him personally, and was averse to risk and risk-takers. It would not persuade him to support greater goals in the future and it failed to garner his enthusiasm for a post-Apollo programme.

At NASA, the struggle for survival would go on as the agency conducted an investigation into what had happened with *Odyssey*, to plan modifications to prevent it happening again and to follow through with remaining lunar landings. On September 2, 1970, NASA had to cancel Apollos 18 and 19 and reset the procedures for determining the best sites to select for the four remaining landing options available.

But first, what had happened to Apollo 13 on the way to the Moon?

Very little attention had been given to the cause of the accident until the mission was safely over. But the flight telemetry and instrument readings quickly uncovered the cause. One of two oxygen tanks in the Service Module had over-pressurised and exploded, rupturing the second tank, which soon vented its contents. The blast had ripped off the outer casing exposing the entire bay.

Records showed that electrical connections to the oxygen tank had not been modified by the contractor as requested by NASA to withstand a higher voltage in ground-based test equipment than the voltage on

SUBSCRIBE TODAY!

Air International has established an unrivalled reputation for authoritative reporting across the full spectrum of aviation subjects.

/collections/subscriptions

Free 2nd class P&P on BFPO orders. Overseas charges apply.

END OF AN AGE

Moon buggies, extended Moonwalks and a large collection of rock samples bring an end to manned lunar landings

Rectifying the problems that exposed Apollo 13 to danger took engineers several months to fix, but scientists believed the Fra Mauro site to be sufficiently important to retain it for Apollo 14 and, with the cancellation of Apollos 18 and 19, to make the next flight the last H-series mission. At NASA, there was a distinct change in management style and a shift toward stronger independence for field centres, which would be given greater autonomy in the drive to diversify and encourage creative engineering for future technologies. In this context, headquarters would have a supervisory role and direct overall policy and planning, but there would be a greater focus on specialisation. George Mueller retired from government service on December 10, 1970, replaced as head of manned space flight by Dale Myers from North American Aviation.

Carrying improved spacecraft back-up systems, nine months after its predecessor limped home, Apollo 14 was launched on January 31, 1971, with astronauts Al Shepard, Stu Roosa and Ed Mitchell on board heading for the third lunar landing. NASA had lost a lot of followers among the general public and the absence of any TV from the surface of the Moon since Apollo 11 in July 1969 did little to encourage people back to their TV screens to watch bunny-hopping Moonwalkers.

The crew named their Apollo spacecraft *Kitty Hawk*, and called the Lunar Module *Antares;* the mission profile was similar

to Apollo 13, but the crew would spend additional time on the surface due to reassessment of the consumables used on Apollos 11 and 12. They would also have a wheeled handcart to carry all the tools and sampling equipment, together with bags for rocks and core tubes. In addition, there was the second ALSEP (Apollo Lunar Surface Experiments Package) to lay out across the surface that would take several hours during the first Moonwalk.

The flight progressed as planned, although there was difficulty docking *Kitty Hawk* to *Antares* to extract it from the top of the S-IVB stage, and the transfer to a non-free-return path was completed at the planned time. A change to the lunar orbit geometry was made for this flight whereby the circularisation burn on the second revolution of the Moon was changed to one in which *Kitty Hawk*'s main engine put the docked vehicles into a path of 67.7 miles (109km) by 10.5 miles (17km). From this orbit, *Antares* could start its descent to the surface directly from that low point rather than having to put itself in that orbit as with Apollos 11 and 12.

That worked as expected, but it was a fine-tuned risk; had the main rocket motor on *Kitty Hawk* burned longer than planned it would have lowered the orbit so much that the docked vehicles would have ploughed into the surface. The main advantage was to provide longer tracking time in the path from which *Antares* would begin its descent, further perfecting a pinpoint landing strategy.

This 20.8 second engine burn on the second orbit was made on the far side of the Moon and as the time neared for the docked spacecraft to reappear, Mission Control began to fill up, the tension among senior managers plain to see. Tracking would indicate if there had been an overburn threatening safety and flight controllers had 12 minutes to verify it had been performed as planned or fire up the motor again to raise the low point.

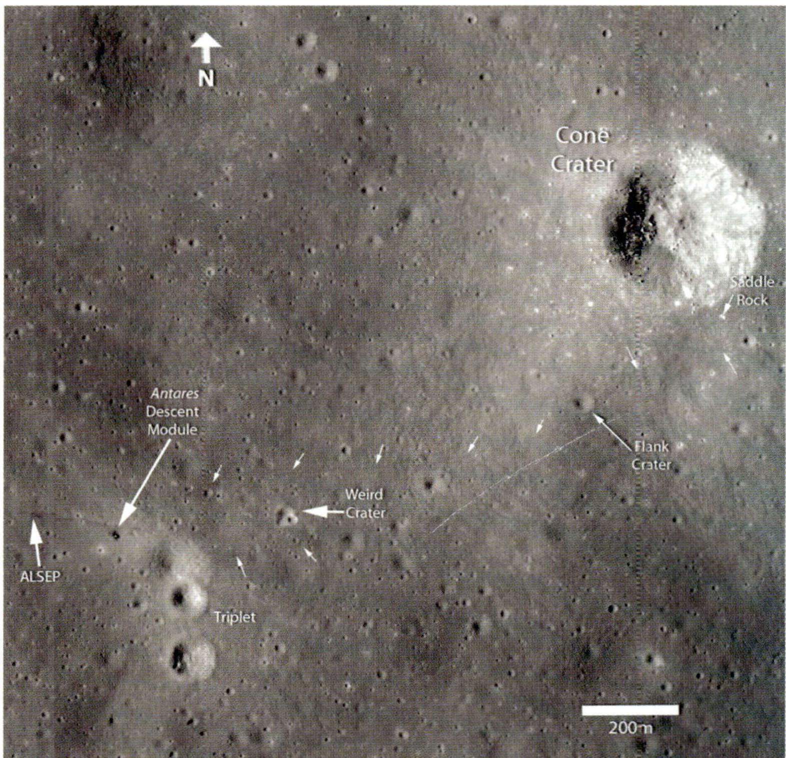

It had worked to perfection and sighs of relief were audible, vindicating the mantra that space flight is dangerous and nothing is achieved without bold confidence in the face of danger. But callouts from the crew acknowledged how close they were getting as Mitchell commented: "Looks like we're getting mighty low here. It's a very different sight [than] from the higher altitudes…as a matter of fact we're below some

ABOVE • A simulation of how the Lunar Roving Vehicle unfolds from its stowed position on board the Lunar Module shows it emerging as a mechanical origami design! (NASA)

The second Moonwalk began after a sleep session aboard *Antares* and lasted four hours 34 minutes, during which the two astronauts tried to reach a place named Cone Crater to sample its rim about a mile (1.6km) east of the Lunar Module. Fatigued by traversing blocky terrain and with high heart rates, they were never sure of precisely where they were and yet came within 75ft (23m) of the rim, sampling as requested at specific station stops on the way out and back.

Antares remained on the surface for 33 hours 30 minutes and lifted off without incident to dock back with Roosa in *Kitty Hawk*, who had spent 39 hours 47 minutes alone orbiting the Moon. After the crew moved back into the Command Module and transferred the 94lb (43kg) of samples, the ascent stage of *Antares* was jettisoned and its thrusters fired to impact the lunar surface. The standard return procedures ensued with the crew ending their nine day two minutes flight with splashdown in the Pacific Ocean.

Public interest in Apollo 14 had peaked during the launch until Shepard and Mitchell landed on the surface, but it lost TV watchers when the astronauts wandered far away from the camera and off toward Cone Crater, viewers switching off in large numbers. The scientific value of Apollo Moon missions was a difficult justification to sell to an audience inured with the belief that Apollo was in essence a political gambit in a race to beat the Russians and having achieved that there was uncertainty as to what repeat visits were all about. It did not help when Shepard, an avid golfer, appeared to tee-off a golf ball with an extension handle, joking that it went "miles and miles and miles" in the one-sixth gravity.

To the Moon in Style

Completion of the two H-series landings cleared the way for the definitive use of Apollo hardware, setting up the scientific investigation of the lunar surface in a way that had been dreamed of by scientists and engineers for a decade since the dawn of the Apollo programme. What the J-series missions represented was the best that NASA could get in the wake of collapsing funds.

Modifications for these fights included a complete bay of the Service Module dedicated to science instruments, enclosed by a door panel jettisoned shortly before getting

of the peaks on the horizon, but that's only an illusion... it certainly is an unusual sensation flying this low."

Shortly after, the two spacecraft undocked and *Antares* prepared to go down to the surface, a problem appeared with the guidance system, which indicated that it would command an abort when the descent programme was engaged. That took some time to sort out and a complex reconfiguring based on rapid simulator tests found a corrective procedure that saw the descent begin four hours five minutes after *Antares* separated from *Kitty Hawk*. In the meantime, as planned, *Kitty Hawk* raised its orbit to an almost circular path 68.4 miles (110km) above the surface.

Antares touched down within 150ft (45m) of the targeted spot, which, given the flexibility for Shepard to manoeuvre away from surface obstructions was certainly a pinpoint landing. The first Moonwalk lasted four hours 48 minutes with the ALSEP array fully laid out and working. But there was an additional task in the form of a seismic profiling experiment involving a string of geophones laid out on a long line extending 310ft (94.5m) from the central data transmission station. Mitchell then walked along the line detonating a series of small charges triggered at the end of a pole he carried to generate seismic waves and provide geologists on Earth with a 'view' some distance below the surface.

Table 2: Apollo and Lunar Module spacecraft specifications

Spacecraft	Apollo CSM	Standard Lunar Module	Extended Lunar Module
Height	36.2ft/11.0m	23ft/7m	23ft/7m
Width	12.8ft/3.9m	31ft/9.4m	31ft/9.4m
Weight	63,500lb/28.800kg	33,500lb/15,195kg	36,200lb/16,420kg
Manned flights	15	6	3

Note: Width of the Lunar Module includes deployed legs

into lunar orbit. On these extended flights, the Apollo spacecraft would be on its own for around 73 hours, almost twice as long as the two preceding missions and the Command Module pilot would conduct detailed and sometimes complex operations operating panoramic and mapping cameras using radar to probe the surface.

Two flights would also carry a small satellite to be released in lunar orbit for data on magnetic fields and particles in the lunar vicinity. J-series flights would last around 12 days and on the return leg the Command Module pilot would conduct a spacewalk to retrieve film cassettes from the science bay in the Service Module.

The much heavier Extended Lunar Module (ELM) would remain on the surface for around 66-72 hours, much more than twice as long as Apollos 12 and 14. Each would carry a Lunar Roving Vehicle (LRV) with expeditionary surveys of the landing site, the crew traversing far greater distances. On each mission the two astronauts would log around 20 hours on the surface compared with little more than eight hours for Apollos 12 and 14, devoting the first of three Moonwalks to laying out the ALSEP instruments before conducting a small surface-sampling excursion followed by two full periods of geological surveys and rock collecting.

Development of the Saturn V had continued apace with weight-saving measures, performance enhancements and operational improvements. The thrust of the first stage had increased and the sum effect of all these changes increased lift capacity from 109,600lb (49,714kg) for Apollo 11 to 116,310lb (52,758kg) for Apollo 17, a relatively small increase of 6%, but sufficient for all the additional changes, upgrades and additional equipment for the J missions. Coincidentally, for the first J mission the increase in weight was divided equally between the Apollo spacecraft and the Lunar Module (LM).

Commanded by veteran astronaut Dave Scott and with rookie crew members Al Worden and Jim Irwin, Apollo 15 was launched on July 26, 1971, less than five months after the last H mission and was sent directly to a non-free-return trajectory by the Saturn third stage, the first time that had happened but with confidence that with the LM's descent engine as a back-up there was minimal risk. In the now standard profile, the two spacecraft decelerated into lunar orbit on the far side of the Moon and changed to the same orbit as that flown on Apollo 14 in which the main rocket motor fired again to place the low point close to the lunar surface from where descent would begin.

The landing site for Apollo 15 was arguably the most visually dramatic of any, a flat bay on the eastern flank of a giant basin caused by a massive impact 3.9billion years ago and now filled with dried lava. Known as the Hadley-Apennine site, the Lunar Module, named *Falcon*, would drop down over the towering peaks of the basin rim and land just short of a giant rille 2,500ft (762m) wide and 1,000ft (305m) deep, at the bottom of which were scattered rocks and boulders, originally from the roof of a now collapsed lava tube snaking just below the surface. As *Falcon* went down to the surface, the Apollo spacecraft, named *Endeavour* in English spelling for the British research vessel it was named after, began three Earth days of science and Mission Control settled in to maintaining operations with two spacecraft.

After landing, the first activity was for Scott to open the top docking hatch of *Falcon* and, standing on the ascent engine cover, to conduct a visual and photographic survey of the entire landing site, lasting 33 minutes, from the dramatic slopes of the Hadley Mountains to the east, to the flat, pock-marked surface of the foreground, like a giant gorge. Both Scott and Irwin conducted their first drive across the lunar surface before deploying the ALSEP, but a problem with drilling the second of two holes in which heat sensors were placed proved difficult.

ABOVE • Cernan and Schmitt conducted three extensive geological surveys of the site area during the last Apollo Moon mission. (NASA)

The opportunity presented by the LRV and its colour TV camera was of immense value to scientists who could watch and advise the astronauts as they worked away at various pre-planned stops to gather samples, take pictures, sink core tubes and provide verbal descriptions. To the public relations people at NASA it was a unique opportunity to show the public a continuous view of events as they were happening, despite how far they roamed across the surface. Only when the rover was in motion did the pictures stop temporarily.

The second Moonwalk took the crew south to the slopes of encroaching mountains while the third had them heading north parallel to the rille that had been subject to a close visit on the first day. The expeditions had been planned so that they were never so far distant from the Lunar Module that the astronauts could not walk back to safety had the LRVs broken down at the most distant point. On all three expeditions, the Apollo 15 LRV clocked 17.25 miles (27.7km) across the lunar surface.

Pioneered on Apollo 14, NASA introduced a buddy system consisting of emergency hoses to connect the two suits together should the backpack for one crew member fail. Thus, there could be a failure to the LRV and a life-support system for one of the two astronauts yet both could still get back in the LM. All the pre-planned excursions on all three J missions were designed with these safety requirements. Biomedical data continuously transmitted to Mission Control provided health checks, heart and respiration rates, and data from the backpacks showed oxygen and water quantities remaining.

The highly successful mission of Apollo 15 came to an end with splashdown at an elapsed duration of 12 days seven hours 12 minutes, the crew returning with 170lb (77kg) of lunar material. During lunar surface activity, as an education lesson, Scott had dropped a falcon feather and a hammer, both falling at the same rate in the absence of an atmosphere and subject only to gravity. He left a small aluminium statuette of an astronaut together with a plaque

RIGHT • With the Lunar Roving Vehicle parked alongside the Lunar Module Orion, Apollo 16 commander John Young jumps off the surface while saluting the flag. (NASA)

carrying the names of US and Russian spacemen who had died in the line of duty.

A Fleeting Moment

The second J mission, Apollo 16 was launched on April 16, 1972, carrying astronauts John Young, Ken Mattingly and Charlie Duke in Apollo spacecraft *Casper* carrying the Lunar Module *Orion*. Targeted for a landing in the Descartes region of the ancient lunar highlands, it was originally selected for Apollo 19 but moved up when that was cancelled, so important was it considered to be. The flight profile followed largely that of its predecessor, but following separation prior to landing some difficulties with actuators on *Casper*'s main rocket motor seriously threatened to end all hope of a descent to the surface.

It did not help when the public affairs officer announced to the world in a dramatic tone: "The atmosphere here in the control room is reminiscent of the period just after the cryogenic oxygen tank incident on Apollo 13." Yet it was true. Assuming *Casper*'s main rocket motor was inoperable as it appeared to be, if Orion went down to the surface using its descent engine the crew would have lost the only motor that could get them back home. After almost six hours delay for tests and deep analysis, it was judged that the landing could proceed because the back-up system was working fine.

Because of the extended day, Young and Duke rested first before conducting their initial Moonwalk, including a preliminary geologic traverse prior to setting up the ALSEP experiments. The second Moonwalk saw an extensive sequence of geological activity at several station stops, viewers seeing continuous coverage at the various sites. The third Moonwalk had further work exploring, documenting and sample collecting for a mission total of 209lb (95kg) of surface material in 20 hours 14 minutes outside traversing a total of 16.5 miles (26.5km) in 71 hours spent at Descartes. The mission ended in the Pacific Ocean after 11 days one hour 51 minutes.

Overly concerned that there should be a disaster in the run-up to the US presidential election on November 7, 1972, and the impact that might have on his campaign, the last manned flight to the Moon had been delayed by President Nixon and in his mind the near-abort during Apollo 16 reinforced that decision. For some reason, Nixon had been advised that Apollo 17 was

more dangerous than any of the preceding missions, but there is no reason that he should have been told that, except by those still trying to get more flights cancelled.

There had been some effort to get the last flight to the Moon adapted as a polar-orbiting mapping mission without a Lunar Module and Dale Myers had tried to persuade the Administrator to have it so, without success. The cycling of the back-up crew of one flight to prime status on the second flight along put astronauts Gene Cernan, Ron Evans and Joe Engle in the seats for Apollo 17, but Engle was replaced by the geologist Harrison Schmitt, one of six astronauts selected in June 1965 for their scientific credentials. There were several convincing arguments to justify the switch, the most weighted being political, although it is doubtful that Schmitt contributed anything more on the lunar surface than Engle would have done.

Launched in the hour after midnight on December 7, 1972, Apollo 17 headed for the Taurus-Littrow region, which, like Apollo 15, was within the arcuate rim structure of an old, eroded basin now filled with dried lava beds. Due to the hour of its flight, sky-watchers along the eastern seaboard saw the slender rocket head for space, the only night launch of an Apollo mission. For those at Cape Canaveral, the night effect produced a spectacular orange ball expanding out with pulsating shock waves rippling through the glow, the shattering sound of the five first-stage engines penetrating the night all the more audible — or so it seemed.

The flight proceeded largely without trouble and because of the need to arch the trajectory in a curving path to position the docked vehicles for the proper lunar orbit necessary to reach the landing site, it took 86 hours to get there compared with 76 hours for Apollo 16 and less than 72 hours for Apollo 15. The landing site was nestled within sloping hills on three sides and situated further east than previous locations, demanding highly precise navigation with Mission Control integrating observations and surface landmarks and markers set by the Lunar Module.

Named *America*, the Apollo spacecraft went about its own tasks after the Lunar Module *Challenger* cut loose and headed down. The three Moonwalks followed the profile of the previous two missions and after laying out the ALSEP array, Cernan and Schmitt conducted two detailed and strenuous Moonwalks collecting 142 samples weighing 243lb (110.4kg)

Table 3: Apollo Lunar Missions

Mission	11	12	14	15	16	17
Moonwalks	1	2	2	3	3	3
ALSEP	x	1	1	1	1	1
LRV	x	x	x	1	1	1
Samples	47.5lb	75.6lb	94.3lb	169.1lb	209.8lb	243.5lb

Note: ALSEP is Apollo Lunar Surface Experiments Package; LRV is Lunar Roving Vehicle

ABOVE • For Apollo 17, the crew of Eugene Cernan (seated), Ron Evans (right) and Harrison 'Jack' Schmitt would visit the Taurus-Littrow valley. (NASA)

while the mapping and panoramic cameras in *America* returned with more than 4,600 frames of selected places on the lunar surface. The three Moonwalks totalled 22 hours four minutes, considerably longer than the previous two missions.

The significance of this last Moon flight was not lost on the crew, accepting that it was uncertain when humans would return to the lunar surface. Gene Cernan had a thoughtful reflection as he paused to ascend the ladder for the last time: "...as I take man's last step from the surface, back home for some time to come — but we believe not too long into the future — I'd like to just [say] what I believe history will record. That America's challenge of today has forged man's destiny of tomorrow. And, as we leave the Moon at Taurus-Littrow, we leave as we came and, God willing, as we shall return, with peace and hope for all mankind. God speed the crew of Apollo 17."

The Lunar Roving Vehicle had performed superbly, completing a record 22.3 miles (35.9km) on the three expeditions of Apollo 17, but one of the most enduring records was the live coverage of lift-off from the Moon. With meticulous precision and perfect timing, on all three J missions each LRV had been parked a convenient distance from the Lunar Module to broadcast live TV of ignition and ascent from the surface, the camera being pitched upward under manual control from Houston to track the ascending vehicle as it departed.

Apollo 17 splashed down at 1.55pm Houston time on December 19, 1972, the mission having lasted 12 days 13 hours 52 minutes. During the J missions of 1971 and 1972, for a fleeting moment in the history of the space programme NASA demonstrated how well purposed the Apollo spacecraft and the Lunar Module were for expanded operations and extended scientific expeditions across the surface.

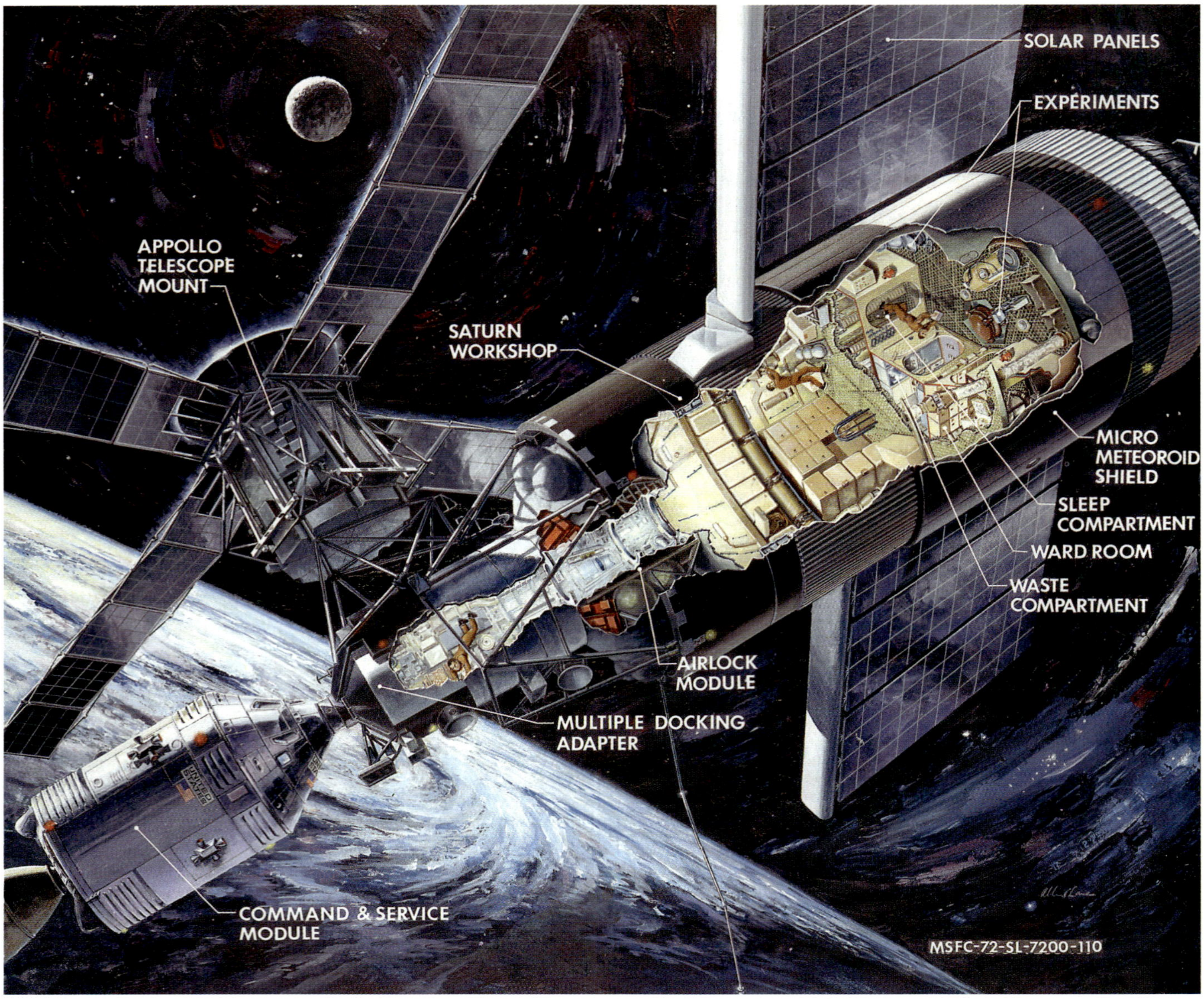

GOODBYE APOLLO

Skylab visits, resident astronauts and the only NASA space station built exclusively in the United States

ABOVE • The Skylab space station provided NASA with unprecedented research opportunities in a spacious and well equipped facility supporting three crews for a total of 171 days – 31 days longer than planned. (NASA)

RIGHT • The lower section of Skylab contained the living quarters with sleep cubicles, galley and exercise area. (NASA)

After the cancellation of three Moon landings, one Saturn V was allocated to the launch of the Skylab space station, which some NASA managers had hoped could be the start of a series of orbiting facilities converted from Saturn S-IVB stages. But that was not to be. The Saturn IBs used for taking crews to Skylab would launch from LC-39B, which had been modified with a trestle platform known as the 'milk stool', the original launch pads for Saturn IBs having been dismantled after Apollo 7.

Skylab represented a change in focus, research embracing Earth science, astronomy, microgravity materials processing and studies into the long-term effects on humans in space. There was an Apollo Telescope Mount (ATM), originally modelled on the descent stage of a Lunar Module, supporting batteries of solar telescopes for studying the behaviour of

LEFT • *The last Saturn V, minus the usual third stage replaced by the Skylab space station, on its way to the launch pad. (NASA)*

the Sun, a research laboratory attached to the forward end of the workshop with Earth-scanning cameras and an airlock module for conducting spacewalks to retrieve film from the ATM and other science packages exposed to the vacuum of space for lengthy periods.

Skylab was unlike anything NASA had flown before, providing a vast interior space for living and working, eating and sleeping in a way impossible with previous vehicles. It was powered by two large solar array wings attached to opposing sides of the cylindrical Orbital Workshop and four solar arrays in a cruciform layout for power to the ATM. The atmosphere would be a mix of nitrogen and oxygen, a 'shirtsleeve' environment similar to that on Earth. Refrigerators would contain sufficient food and there would be enough clothing for the one period of 28 days and two of 56 days.

Materials processing was a new technology for space applications, embracing the preparation of different semiconductor crystals in an environment where there was an absence of convection and in the preparation of new pharmaceutical products with higher levels of purity than could be achieved in large quantities on Earth. For the first time, NASA would have the chance to fully evaluate these processes over extended lengths of time, demand in Earth-based industry rising with the evolution of computers and advanced processing systems. It was for all these different studies that NASA wanted to invest in future-proofing its programmes directed specifically to the advantage of industries and people on Earth.

The Skylab programme represented the shift from deep-space exploration to one serving science, engineering and technology, the use of space applied to programmes bringing benefits to people on Earth. By 1972, there was no possibility that NASA would be able to return to manned operations beyond Earth orbit soon. Much of what would be accomplished in lunar and planetary exploration over the next several decades would be done with unmanned space vehicles visiting every other planet in the solar system and sending robotic explorers beyond and toward the nearest stars.

Interest in getting a close look at the Earth's natural resources from space had been stimulated by photographic coverage of the planet during the manned Gemini missions

of 1965. Scientists at NASA's Goddard Space Flight Center developed a programme for Earth-observing cameras going by the clumsy title of Earth Resource Technology Satellite (ERTS), eventually changed to Landsat. Attracting opposition from government financiers who believed it would be more expensive than using aircraft to photograph the surface and from the military fearing that it would reveal details held by spy satellites, it eventually got permission to proceed.

Landsat 1 was launched on July 23, 1972, equipped with cameras of relatively low resolution so as not to overstep the boundary into classified spy satellite imagery, a restriction that would remain in force for non-military Earth-observation US satellites. The government opened the Landsat programme to international access, which was why there was sensitivity to how belligerent foreign powers could use enhanced imagery for surveillance purposes. It was in support of the wide-scale development programme for Earth-imaging cameras and sensors that the Skylab remote-sensing instruments were carried so that scientists could evaluate the results from a range of optical and infrared sensors.

The crew for the first manned Skylab flight was selected in February 1972 with Pete Conrad, Joe Kerwin and Paul Weitz assigned to the first visit planned for the following year. The crew played a major role in designing the interior and configuring the way supplies were stored, coded and tagged for use and how operational procedures were designed. Mission Control would be controlling operations for several weeks on each visit, a new and challenging role for teams used to measuring mission duty in days and a lot of training involved both ground and flight crews.

Three to Go

The launch vehicle for Skylab (AS-512) consisted of the first two stages of a Saturn V, the S-II second stage being responsible for placing the assembly in orbit, which comprised the Orbital Workshop, the ATM (Apollo Telescope Mount), the Docking Module, the Airlock Module and a large payload shroud that would be separated into two halves and jettisoned in space. On previous Saturn V launches, the active S-IVB third stage placed itself into orbit with sufficient propellant to fire again and push the Apollo payload to the Moon. On this flight it was just a space station.

Overall, the weight delivered to orbit by the first two stages of Saturn V was approximately 377,716lb (171,330kg), the heaviest

BELOW • *During ascent, the micrometeoroid shield tore loose taking with it the thermal barrier and on reaching orbit one of the two massive solar array booms was torn away. (NASA)*

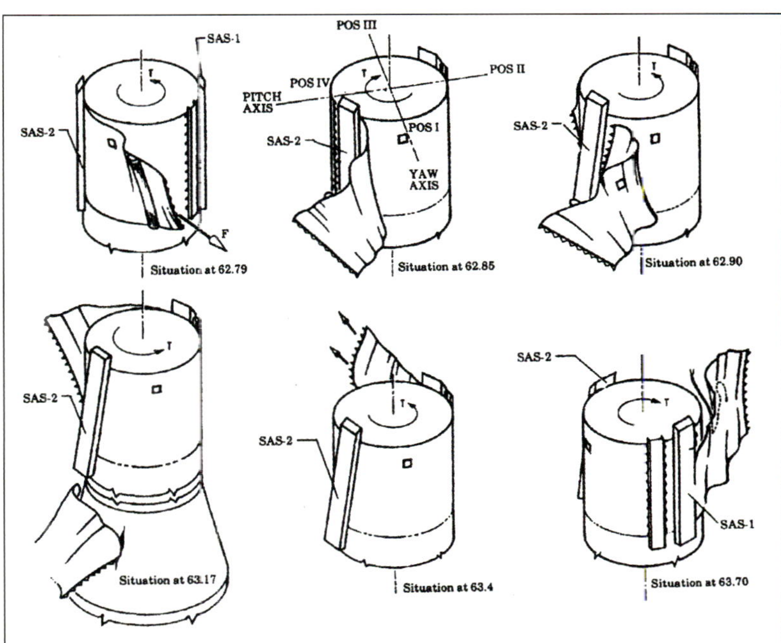

RIGHT • Above the crew area, sealed by a grid ceiling with an access aperture, was a cavernous experiment void, also containing consumables and supplies. (NASA)

BELOW • Materials processing experiments in the Multiple Docking Adapter to which the Apollo spacecraft was attached. (NASA)

load placed in Earth orbit by any Saturn V, which averaged 308,000lb (139,700kg) for the J-series Moon landing flights. It also included the S-II second stage that had never been placed in orbit before — this would be the heaviest load placed in orbit by a single launch vehicle and remains so to this day. Purists may say that the SpaceX Starship weighs more, but at the time of writing that has only been launched to a suborbital trajectory, returning before completion of the first orbit.

Never very good at assigning flight numbers, confusingly NASA designated the launch of the unmanned Skylab as SL-1, the first, second and third crew visits becoming SL-2, SL-3 and SL-4. The orbital assembly was launched on May 14, 1973, and almost immediately things began to go wrong. The cylindrical exterior of the Orbital Workshop had a thin protective barrier against micrometeoroid impacts, which was engineered to be held tight against the hull until it reached orbit. Incorrect design allowed air to enter the meteoroid shield, tearing it loose and partially deploying one of the two solar array wings folded down along opposite sides of Skylab.

But this was just the beginning. When the S-IC stage shut down and separated, ignition of the five engines in the S-II upper stage should have been followed by separation of a cylindrical skirt, or adapter, connecting the two stages together, but it failed to detach itself. Still connected, the J-2 engines were shrouded and heat began to build up, temperatures soared to levels never seen before and when the stage shut down as planned, delivering itself and Skylab into orbit, it was seconds away from rupturing critical lines with a catastrophic explosion.

It was not over yet. The adapter connecting the S-II stage to the base of the Skylab workshop carried forward-firing retro-rockets, which ignited to shunt the inert stage away and prevent a collision. The thrust from those solid-propellant rockets tore loose the massive unhinged solar array wing from the hull of Skylab to send it cartwheeling away into space, electrical wires dangling from the side of the workshop.

With the meteoroid shield ripped away, taking with it a thermal barrier protecting the hull from the fierce rays of the Sun, temperatures quickly began to build, threatening food and other consumables inside the capacious hull. The mission plan had been to launch the first crew the following day, but that was now out of the question, with temperatures rising the workshop was uninhabitable and a rescue plan was necessary if it was ever going to support a crew. By the eighth day, the internal temperature had reached 125°F (51.7°C).

NASA's Marshall Space Flight Center had management of the Skylab programme and a uniquely co-operative work schedule was organised with the Manned Spacecraft Center in Houston developing equipment for the first crew to make repairs to the space station and set up a sunshade. An added problem was that debris from the damaged meteoroid shield had snagged the remaining solar array preventing it from opening and starving the workshop of electrical power, only the ATM arrays having been deployed successfully.

Timing was all important. NASA wanted the SL-2 crew to carry a shade in the form of a folded umbrella that could be deployed from inside Skylab through a small airlock no larger than a cat-flap, which was already built in to the wall of the workshop facing the Sun. That would buy time for a more robust form of shade to be installed by the second crew. NASA also asked the National Reconnaissance Office to use the 38th KH-8 Gambit III spy satellite launched on May 16 to take pictures of the damaged Skylab.

Launched on May 25, 1973, Conrad on SL-2 flew the Apollo spacecraft around Skylab to assess the state of the exterior and to provide verbal evidence of its state before moving around to dock with the station. After a meal inside Apollo they undocked and flew around to where the sole remaining solar array arm was fouled by debris from the ripped meteoroid shield and, during a spacewalk, Weitz unsuccessfully tried to free it so that an arm supporting the solar cells could deploy. Back inside Skylab, the umbrella was deployed through the airlock and unfurled like a sunshade; temperatures began to fall. A lot of work remained to examine the interior, to verify that food was unaffected and that Skylab was inhabitable after all.

Although they were still relying on power from the ATM arrays, a second spacewalk during the third week was conducted to free the solar array arm and that was a success, the giant arm swinging open with such force that it sent Conrad and Kerwin spinning off the hull to the extent of their tethers. Further work was necessary to get the station fully operational, despite which a considerable amount of science work was completed.

Rescued from a potential disaster, the mission went its full 28 days, doubling the time US astronauts had spent

in space previously achieved by Frank Borman and Jim Lovell in December 1965. The flight ended on June 22 with splashdown in the Pacific Ocean only six miles (9.6km) from the recovery ship, the USS *Ticonderoga*.

Return Visits

Planning for the second crew visit on SL-3 was already well under way, Skylab being left unoccupied for more than five weeks as a full programme of science was planned for the anticipated 56-day stay flown by astronauts Owen Garriott, Jack Lousma and Alan Bean. Launched on July 28, 1973, the Apollo spacecraft had thruster problems during manoeuvring and, after successfully docking, a leak developed in another thruster quad. This activated the rescue plan with the launch of the Saturn IB/Apollo reserved for the third visit and piloted by Vance Brand and Don Lind.

As preparations for the rescue flight went into high gear, but with the SL-3 crew in no danger, the Skylab astronauts prepared for their first spacewalk to deploy a more permanent shade in the form of a full-length awning laid out along the entire length of the Sun-facing side of the workshop over the top of the parasol-like umbrella set

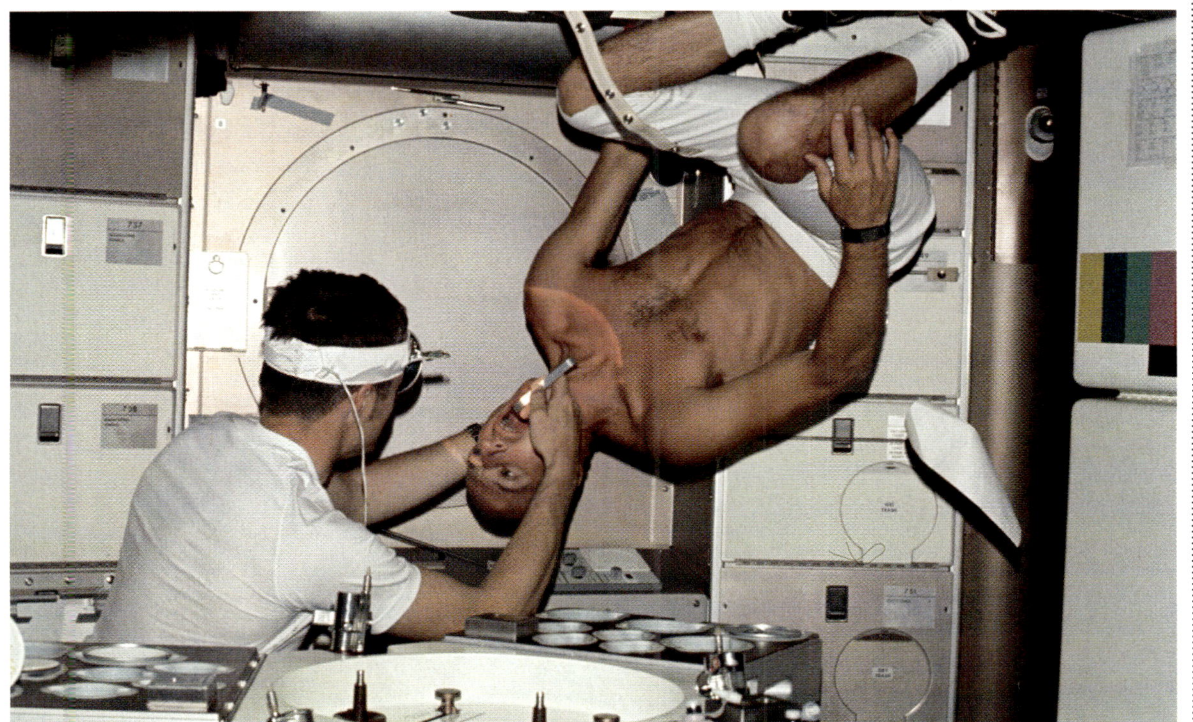

RIGHT • An overhead view of Skylab showing the one remaining solar array arm, the initial parasol shield and the cover set out by the second crew to maintain a habitable environment. (NASA)

up by the first crew. Not without difficulty and held taut by two poles down each side, that was achieved by Garriott and Lousma on August 6, a spacewalk lasting six hours 29 minutes. after which it was back to the usually crowded days of science experiments and observations.

Medical measurements were a priority, the duration of the second visit doubling the record of the previous visit, but detailed observations of the Sun, the Earth and materials processing experiments kept the crew fully occupied. Mission Control too was on a learning curve, with shifts maintaining a crew work day aligned with that in Houston, Texas, ensuring

continuity in their pre-flight circadian body rhythms. With hopes of a permanently manned space station, Skylab was effective in testing work/rest cycles and the ability of astronauts to maintain pre-planned workloads.

Physical exercise was important, with a bicycle ergometer provided for musculoskeletal conditioning and exercise regimes for cardiovascular analysis in weightlessness. A special device was provided to lower pressure in the lower torso and legs to evaluate the flow of blood, and blood samples were routinely taken for analysis back on Earth after the flight. Two more spacewalks were made, by Garriott and Lousma for four hours 30 minutes on August 24 and by Bean and Garriott for two hours 45 minutes on September 22, to retrieve film cassettes from the solar telescopes. When it was judged that a rescue was unnecessary, the crew came home in their original spacecraft on September 25, ending their 59 day 11 hour nine minute mission.

Although the second crew had remained in space three days longer than originally planned, while publicly declared as a 56-day mission there was an intention to let the third and final visit run as long as was prudent, within the limitations of food and consumables on Skylab. What was being learned was vital for the future development of space stations, fast becoming NASA's new objective for the next decade, and it was important to extract as much value as possible from what was already turning into a highly successful programme, notwithstanding its perilous start to operations.

After some concern over stress cracks in fins on the first stage of the Saturn IB assigned to SL-4, a rocket already more than seven years old and recently removed from storage, the third crew of Gerald Carr, Edward Gibson and William Pogue were launched on November 16, 1973. As

RIGHT • A depiction of the Apollo spacecraft (left) attached to the Soyuz spacecraft (right) by means of the Docking Module.

the mission progressed it was extended until achieving a duration of 84 days one hour 15 minutes at splashdown with much learned, a lot of it unanticipated and reorganised work schedules, task levels and flight plan assignments. For the first time, Mission Control was learning how to run a complex, multi-faceted timeline in which daily routines were planned while the crew were still in space.

This was a significant turning point in how interactions between flight controllers and crews worked together, SL-4 producing some difficulties in ground operations synchronising with activities in space, because what worked in theory never quite seemed to work that way in practice. There were brief periods when the crew had to reconfigure workloads themselves and withdraw from daily briefings on routines and flight plan changes, but always to the benefit of both Mission Control and the crew, none of whom had flown in space before.

This third and final Skylab visit had achieved much, with four spacewalks for retrieving film and for other experimental purposes, together with a vast array of data and imagery of the Earth and its environmental resources.

The station itself had responded well to technical problems, although it was beginning to fail in several areas, still NASA retained hope that it could be visited by an early Shuttle flight. After the last crew departed, engineers continued to operate several systems remotely and to glean additional information. But on July 11, 1979, it tumbled back through the atmosphere where the majority of the structure burned up, although large chunks survived to fall to Earth across a wide area of southwestern Australia. There was an additional legacy. In the event a rescue was needed to bring the last crew back home, a Saturn IB had been reserved to make that flight. It was of course never required and it resides today at the Kennedy Space Center.

The achievements of the Skylab programme had been immense, the one and only space station 'made in the USA' as its successor, the International Space Station, would be an assembly of modules built by the United States, Russia, Europe and Japan with mobility systems provided by Canada. But that would not receive astronauts for another 21 years at the end of a long and sometimes troubled transformation at NASA in which the focus had redirected attention from exploration to application — of the near-Earth environment for study, analysis and research in which humans would play a central role.

ABOVE • Stafford (right) and Leonov greet each other in space to end the competitive and sometimes confrontational space race between the United States and the Soviet Union. (NASA)

Bridging the Divide

As noted later, President Nixon was keen to add an arms control agreement to his political record and to consolidate that he agreed a deal between NASA and the Russian government for a joint flight in orbit, the Apollo-Soyuz Test Project (ASTP). It had been an early aspiration of the Nixon presidency to sound out a mission bringing together in space astronauts and cosmonauts to cement a gradually warming relationship with the Soviet Union.

A Soyuz spacecraft would be launched into orbit followed by an Apollo spacecraft that would carry along with it a docking module attached to the nose of the Command Module to which Soyuz would dock. With hatches at each end, the module would serve as an airlock to provide an environmental match between the pure oxygen of Apollo and the nitrogen/oxygen atmosphere of Soyuz by lowering the pressure inside the module from 14.7psi (101.36kPa) of Soyuz to 10psi (68.95kPa), thus avoiding the need for lengthy pre-breathing to purge nitrogen from blood vessels and avoid the 'bends'.

Largely uncommented on at a general public level, agreement had been signed in 1962 for co-operation over weather satellites and Earth science data, and in 1965 for the exchange of information on space biology and medicine. The ASTP was a further step, but it had its critics as well as many advocates. For Nixon, it would unplug the space programme from a Cold War confrontation and reduce the need for decisions made purely on the grounds of political ideology and technological competition.

Carrying Alexei Leonov and Valery Kubasov, Soyuz was launched from Baikonur on July 15, 1975, followed less than eight hours later by the Apollo spacecraft carrying Tom Stafford, Deke Slayton and Vance Brand on a Saturn IB from the 'milk-stool' platform at LC-39B, docking two days later. After formal ceremonies and exchange of mementoes to mark the event, the two spacecraft separated after a duration of just over 44 hours, tested re-docking and undocking before Soyuz returned to Earth on July 21. Apollo remained in space for a further three days conducting science experiments before splashdown near Hawaii.

After 15 manned flights in almost seven years, the Apollo programme was over and on its final mission had demonstrated a level of co-operation that would have been unthinkable at its inception. It had been to the Moon nine times in which 12 astronauts had explored the surface on six landings, sent three teams of astronauts to the Skylab space station and shaken hands with cosmonauts in orbit. In every essential aspect, it was the end of an era.

LEFT • The Apollo-Soyuz crew consisting of cosmonauts Leonov and Kubasov (from right) with astronauts (from top left down), Brand, Slayton and Stafford. (NASA)

EXPLORING
THE PLANETS

Although human space flight had dominated NASA, the exploration of the planets began to flourish with the end of Apollo

Following its establishment in October 1958, NASA had just 32 months before the White House decided its priority for the next decade — a manned landing on the Moon. In the interim period it had set out a balanced programme of science, exploration, research and development in both space and aeronautics, working with science institutes and educational establishments.

Uppermost in the long-range plan were exciting missions for exploring the Moon with Ranger probes to impact the lunar surface after taking photographs during the approach phase, Surveyor spacecraft to land on the surface and sample the soil and Prospector landers to roam around taking pictures and digging the surface. The general plan envisaged manned lunar orbit reconnaissance missions followed by lunar landings when appropriate.

With justification, scientists were excited by the prospect of engaging with a legitimate government agency providing money and support for research that previously had struggled for acceptance in the wider community. Space research was now a credible, scientific undertaking with funding and a planning agenda, attracting proposals for experiments and mission profiles. At the time, there was no precedent for how to design and build such spacecraft and no parallel with which to compare prospective engineering designs.

The planets beckoned through detailed observational records dating back several decades where, in the late 1950s, there was still uncertainty regarding the possibility of life on Mars and the precise nature of Venus, an enigmatic, cloud-shrouded world in which verdant pastures and warm, tropical seas were considered possible. It was, therefore, an exciting prospect to plan early flights near these worlds and take measurements for transmission back to Earth, setting a baseline for future missions including orbiters, landers for sampling and roving vehicles for surface exploration.

The Jet Propulsion Laboratory (JPL), an arm of the California Institute of Technology (Caltech), seized the opportunity for a leading role in planetary exploration through deep research into science instrumentation, solid rocket propulsion and long-range telecommunications. In May 1960, Edgar Cortright at NASA's Office of Space Flight Programs was a strong supporter of the JPL programme of common spacecraft 'bus' designs to which could be attached bespoke instruments, payloads suited to each target planet. He named the concept Mariner to invoke a sense of "sailing on the ocean of space", a phrase picked up by President Kennedy.

Through commonality, money would be saved by using a production-line approach to spacecraft assembly and initial plans envisaged a flight to Venus in 1962 and a flyby mission to Mars in 1964. Because of the relative geometry of the planets, launch windows to Venus open every 19 months and to Mars every 26 months or so. Built to a common bus design, Mariner 1 and 2 would be assigned to Venus, Mariners 3 and 4 to Mars.

Originally planned for launch on an Atlas-Centaur, when the Centaur stage ran into delays the JPL reconfigured the Venus mission to go on a less powerful Atlas-Agena, which switched engineers to base the bus on the smaller Ranger platform, thus did Mariner-R become the name of the initial planetary probes. Mariner 1 was launched on July 22, 1962, but the Atlas-Agena veered off course and had to be destroyed.

Its twin, Mariner 2 was launched successfully on August 27 and flew by Venus at a distance of 21,660 miles (34,854km) on December 14, sending back information that gave an astonishing indication the planet had a surface temperature of 932°F (500°C). This ran contrary to standard expectations of the time and dashed hope of a surface supporting Earth-like conditions with the high possibility of life. Nothing understood to form a living form could exist and evolve under such extreme temperatures.

In the wake of Mariner 2 results, preparations moved ahead for the flight of two Mariners to Mars in the 1964 launch window. Equipped with four solar panels compared with two on Mariner 2, the Mars-bound spacecraft weighed 575lb (261kg) compared with 449lb (203kg) for the Venus probes. On this mission, each spacecraft would carry a TV camera designed to send 21 pictures back to Earth as well as a spectrometer and a radiometer for environmental data to significantly improve on measurements taken directly from Earth.

Mariner 3 suffered a launch failure but Mariner 4 was launched successfully on November 28, 1964, and flew by Mars on July 14, 1965, at the closest distance of 6,118 miles (9,846km) sending 21 pictures back to Earth. As with Mariner 2 at Venus, Mariner 4 turned up some surprises at the Red Planet. Sent back at the slow data rate of 8.5bits/sec, it took a couple of days to assemble all the images back on Earth.

Both missions had been as much a test of the communications systems and the tracking stations, for which NASA was building a Deep Space Network of large dish antennas located at one-third revolutions of the Earth: Goldstone, California; Johannesburg, South Africa; and Canberra, Australia. The Johannesburg tracking station would be replaced by one at Madrid, Spain, in June 1974, equally suitable as it was on approximately the same longitude, all three stations providing planetary spacecraft with a continuous view of Earth from wherever they were in the solar system and thereby maintaining unbroken communications.

Using the back-up spacecraft for Mariner 4, NASA tasked the JPL with assembling a spacecraft for carrying more advanced science instruments back for a second flyby of Venus with Mariner 5. Launched on June 14, 1967, it passed the planet on October 19 at a distance of 2,480 miles (3,990km) and verified the surprising results from Mariner 2, but it would be a long while before NASA went back. At the time Mariner 5 was sending its results back to Earth, Russia too was engaged in a series of successful flights to Venus and the international scientific community shared findings, forging professional relationships.

With only minimal modifications, and with a different suite of science instruments, Mariners 6 and 7 were launched by Atlas-Centaur to Mars in February and

March, 1969. While all eyes were on the advancing Apollo missions, each achieved flybys on July 31 and August 5. With the attention given to Armstrong, Aldrin and Collins, few noticed and were little aware that this concluded the initial set of Mariner missions While the name would continue, further Mariner flights would build on the flybys with orbiters to conduct detailed surveys of Mars.

In the language of planetary scientists, flybys conducted spatial surveys — scans of limited sections of the surface as spacecraft sped by the planet and went on their way, images providing only a quick snapshot of what the surface looked like. Orbiters continually surveying the surface would provide not only a total spatial survey, but also remain in orbit for what scientists called temporal analysis — observations of changes across the surface over long periods of time, as might be conducted observing the seasons on Earth.

Digging the Dirt

Emboldened by ambitious plans for Moon landings and a general expansion of the space programme, scientists hoped to get orbiters around Mars and landers on the surface for

that prospect alive and by the mid-1970s it was a funded programme at the JPL for a spacecraft comprising an orbiter and a lander weighing a total 6,500lb (2,948kg) at launch. It was ambitious, with high-resolution telescope-cameras on the orbiter and TV cameras, surface samplers, seismometers, meteorology sensors and other science instruments on the lander. But the driving imperative was to search for organisms and Voyager would also carry biological instruments for testing samples for evidence of life – past or present.

As the launch dates for what had grown into a series of Voyager missions were refined and the costs matured, senior NASA managers were aware that the agency was in trouble and it was during the second half of 1963 that significant changes were put into effect when George Mueller, Sam Phillips and others were brought in to take control of the manned Moon programme. The next effect was to slash both lunar and planetary research to the bone, elevating all priorities to the Apollo effort.

There was sufficient money for two more Mariner missions, one each to Mars and Venus. To get the temporal view of Mars, after a launch failure with Mariner 8, Mariner 9 was launched during the May 1971 window. The 2,200lb (998kg) spacecraft entered orbit of Mars six months later and over almost a full year returned more than 7,300 pictures showing canyons so vast they would span the North American continent, massive volcanoes dwarfing anything on Earth and clear evidence of seas and oceans in the distant past.

Voyager had been cancelled in 1967, in part because Mariner 4 results indicated the atmosphere was much thinner than expected, requiring greater reliance on rockets for slowing down to a landing and that raised the weight considerably, calling for a much larger rocket to launch it. The programme was resurrected in 1968 as Viking and this slimmed-down version of Voyager put two orbiters around the planet and two landers on the surface in 1976 where

those temporal observations. Following studies that began during 1960, planetary scientists wanted to send a biological laboratory to Mars on a lander that would be launched by Titan, Saturn IB or Saturn V. But that was before the results from Mariner 4 showed a barren and Moon-like surface, which dissuaded some politicians from voting to fund the idea of a search for life using expensive spacecraft.

Acquiring the name Voyager, as a part of the Cold War race with Russia, Congress was just willing to keep

they operated for several years, manipulator arms digging trenches, putting samples in biology instruments and taking seasonal readings of the trace atmosphere.

Surface samples revealed the possibility of past life, but there was nothing conclusive and the expensive Apollo flights had drained NASA of the funds sought by planetary scientists to continue the search. Not until 1996 would NASA get another spacecraft into Mars orbit, a year in which the first rover was put down by Mars *Pathfinder*, albeit only the size of a microwave oven and with limited scope for moving around. But it was a 'first' for NASA and would trigger an extensive campaign to get bigger and better roving vehicles on the surface.

While Mars exploration was placed on hold, the outer planets beckoned and, seeking a balanced programme of planetary exploration, NASA did receive funds for missions to go beyond Mars, cross through the boulder-strewn asteroid belt to explore the gas giants Jupiter and Saturn and eventually the ice worlds of Uranus and Neptune. Being so distant to the Earth, using conventional trajectories and available propulsion systems, these worlds would take a very long time to reach, Jupiter being five times as distant from the Sun as Earth, Saturn almost ten times, Uranus about 20 times and Neptune more than 30 times.

In 1964, while studying different trajectories, JPL engineer Gary Flandro fell upon a rare alignment of Earth and all the outer planets that occurs once in 175 years, a period between 1975 and 1980 in which a spacecraft would be accelerated by the gravitational energy of Jupiter and thrown on course to Saturn, where it could undergo the same effect at Uranus to reach Neptune. Permutations of these slingshot manoeuvres would require precise targeting and there was an opportunity to launch a precursor trial with the Pioneer programme.

With the window of opportunity fast approaching, NASA managed to secure funding for an initial slingshot to Saturn by way of Jupiter, which would be made for only the second of two spacecraft, both developed at the Ames Research Center and launched in 1972 and 1973. Sent first, Pioneer 10 became the first man-made object to pass through the asteroid belt, finding it less threatening than some had feared, and performed a close flyby of Jupiter in December 1973, flying to within 82,178 miles (132,252km) of the cloud tops, which was about one planetary diameter away.

With a satisfactory set of science data in the bank, in December 1974 Pioneer 11 made a 27,000 mile (43,000km) flyby of Jupiter, optimised for a slingshot to Saturn where it came within 13,000 miles (21,000km) of the ringed planet in September 1979. Both spacecraft are now departing the solar system and will journey on in the galaxy for ever, Pioneer 10 encountering the star Aldebaran in about two million years while Pioneer 11, heading in a different direction, will reach the vicinity of the star Aquila in about four million years. For perspective, modern humans appeared only around 250,000 years ago.

The Pioneer probes gathered a lot of information about the two giant planets and some of their moons, and the results helped build a programme based on the Mariner spacecraft but with significant changes resurrecting Voyager as the most appropriate name for this next generation. The flight paths selected for these two spacecraft were complex and interdependent, great effort being made to obtain a close flyby of Saturn's moon, Titan, which Pioneer 11 would indicate to have a dense atmosphere.

The Outer Limits

Weighing 1,592lb (722kg), Voyager 2 was launched first in August 1977 followed by Voyager 1 a few weeks later on a faster track that got it to Jupiter in March 1979, four months ahead of Voyager 2. It had been arranged that way so that if Voyager 1 were a success, Voyager 2 would be targeted for a flight path that would set up a close flyby of Titan when it arrived at Saturn. Only Voyager 1 would make what was dubbed the Grand Tour of all the outer planets.

ABOVE • The Viking Lander 2 site on Mars where the spacecraft would sample the surface and conduct scientific tests for signs of life. (NASA)

LEFT • Pioneer 10 flew through the asteroid belt and by Jupiter for the first time, opening the possibilities of reaching the outer worlds in the solar system. (NASA)

FAR LEFT • Gary Flandro designed mission trajectories to the outer planets using slingshot flybys to dramatically reduce the time taken to get there. (NASA)

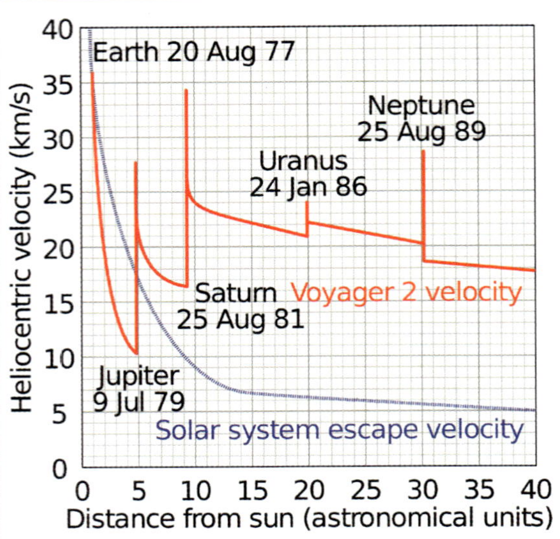

Voyager 1 passed Saturn on November 12, 1980, at a distance of 77,000 miles (124,000km) on the day in which it also came within 4,030 miles (6,490km) of Titan, the second largest moon in the solar system. Voyager 2 came within 63,000 miles (101,000km) of Saturn on August 26, 1981, and sped by Uranus at a distance of 50,600 miles (81,500km) on January 24, 1986, closing to within 3,076 miles (4,951km) of Neptune on August 25, 1989.

The two Voyager spacecraft joined the two Pioneers in starting their journeys into the galaxy and beyond the influence of the Sun, making observations and reporting back as they went. Having provided scientists with data that still continues to unlock secrets about these enigmatic worlds, the moons of Jupiter and Saturn continued to amaze scientists with their variety and possibilities for supporting oceans that may contain living organisms, tipping the scale away from a presumption that Mars was the only harbinger of life.

Such was the level of interest in the gas giants that the scientific community successfully pressed for an orbiter to remain at Jupiter and extensively survey the giant planet and its many moons. That was realised with Galileo, launched on October 18, 1989, by the Space Shuttle *Atlantis* which, after release from the payload bay, was boosted out of Earth orbit by a solid propellant rocket motor. Weighing 5,640lb (2,560kg), the orbiter carried a probe that was released into the atmosphere of Jupiter, sending back information as it plunged down to destruction on December 7, 1995, a day before Galileo put itself into orbit. Conducting surveys of the planet and several of its larger moons, the spacecraft ended its mission on September 21, 2003 when it was directed to a deep dive into the denser layers of Jupiter's thick atmosphere.

A similar mission profile was flown by the 12,593lb (5,712kg) Cassini-Huygens launched by a Titan rocket on October 15, 1997. Following a circuitous path using multiple flybys of Venus, Earth and Jupiter to gain energy, it reached Saturn on July 1, 2004, sending the European Huygens probe down to a landing on Titan on January 14, 2005. Surveys and close flybys of Saturn's moons occupied the next several years before the spacecraft was intentionally sent to its grave within Saturn's atmosphere on September 15, 2017.

Engineered at the Johns Hopkins University Applied Physics Laboratory, the New Horizons mission was designed to explore distant Pluto, once considered a planet and now allocated as a dwarf planet, a prominent member of the Kuiper belt of objects orbiting the Sun at great distances beyond the outer planets Uranus and Neptune. Because of its highly elliptical orbit, Pluto comes within the orbital radius of Neptune during a ten-year period as it orbits the Sun once every 248 years, the most recent being 1979-1999. Not until the year 2,277 will it be that close again.

Albeit with the destination not at its closest, but taking the opportunity to reach Pluto within a reasonable time, weighing 1,054lb (478kg) the New Horizons spacecraft was launched on January 19, 2006, on an Atlas V rocket that accelerated the probe to 36,373mph (58,536km/h), the fastest ever achieved by an object made by humans. Using Jupiter for a gravity-assist slingshot in February 2007, it passed to within 7,800 miles (12,500km) of Pluto on July 14, 2015, 4.67billion miles (7.5bn km) from Earth, almost 1.9bn miles (3.06bn km) beyond the mean orbital radius of Neptune.

New Horizons discovered much about the Kuiper belt and observed other objects, including Arrokoth, the only object subject to a flyby discovered after the spacecraft's launch, which it flew by in January 2019, together with other icy bodies orbiting the Sun at the outer fringes of the solar system. New Horizons explored Pluto's moon Charon, which had been discovered in 1978, and active geological features that posed many questions about the origin of this tiny world orbiting at such a distance that the Sun only appears as a bright star. The spacecraft will leave the Kuiper belt in 2028 as it continues on its way out of the solar system.

The United States is the only country to have explored the solar system beyond Mars and on August 5, 2011, NASA's Juno spacecraft was launched to Jupiter, entering a polar orbit around the giant planet on July 5, 2016, where it operates today in its survey of planetary characteristics,

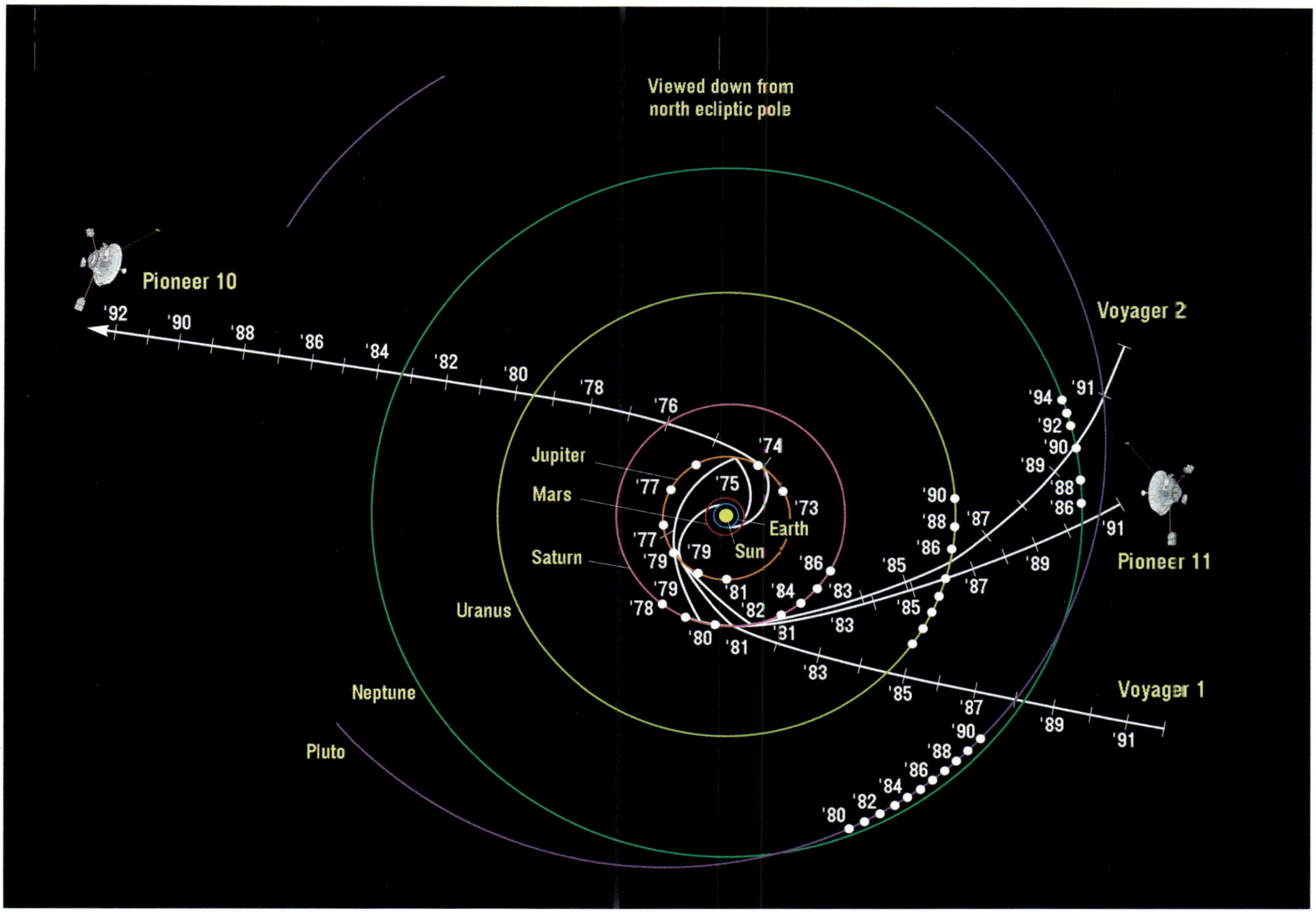

ABOVE • This chart displays the directions in which Pioneer and Voyager spacecraft exiting the solar system are headed. (NASA)

LEFT • Three generations of NASA Mars rovers with Pathfinder of 1997 (foreground), Spirit and Opportunity (left) of 2004 and the Mars Science Laboratory vehicles, of which Curiosity landed in 2011 and Perseverance in 2021. (NASA)

quantities of water beneath ice-encrusted surfaces. There are strong possibilities for life in these subsurface oceans warmed by thermal energy, possibly of a type that scientists have discovered supports life around ocean vents on Earth.

Over the last several years, the pivot of attention has shifted from Venus and Mars to Jupiter and Saturn, with the latest launch sending the heavyweight Europa Clipper, weighing 13,371lb (6,065kg), in October 2024 to a rendezvous with Jupiter, where it will enter orbit in April 2030. Arriving before JUICE due to its faster flight path after being launched on a SpaceX Falcon Heavy rocket, the spacecraft will conduct 44 close flybys of Europa, considered by many scientists to be a likely candidate for microbial life, down to around 16 miles (25.7km) where it will conduct remote sensing of the surface.

For the future, NASA is planning to launch a flying machine to Saturn's moon Titan in 2028. Arriving in 2034, the Dragonfly spacecraft will land on the surface and release a helicopter powered by rotary blades drawing energy from batteries charged by a radioisotope generator. With science instruments and cameras, Dragonfly will move around from site to site providing detailed information on a surface first visited by the Cassini-Huygens probe in 2005.

The New Mars

While NASA directed considerable effort to advanced space exploration at the outer planets, missions to Mars ran into problems after *Pathfinder* put down its small rover in 1997. There was a period when a determined effort was made to use commercial off-the-shelf (COTS) products to assemble and fly low-cost spacecraft, but that proved too simplistic and brought a period of failures, which prevented a successful mission to Mars before Mars Odyssey, an orbiter launched in April 2001, which is still operating there.

Two years later, in 2003 NASA launched two spacecraft in the Mars Exploration Rover series, each (*Spirit* and *Opportunity*) about the size of a shopping trolley festooned with science instruments, cameras and fundamental autonomous navigation equipment all powered by solar cell panels. Their performance was spectacular, *Spirit* trundling 4.8 miles (7.7km) across the surface and operating for six years from January 2004 until its last signal was sent in March 2010. Its twin, *Opportunity* travelled a distance of more than 28 miles (45km) and operated from landing in January 2004 until June 2018.

The information these two roving vehicles sent back on a continuous basis for a period of more than 14 years greatly exceeded expectations and their lifetimes went far beyond the 90-day design requirement, sending to Earth more than 330,000 images of soil, pebbles, rocks, craters, canyons, arroyo, sand dunes and new features never seen on any other world. In concert with Odyssey in orbit, their work was supplemented by Mars Reconnaissance Orbiter, which arrived in orbit in March 2006 and is still operational. But this was just the beginning.

With a launch weight of 8,462lb (3,893kg), the Mars *Curiosity* spacecraft was sent on its way to Mars by a powerful Atlas 5 on November 26, 2011, a radical concept including a rover the size of a compact car and weighing 1,982lb (899kg). Arriving in the vicinity of Mars on August 6, 2012, it was set down on the surface lowered by a sky-crane hovering over the touchdown site until *Curiosity* was on all six wheels, at which point the sky-crane sped away and crashed to the surface at a safe distance. Carrying a diverse and complex suite of instruments, cameras and scientific tools, it continues to examine the surface at a place called Gale crater and has so far travelled a distance of more than 20 miles (32km).

the first outer-planet spacecraft powered by solar cells, previous spacecraft having radioactive thermoelectric generators of the type used to power Apollo Lunar Surface Experiment Package (ASLEP) experiments left on the surface of the Moon.

Improvements to solar cell technology meant this mode of electrical energy production was applied to the next NASA mission to Jupiter, the JUICE – Jupiter Icy Moons – programme launched by a European Ariane V rocket on April 14, 2023, the first outer planet mission not sent on an American rocket. With an anticipated arrival date of July 2031, it will enter an orbit that allows a detailed survey of Ganymede, Callisto and Europa, moons that scientists have identified as having large

A second rover named *Perseverance* was launched on July 30, 2020, with some improvements and with a helicopter called *Ingenuity* for demonstrating the ability of winged flying machines to assist with reconnaissance and route planning. A prime purpose for this mission was to collect samples for return to Earth on a subsequent mission. *Ingenuity* successfully demonstrated powered flight in the thin atmosphere of Mars, accumulating almost two hours nine minutes on 72 flights logging a total distance of 10.7 miles (17.2km) before it was grounded due to damage to its rotor blades.

Over time, NASA had focused planetary research on Mars, Jupiter and Saturn, while during the period of the Cold War Russia had sent orbiters and landers to Venus. NASA sent the last of the Mariner-class spacecraft to Venus in November 1973 when Mariner 10 conducted a flyby on its way to Mercury followed in May 1978 by Pioneer Venus 1 to orbit the planet and Pioneer Venus three months later to send a series of probes through the atmosphere. The orbiter Magellan was launched in May 1989 with plans to send another orbiter and a separate lander mission in the early 2030s.

NASA has sent only two missions to the innermost planet Mercury, first with Mariner 10 launched in November 1973 followed by Messenger in August 2004 and both were an outstanding success. As noted, Mariner 10 conducted a fast flyby of Venus gathering data and using gravity-assist to modify its orbit around the Sun so that it completed three close flybys of Mercury before completing its mission in March 1975. However, synchronised with the rotation of Mercury, the visits only imaged 45% of the surface.

Entering orbit around Mercury in March 2011, seven years after launch due to multiple flybys of Earth, Venus and Mercury, Messenger operated for just over four years, returning more than 300,000 images and mapping all the surface features to provide unprecedented science that continues to provide fresh insight to the origin and evolution of this strange world. Mercury has attracted the interest of the European Space Agency, which sent its BepiColombo mission to Mercury in October 2018 and which it is expected to reach in December 2025.

BepiColombo is a co-operative venture with both the European Space Agency (ESA) and Japan, each providing an orbiter for unique studies of the planet and its environment, epitomising the international nature of planetary exploration. Only NASA has sent a probe to every planet in the solar system and to the Kuiper belt, while Russia has focused on Venus and Mars and ESA has sent spacecraft to Mars, Venus and Mercury, joined now by India, Japan and the United Arab Emirates with its Mars missions.

More could have been accomplished had a broader base of manned and unmanned flights of exploration and discovery been funded, but first the race to get astronauts on the Moon starved planetary science of much that could have been achieved and then the drive to develop the shuttle prevented many missions that could have flown. It was the urgent pressure to retain a manned flight programme within diminishing budgets that prevented more ambitious goals such as returning samples from Mars or exploring the subsurface oceans on the moons of Jupiter.

THE SPACE SHUTTLE AND AN OLIVE BRANCH

NASA wanted a Space Shuttle, a Space Station and bases on the Moon and Mars, but it was all too much to ask for, while the Russians were invited to further co-operation

I t had been in London on August 10, 1968, that NASA chose to talk publicly about a reusable shuttle for the first time, when its head of manned space flight George Mueller presented a paper to the British Interplanetary Society (BIS). Formed in 1933, this organisation had been a founding member of the International Academy of Astronautics, the prestigious world body representing space and rocket engineers and scientists. The BIS gave Mueller an award for his work on Apollo and it was then that he chose to articulate what had already been part of NASA planning for at least two years.

NASA's plans for a reusable shuttle had humble origins and grew more ambitious as partners pledged support in return for a bigger vehicle. Initial Phase A feasibility studies relied heavily on NASA's existing work on lifting-bodies and hypersonic research, envisaging a reusable orbiter propelled into space on the wings of an equally reusable 'fly-back' booster. To help share the cost, when contracts for Phase B definition studies were issued to competing teams led by North American Rockwell and McDonnell Douglas in July 1970, NASA wanted the military to endorse the Space Shuttle as a vital national asset.

The Phase B contracts specified a two-stage fully reusable shuttle with the orbiter carrying 15,000lb (6,800kg) of cargo. NASA anticipated up to 75 flights a year with a turnaround time of just two weeks and for it to be operational by the end of 1977. It wanted the lowest cost-per-flight to encourage extensive use of the vehicle. Because the fully reusable system was expensive to develop, annual costs spread over the seven or eight years of development could grow beyond NASA's annual budget. But in the summer of 1970, NASA raised the payload capability to 25,000lb (11,340kg).

The fully reusable system involved a 1,700-ton piloted fly-back booster, bigger than a Jumbo Jet and powered by 12 rocket engines, launched vertically with the 380-ton orbiter on its back. The mated stack would reach a speed of 7,000mph (11,260km/h) whereupon the booster would separate and fly back leaving the orbiter powered by two rocket motors to reach orbit at a speed of 17,500mph (28,157km/h). The orbiter alone was more than 200ft (61m) long and as it stood on the launch pad the mated stack would be 276ft (84m) tall.

The colossal cost of developing a booster and an orbiter was too great to fund and in May 1971, NASA learned that it would have to cope with the reduced budget it already had.

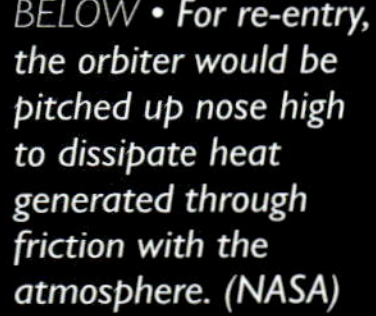

BELOW • For re-entry, the orbiter would be pitched up nose high to dissipate heat generated through friction with the atmosphere. (NASA)

A year earlier NASA had learned that it would not be able to afford both shuttle and space station, the latter having to wait until the shuttle was built and paid for. Now, on top of that, it appeared there would be insufficient money to build both booster and orbiter.

One solution was not to develop a manned fly-back booster at all, simply to reduce the size of the orbiter so that it could be launched by an expendable rocket stage thrown away on each mission. It was a far cry from the original idea of a fully reusable Space Shuttle! Without the reusable booster the low-cost goal of cheap flights was an impossible aspiration. But even if NASA opted for a conventional booster, how could the size of the orbiter be reduced?

A solution suggested itself from Phase A studies conducted by the US Air Force. Instead of carrying all the hydrogen fuel for its rocket motors inside the orbiter, why not carry it in two jettisonable over-wing tanks? The physical size of the orbiter could be reduced because liquid hydrogen has 75% of the volume and less than 20% of the weight of the two propellants (hydrogen and oxygen). Moving it outside in separate tanks would substantially cut the size, and the cost, of the orbiter.

Since July 1970, NASA had funded studies of alternative shuttle configurations and employed the consultancy firm Mathematica to calculate the financial advantages in having a shuttle at all. NASA was wedded to the concept of low-cost space transportation and wanted sound economic analysis as a useful justification. For previous manned programmes, the Russians had triggered the idea of putting Americans in orbit or on the Moon. This time, there was no direct challenge or reason to build it. But without the Space Shuttle, US manned space flight would have been killed off at the end of the Apollo missions and the short-lived Skylab space station.

The value of the shuttle as a potential workhorse, rather than a ferry to a space station, began to take hold. With economists looking at costs and NASA looking at technical innovation, 1971 was a seminal period in the development of its future manned space vehicle. Only by launching several of them on each mission could the cost per flight fall to a level that would attract its use as a satellite launcher, the shuttle's flexibility and carrying capacity more than offsetting the high price per flight. Moreover, this price could be spread among

ABOVE • Existing Apollo facilities would be used to launch the combination booster/orbiter, both elements piloted for return to Earth. (NASA)

several customers with each paying less than they would for a dedicated expendable launch vehicle.

But even with these measures, still the development cost was too high, so NASA took the engineering a step further, proposing that both hydrogen and oxygen propellants be carried in a big external tank. The winged orbiter would be attached to the side of the external tank and the tank itself fixed atop a rocket booster taking the place of the winged, fly-back booster in the original Phase B study. Although the external tank would be thrown away after reaching orbit, the simplicity and relative low cost of the tank itself would offset the price of a new one each time. As for the original fly-back piloted booster, that might be a legacy candidate from existing rocket stages such as a reusable version of the S-IC first stage of the Saturn V, fitted with wings as proposed by Boeing.

Second Guess

In a series of Phase B extension studies throughout 1971, NASA refined the Space Shuttle concept and Mathematica took each option and worked out the development cost versus the price per flight. NASA had wanted to push for the lowest launch cost, but that would bring the highest development price, which was way out of reach. However, making the shuttle cheaper to develop meant it would be more expensive to fly. A classic Catch 22 situation. The only way out of this dilemma was to look not for super-efficient liquid propellant booster stages, but to less efficient, but very much cheaper, solid propellant rockets.

By the autumn of 1971, teams conducting Phase B Shuttle extension studies were working to find a solution to the cost problem. The government had received word about the proposed development cost of the shuttle and it

RIGHT • Two Phase B contenders, North American Rockwell (NR) and McDonnell Douglas (MDAC) propose different configurations for the Space Shuttle contract. (NASA)

was too high, well above what the Nixon administration was prepared to take to Congress for approval. By moving all the orbiter propellant to an external tank, the size of the winged spaceplane had shrunk to 110ft (33.5m), significantly cutting the cost. Now a decision had to be made about the booster, at best now only a partially reusable system, but it was not certain that NASA would go with solids.

With their uncontrollable operating profile, once lit they were very difficult to shut down and NASA had always said it would not use solid propellant rockets to launch people into space. Being simpler and cheaper to build, the economics argued otherwise, but NASA examined a wide range of liquid propellant concepts and had Mathematica do a cost/benefit analysis of all these different types of booster. Plus there was the question whether series-burn or parallel-burn configurations were more effective and at what cost for each concept.

Series-burn was the conventional layout whereby the orbiter would be stacked on top of the booster in a conventional rocket configuration. But that pushed up the required thrust of the booster to 3,000 tons to lift the fully fuelled shuttle weighing a projected 2,200 tons. A parallel-burn arrangement had two boosters either side of the orbiter so that all three elements could fire up their rocket motors to get off the pad, for which each booster would have to produce only 1,300 tons of thrust in addition to about 500 tons of thrust from the orbiter's liquid propellant motors. Whichever type was chosen, NASA insisted that the boosters must be recovered from splashdown for reuse.

But there was a further impediment to cost savings, which originated when the air force was encouraged to get behind the shuttle as a concept and support its development in Congressional budget hearings. If the air force was to use the shuttle it would have a big say in the orbiter's payload capacity. Initially, NASA had wanted a Space Shuttle capable of putting 25,000lb (11,340kg) of cargo 200 miles (322km) above Earth out of Cape Canaveral in Florida. The air force wanted to place 40,000lb (18,144kg) in a polar orbit from Vandenberg Air Force Base in California. But the increase was more than that implied by the numbers.

NASA's mission would take it due east on a path using the spin of the earth as it rotated on its polar axis. The air force wanted to send satellites into space that would head due south and circle the earth at 90° to the equator, passing over both poles. That meant the energy needed to get it into orbit had to be that much greater because it could not get energy from the Earth's spin, which adds just over 1,000mph (1,609km/h) to the launch speed at the equator. A lift of 40,000lb (18,144kg) to polar orbit was equivalent to 65,000lb (29,484kg) out of Cape Canaveral, more than four times NASA's original reference mission.

A larger payload means a bigger rocket, more thrust to launch it and higher cost. It was a price that had to be paid because accommodating the air force was essential to getting the shuttle approved. In addition, the air force wanted the shuttle they used to return to a runway near the launch site within one orbit of the Earth. In the 90 minutes it takes to circle the Earth, the launch site would have moved 1,500 miles (2,413km) to the west, which required the returning orbiter to

BELOW • When costs for a fully reusable system proved too high, NASA looked at removing fuel from the orbiter fuselage to over-wing tanks. (NASA)

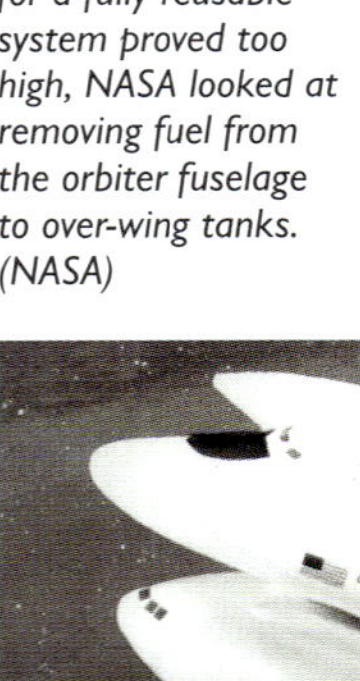

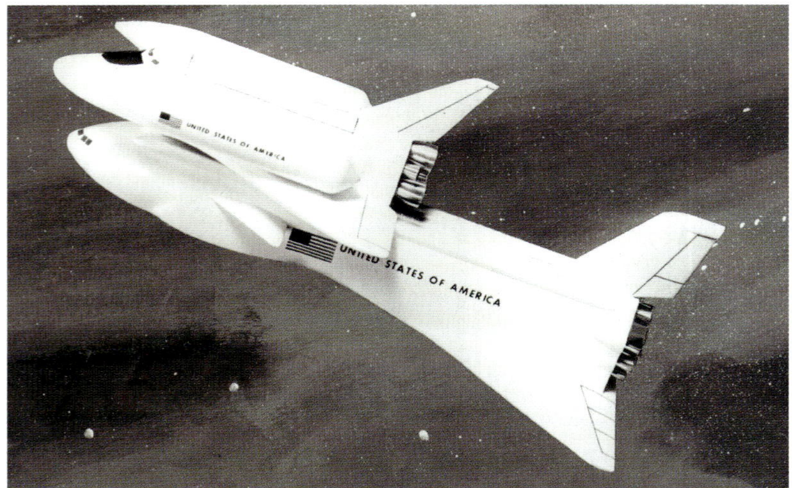

fly back east as it descended though the atmosphere and to do that it required a very big double-delta wing.

Initially, NASA had lobbied for a simple orbiter with a straight wing like a conventional aircraft needing relatively simple protection in the form of a heat shield when returning to a landing. All these additional requirements, the majority driven by the air force, required a bigger, heavier and more costly shuttle with an advanced thermal protection driven by the need for a cross-range capability.

Ironically, it was reusability that pushed the air force to specify these demanding requirements, a use that could not be publicly declared at the time. It wanted to launch a very large spy satellite the size of a school bus that could remain operational by Space Shuttle orbiters periodically refuelling it in space. But to avoid detection by Soviet snoopers it would have to do that within one revolution of the Earth. In a further irony, although NASA had hoped to split the cost of the Space Shuttle with the air force, that was never possible, neither did the spy satellite refuelling task that pushed the specification so hard ever take place.

The price of developing even a partially reusable launch system was high and it was becoming a hard sell to President Nixon. But there were other factors too that bore down on NASA as it struggled to find a way to preserve manned space flight in the dying months of lunar exploration with the last of the Apollo Moon flights. In its reports, Mathematica had assessed the overall cost of a space programme operated with conventional expendable rockets and one wholly supported through reusable shuttle missions.

By 1971, it was clear that instead of being a supply ship for crew and cargo to a space station, a task for which it had originally been envisaged, without a space station it could only be justified if it became the sole means of sending anything into space. Mathematica reported that the shuttle would be cheaper only if it operated around 60 flights a year. It would not be cheaper if there were less, fewer flights failing to pay over time the cost of development through lower launch costs.

The Nixon government stipulated a binding requirement that a partially reusable Shuttle had to cost less than

ABOVE • When a fully reusable booster was too expensive, liquid or solid propellant side-boosters were proposed for the orbiter with its propellants in an external tank. (NASA)

LEFT • McDonnell Douglas presented its Phase B Shuttle proposal with solid rocket boosters in late 1971. (McDonnell Douglas)

$5.15billion to develop compared with NASA's original fully reusable system at $10bn. That more ambitious concept would pay for itself only with a much larger space programme than NASA could support on the money it had. The annual budget was continuing to fall and the break-even mark of 60 Space Shuttle flights a year was only marginally capable of paying back development costs of $5.15bn over a 12-year period.

A persistent myth has been entrenched in retro-analysis of the Space Shuttle that it failed because it never reduced the cost of space transportation to the levels claimed and used at the time to justify its development. When presented to Nixon, NASA received support from his advisors on the basis of a jobs programme, one too that would bring money and work to the President's California state.

A Different Direction

The pivotal changes in NASA planning made during 1971 transformed the agency from a research and development organisation operating satellites and spacecraft across the solar system while simultaneously advancing human space flight through expanding capabilities and scientific research on the lunar surface. Instead, NASA would fund development of what was framed as the Space Transportation System (STS) and whose initials underpin a core programme from which all else would emerge. But only when funds permitted.

It was a significant and transformational time for the storied agency and one that was stressed continually by declining budgets and political opposition, many members of Congress seeking to redefine the world in which a new period of détente and co-operation with the Soviet Union opened a glimmer of hope and optimism. While NASA and the White House were struggling to find a way to sustain manned space flight, diplomats were redefining the relationship with Russia and writing rule books on nuclear arms agreements of a type that had never been put together before.

The first Moon landing was little more than a year old when NASA Administrator Thomas Paine wrote to Mstislav Keldysh, President of the Soviet Academy of Sciences, in October 1970 to open discussions about possible co-operation in manned space flight. By early 1971, Nixon was actively encouraging such a proposal, egged on by foreign policy advisor Henry Kissinger who saw in this an opportunity to forge better relations and cement ties already being defined through arms agreements.

There was an unexpected connection between the arms agreements and the possibility of mounting a joint flight with the Russians. In Nixon's view the United States could not afford to slow down its premier flagship achievements in space while simultaneously discussing a space venture with the Kremlin. Agreement on the joint venture would have to come quickly as it relied on availability of a Saturn IB and an Apollo spacecraft. In Nixon's view — "I want symbolism" — the impending arms

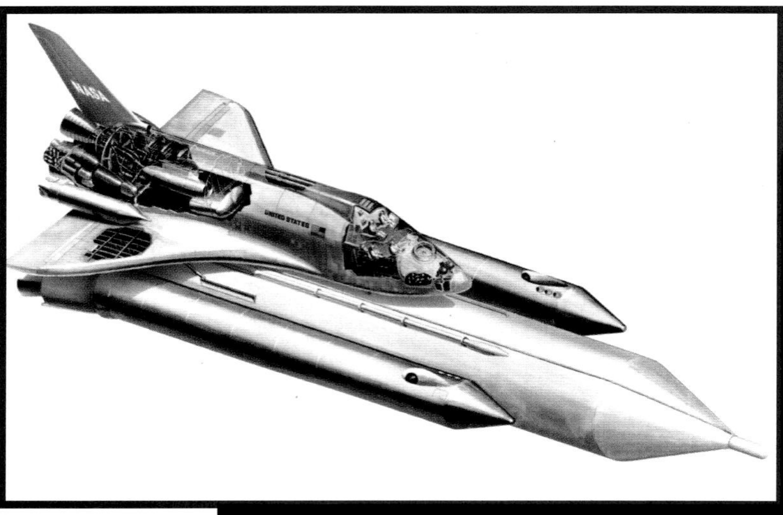

ABOVE • The North American Rockwell proposal with turbofan engines in the aft section of the payload bay and two solid rocket abort motors above each wing adjacent to the fuselage. (North American Rockwell)

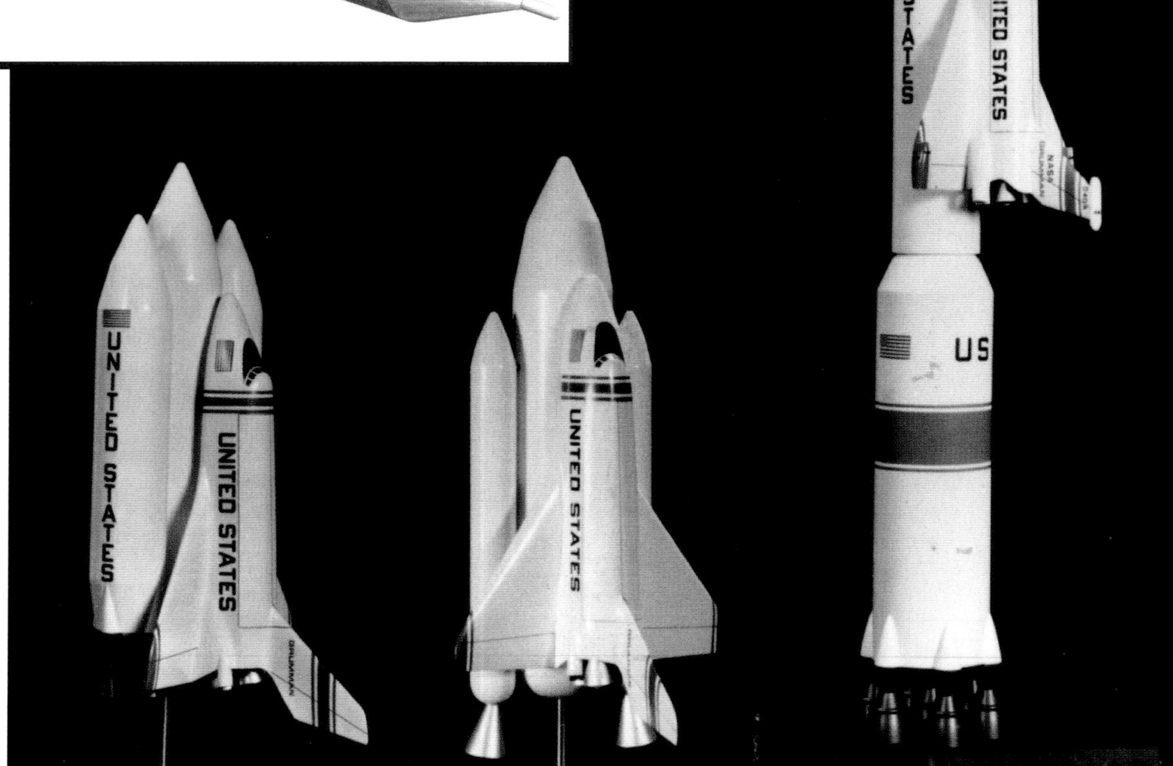

RIGHT • Three contenders for booster configurations including liquid propellant, solid propellant and a series-burn stack (right). (NASA)

agreement and the space offer to the Russians would give his presidency a boost in the 1972 re-election bid.

It was for all these reasons that Nixon finally agreed to support the Space Shuttle and to bring that to Congress for approval. For him, the shuttle was a jobs programme made valid by Congress's cancellation of the Supersonic Transport and the loss of workers resulting from that, while the joint flight with the Russians boosted his credentials for strategic decisions while bolstering geopolitical diplomacy through the arms agreement.

Thus, when the Space Shuttle announcement was made from the Western White House at San Clemente, California, in January 1972, it was the product of a complex interplay between funding new jobs, brandishing a new challenge to the Russians and keeping NASA in the manned space flight business while constraining its ambitions through limited funding and a tight rein on those long-term projects calling for sustained expenditure. Nixon was adamant he would not preside over programmes with runaway budgets like Apollo.

By this date, too, Russia had re-orientated its own space programme toward Earth-orbiting space stations with the Soyuz spacecraft, but the occupation of its first facility, Salyut 1, in June 1971 had resulted in the deaths of cosmonauts Georgy Dobrovolsky, Vladislav Volkov and Viktor Patsayev when their spacecraft depressurised. It was not a good omen for future co-operation where the engineering practices and techniques of both Russia and the United States were very different and it would be more than two years before the Soyuz/Salyut programme resumed.

And the Space Shuttle decision had another significance, too. Nixon was influenced by programmes and actions pursuant to his foreign policy initiatives — ending the war in Vietnam, improving relations with the Soviet Union and opening China to dialogue. In February, he visited Beijing and met with Mao Zedong. All these factors were conducive to supporting geopolitical initiatives and within this frame it was quietly mooted that the United States and the Soviet Union might extend the joint docking flight planned for 1974 into the Space Shuttle era, this winged spaceplane docking perhaps with the Salyut space station.

It had taken the connection between development of the shuttle and national security credibility to the programme, tipping the Congressional vote in support of this exciting new venture, but it had its price. In trying to reduce costs, NASA had suggested a unique arrangement in which the then British Aircraft Corporation was invited to build the wings for the shuttle, thereby gaining access to US space technologies as a result. The idea was scotched when the air force declared that it would embed the Space Shuttle as a launch system for its own operations, de facto preventing any hardware element for national security being provided by a foreign manufacturer.

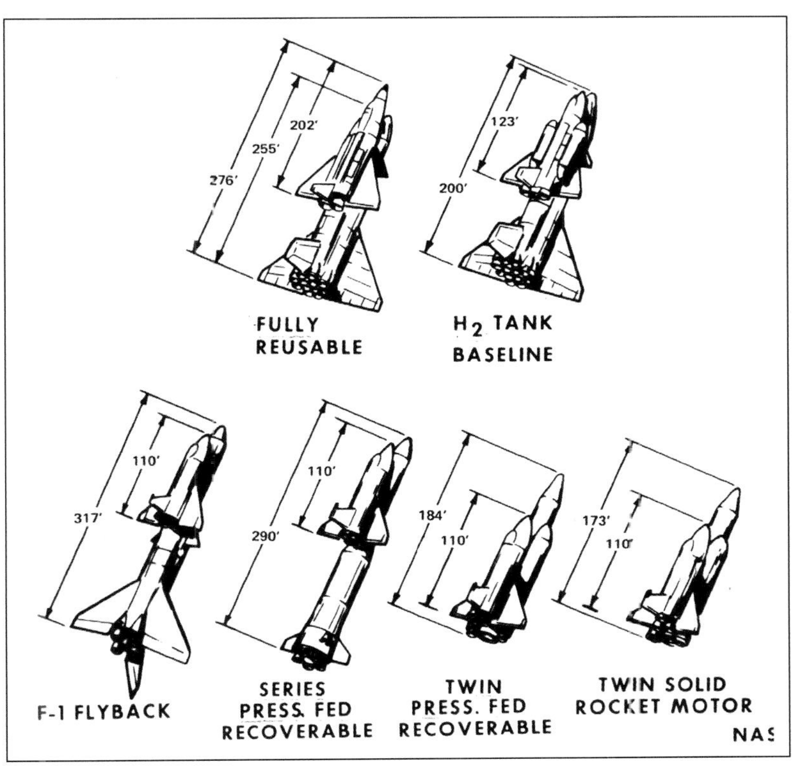

A NEW WAY OF FLYING

NASA develops a Space Transportation System and faces challenges that transformed an industry

ABOVE • The Space Shuttle concept envisaged a future of reusable vehicles plying back and forth to space supporting beneficial research for humans on Earth. (NASA)

At the time the Space Shuttle was formally declared as the next major manned space flight programme for the United States in January 1972, the precise configuration had not been decided, but it would not take long to recognise the economic value of the Solid Rocket Booster (SB), despite NASA's historic reservation regarding the use of solid propellants launching astronauts. Overall, the Space Transportation System would form the core of America's launch infrastructure and that still assumed the use of a Space Tug to move satellites and spacecraft around to different orbits above and beyond the maximum altitude the Space Shuttle could reach, usefully around 500 miles (804km).

Early hopes of a first flight in 1977 quickly evaporated and by 1973 the general configuration of the Orbiter had been agreed. Attached to an external tank and straddled by two solid rocket boosters (SRBs), the Orbiter would be powered by three main engines each delivering a thrust of 450,000lb (2,000kN), throttled over a range of 50-100%

and a combustion chamber pressure of 3,000lb/psi (8.95kg/cm²), three times that of most other rocket motors. While Rockwell International (formerly North American Aviation and then North American Rockwell) got to build the Orbiter, its subsidiary Rocketdyne would build the main engines.

The two SRBs were each 149.16ft (45.46m) long, with a diameter of 12.16ft (3.7m) and although those used for the first seven flights had a thrust of 2.8million lb (12,454kN), from the eighth flight on they had a thrust of 3.3million lb (14,678kN) at lift-off. They would provide 71% of the total launch thrust for around two minutes three seconds, when they would burn out at a height of about 28 miles (45km) and separate from the external tank, firing clusters of solid propellant thrusters at each end to move them away from the rest of the stack.

The SRBs were partially reusable by parachuting into the ocean from where they would be recovered by special vessels towing them back to Port Canaveral for cleaning and the individual segments comprising long cylindrical cases used again. Fitted with replacement electronic

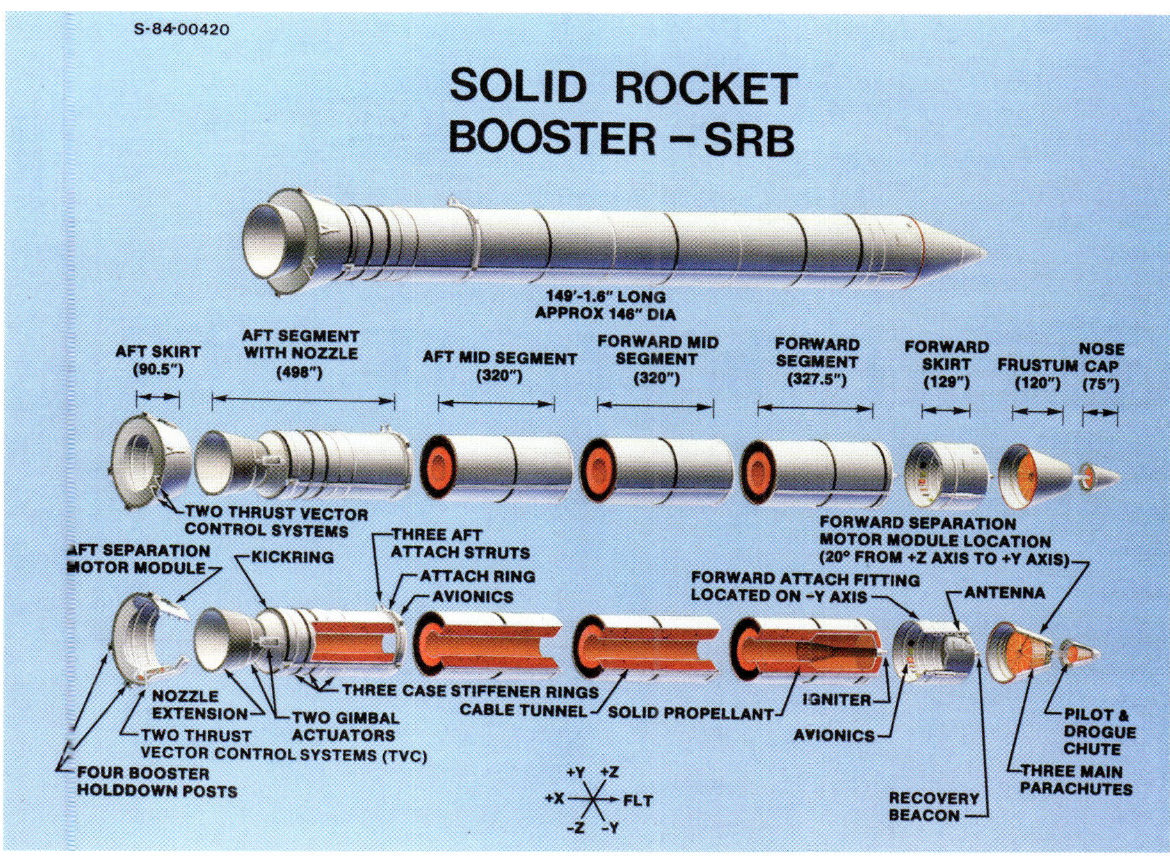

control systems, nozzles and all support equipment, it had been hoped that refurbishment would not add greatly to the overall launch cost of each Space Shuttle, but that would not prove to be the case, reuse of the Space Shuttle SRBs being significantly higher than expected.

The Orbiter was designed to support a crew of six or seven for up to ten days in space in a comfortable, 'shirt-sleeve' environment of an oxygen/nitrogen atmosphere. It had a total length of 122ft (37.2m) and a wing span of 78ft (23.7m). Empty, it weighed 172,000lb (78,000kg), or up to 240,000lb (110,000kg) fully loaded for flight. During aerodynamic flight, control was achieved through elevons on the trailing edge of the wing and a rudder while attitude control in space was by way of thrusters in the nose area and on the two blisters supporting the orbital manoeuvring rocket motors either side of the aft fuselage.

The payload bay was sized specifically to carry a spy satellite (which it never did) and had a length of 60ft (18.18m) and a diameter of 15ft (4.5m), with the maximum weight capability of 65,000lb (29,484kg). Closed by two lengthwise doors, the bay was set along the entire length of the mid-fuselage between the nose section and the aft assembly, which carried the vertical tail and the three main engines. Weight growth in the Space Shuttle never did quite achieve that payload capability. A remote manipulator arm the length of two telegraph poles end to end, was carried down the left side of the bay for moving loads in and out of the Orbiter in space.

Propellant for the Orbiter's three main engines was carried in the external tank, a cylindrical structure 153.8ft (46.8m) in length with a diameter of 27.6ft (8.4m), the liquid oxygen tank being above the tank containing liquid hydrogen. Separate feed lines, each 17in (43cm) in diameter would supply propellants to the three Orbiter main engines from just before launch to shortly before orbit insertion, the added velocity being made up by the two manoeuvring engines also used for changing obit and for returning from space.

With main engine cut-off just before reaching orbit, the tank would separate and arch back down through the atmosphere where it would be destroyed. At first, the flight profile had the Orbiter's main engines operating all the way into orbit, the external tank being separated and de-orbited using a small solid propellant rocket in the nose. But that was wasteful on propellant, the removal of the small nose rocket saving weight.

Some had proposed using the external tank as a space station in much the way Skylab had been envisaged as a 'wet' workshop fitted out for habitation before NASA adopted the 'dry' concept fully equipped before launch. By having the external tank separate just before orbital speed and tumble back down of its own accord, some were grateful that it prevented NASA getting a space station the cheap way, one which would in any event have been limited in concept. With its eye on a permanently manned station, the agency was not going to be short-changed.

While traditional in its construction and materials, the Orbiter was technically challenging in its operating environment, a thermal protection system being required

that could be used many times over. No manned spacecraft had been reusable, heat shields being of an ablative material that would partially burn away to carry thermal energy in a charring process. Ablative heat shields had stood the test of time and that used on Apollo consisted of a stainless-steel honeycomb matrix into which was poured for solidification an epoxy resin. But it was not reusable and that was a limiting factor in using a spacecraft more than once.

The Orbiter's thermal protection would come in the form of more than 30,000 porous silicon tiles, a very light heat sink material that was highly heat resistant and would come in two types, black for the hottest regions and white for less hot areas. Places subject to the highest temperatures on re-entry, such as the nose cap and the leading edge of the wings, were covered in a reinforced carbon-carbon, a matrix of carbon-fibre and graphite.

As NASA examined ways to save money while refining the design of the Orbiter, it deleted two elements in the original requirement. One of which was to carry two conventional turbofan engines in the aft area of the payload bay, each with individual doors so they could be deployed in the atmosphere providing power for the spaceplane to fly from place to place. That was deleted due to excessive weight and the risk of carrying aviation fuel all the way to space and back.

The second element deleted was more contentious and with safety implications. As conceived, the Space Shuttle as a total system was designed to a theoretical concept of fail-operational/fail-operational/fail-safe, under which it could experience two consecutive single-point failures and still conduct its mission, only returning to a safe recovery and landing should a third tier system malfunction. Airliners are designed with that capability and NASA believed it could build the shuttle with the same level of triple-redundancy, failing to recognise that no aircraft has ever been built to that demanding requirement that has not crashed.

Previously, Mercury, Gemini and Apollo spacecraft had launch escape systems, a completely separate method of getting astronauts away from danger without requiring the failing stack to correct itself and bring the crew home. Mercury and Apollo had escape rockets mounted on top of lattice towers and Gemini had ejection seats, all wired to a 'malfunction detection system' that merely sensed something was outside acceptable constraints of safety and fired the escape mechanism.

The Space Shuttle had no such system and a belief in the 'airliner hypothesis' of crew safety encouraged design

engineers to remove two abort rocket motors that had been designed to fit above the delta wings, either side of the vertical tail and at the juncture with the rear fuselage. The abort motors would be jettisoned outside the atmosphere where the Orbiter could separate and return to base in an emergency. The argument for removing the abort motors was a little more nuanced, in that to allow those to do their job the Orbiter would have to be stressed above the level required for accommodating launch loads. Also, eliminating the abort capability saved weight.

Development and Delay

NASA ordered five Orbiters and a rolling contract for the external tank and SRBs with the intention to fly an initial series

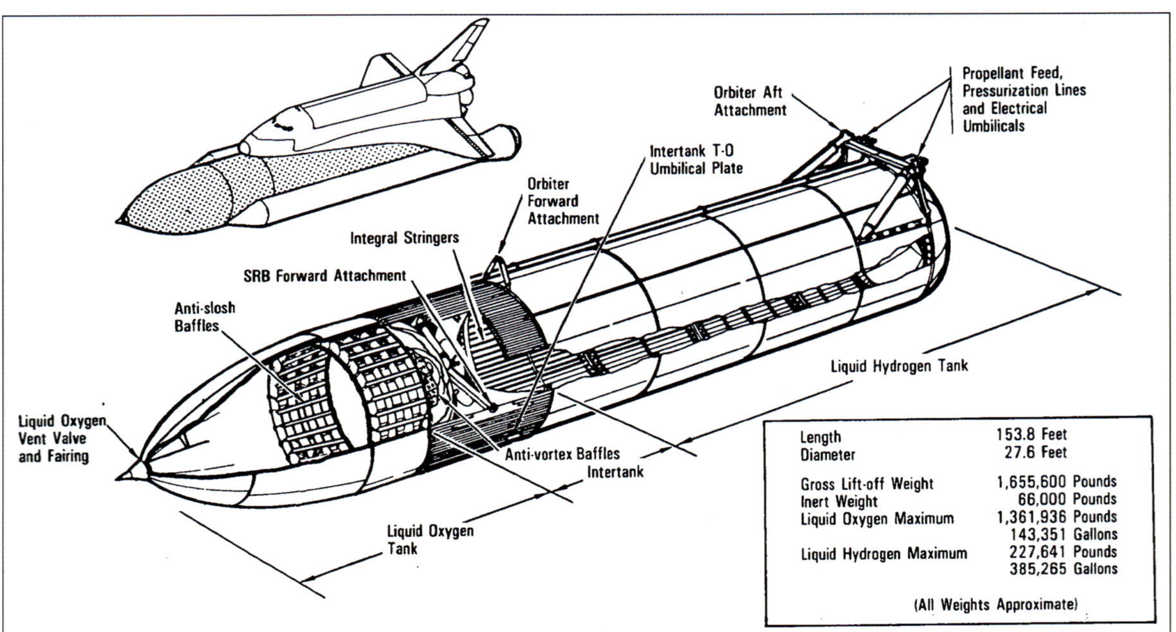

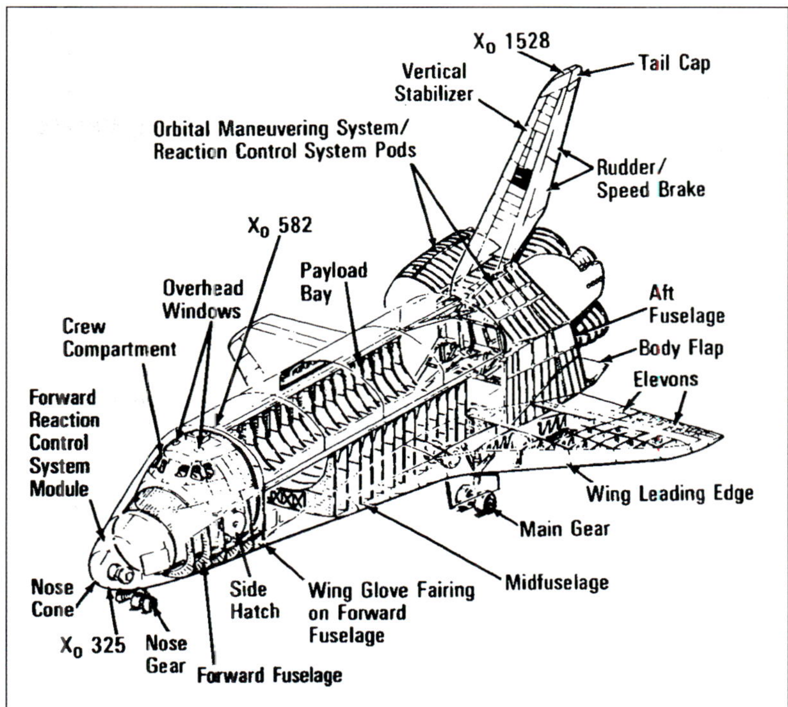

of flight tests to demonstrate aerodynamic efficiency and to gather basic fight performance data. Shuttle Orbiters would be in an OV-series beginning with 01. A competition run to find a name for the shuttles selected *Enterprise* for the first (OV-1), after the famous fictional spaceship in the TV series *Star Trek*. The intention had been to refurbish *Enterprise* for space flight, but that never happened due to weight and engineering issues.

Between August 12 and October 26, 1977, *Enterprise* made five drop-flights from the top of the NASA Shuttle Carrier Aircraft, a converted Boeing 747 that was also used for ferrying the Orbiters around and carrying them from landing locations back to the launch site, LC-39 at the Kennedy Space Center. The first shuttle configured for space flight, OV-102 *Columbia*, experienced several delays and technical issues, including difficulties with fixing the thermal protection tile and an unacceptable number were lost in flying the Orbiter from California to its Florida launch site on the back of the 747.

Delays drifted the launch from 1979 to 1981, with the flight crew of John Young and Robert Crippen assigned to this first flight. The configuration and the flight profile were unlike anything any space-faring organisation had attempted before and there was an air of anticipation and uncertainty as there was no way to practise this without a crew on board.

Throughout the programme, there had been considerable debate about the wisdom of eliminating a unique escape system and designs had been proposed for a crew pod that could survive a catastrophic explosion. Several examples already existed, the Convair B-58 Hustler and the General Dynamics F-111 had crew escape capsules. While there was a justifiable reason for such a system in an aircraft, a spacecraft has a diverse range of environments for which no single design is appropriate. Advocates pointed to the highest risk being in the period between launch and the separation of the SRBs, where an escape pod would have been relevant.

In theory, it would have been possible to instrument the shuttle for automatic operation for the early development flights and the complexity and cost of that would not have realistically modelled the way the Orbiter operates with a crew on board. So there was no alternative but to fly it and see. As a precaution, initial flights would carry a crew of only two and each would wear pressure suits (not suitable for a spacewalk) and have an ejection seat with a special blow-out panel above their positions on the flight deck.

The Computers Take Control

To reduce the overall risk of failure, the shuttle had a unique computer system that borrowed much from the aviation industry, differing from previous programmes such as Gemini and Apollo where bespoke systems were developed. Moreover, there were separate control and processing systems for the launch vehicle and the spacecraft whereas the shuttle integrated both into a single entity. In common usage today, the word 'avionics' was new in the 1960s when the Space Shuttle had its genesis. Combining aviation requirements with electronics, it merged mechanical and analogue equipment, and later digital solid-state electronics into a single coherent system.

The first generalised application of avionics in a military aircraft had been the FB-111 tactical bomber equipped with an avionics system built by Rockwell just before it began work on the shuttle. That concept was applied to the F-15 tactical fighter with the AP-1 computer, the basis for the AP-101 used in the shuttle. Unusual for its time and

ABOVE • Air-launched Test (ALT) flights in 1977 involved unpowered descent off the back of a converted Boeing 747 for evaluating aerodynamic characteristics. (NASA)

that would lead to open-architecture avionics so effectively applied to combat aircraft such as the F-117, the F-22 and, eventually and in much more developed form, the F-35, which is a systems management and sensor integration platform.

There is a direct evolutionary line between the shuttle computer system and the manned/unmanned integrated combat platforms now being planned for future battle management protocols involving mission control being in the cockpit of the pilot in the war zone itself rather than in a separate, remote room.

To get what it needed, Rockwell opened a joint endeavour with IBM, integrating lessons from the Saturn and Apollo programmes based on experience with Gemini computer programmes, and used Draper Laboratory as consultant to form the concept and develop a work strategy. Previously restricted largely to guidance and navigation, shuttle computers would have to accommodate a much wider range of tasks distributed throughout different systems and sub-systems, all integrated with a greater number of on-board crew members each operating complex equipment for longer periods.

Attention to easing the way the astronauts operated the computers would be crucial to how the whole system worked. If developed as a linear progression from Gemini and Apollo operations, the astronauts would be overloaded with time-consuming keyboard activity. To prevent this, the system was designed to reduce the number of operations required to achieve a given purpose and thus began the revolution to a user-friendly computer interface where much of its operation was determined internally, the user making selections from options.

One mythical link between high-level language programmes examined at the time concerned the proposed HAL system, which emerged at the same time as Stanley Kubrick's classic film *2001: A Space Odyssey*, in which a demonic computer of the same name was the key player. In reality, the acronym emerged from the full title, Higher Avionics Language, but may well have been suggested to Kubrick who picked it up as a fitting connection to a 'living' entity, a precursor to today's AI.

unlike aircraft where computers were centred on a single set of machines, the AP-101 had to interconnect with other computers managing different functions such as rocket motor controllers.

Because every aspect of the shuttle's function relied exclusively on its computers, the prime focus was dedicated to multiple redundancy, in some cases up to four levels of consultation to arrive at a judgement. Significant proportions of the computer code were for easing the interface between the crew and the machine and the software development programme was an innovation for NASA, in both ground and space-based systems. It alone changed the entire culture of what was possible and what was not, opening new opportunities for autonomous operation of unmanned spacecraft.

To achieve this pioneering shift in avionics and computer-control, NASA developed new and outstanding capabilities in four key areas: digital avionics, redundancy management, the interconnections between computers and real-time software development. It was these new and exciting possibilities

RIGHT • The cavernous payload bay with doors carrying radiators for the cooling system. (NASA)

The pattern for all future avionics evolution was set when the Space Shuttle system was broken down into four components: the general-purpose computers; data bus network; multifunction displays; and mass memory units. The five AP-101 central processing units were connected to a bespoke input/output processor and this system was adopted for the Boeing B-52 and the Rockwell B-1B strategic bombers. The average number of instructions was 480,000/sec compared with 7,000/sec for the Gemini computer.

A key decision was the exact number of computers to provide for effective redundancy. Working to the requirement for fail-operational/fail-operational/fail-safe, five were required. Two failures would ensure continuity because three would prevent a stand-off where two of four fail. There had to be an odd number for a voting solution, or so it was thought, which was why NASA bought five. But were five really necessary?

The agency had funded five, but reduced the reliability assurance it aimed for to fail-operational/fail-safe. The fifth computer was left in as a back-up so it could conduct a safe return to Earth in the event of a malfunction or a tied vote with the four primary computers. It had validity because triplex systems caused a loss of three in a million while quadruple systems showed a loss of four in a billion.

In fact, Arnold Aldrich at the Johnson Space Center (renamed from the Manned Spacecraft Center) argued for a sixth computer, which was installed with preloaded software so it alone could conduct a return to the Earth while the others were brought back on line. It was carried on the first few flights for just such a function.

During the initial stages of operation, the AP-101B computers were each equipped with 106,500, 32-bit words, but later the P-101S was introduced with a new 256,000, 32-bit RAM that had evolved from the computers fitted to the B-1B. Using the same central processing unit, they were highly reliable with a failure rate of one in 6,000 hours, six times the original requirement and also allowed the new software to operate with the same set of instructions.

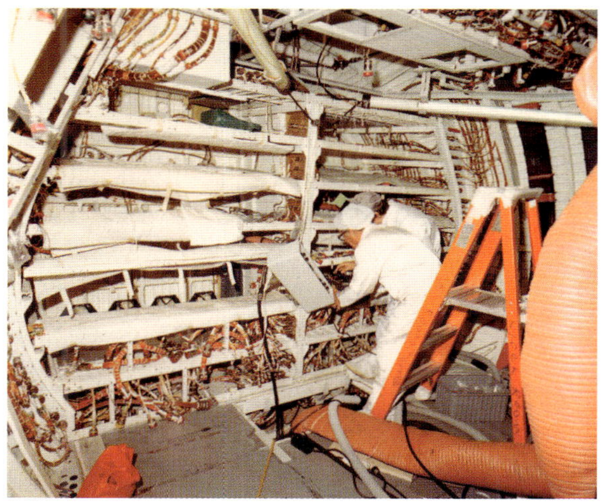

Overall, the Space Shuttle Orbiter incorporated 300 miles (483km) of wiring linking systems through 6,500 connections to more than 6,000lb (2,722kg) of computers, guidance and navigation equipment and a host of systems and sub-systems. To control and navigate the shuttle as both an aircraft and a spacecraft at key points in its operation required a new approach to spaceflight.

Development of the computers, the software, the test and verification of code and the range of simulators required to prepare for development and then operational support for Space Shuttle missions took a greater quantity of resources than anything the agency had supported before. It took the full resources of the separate organisations identified above to provide the necessary avionics, a new architecture being written along with the hardware.

Many devices and spin-offs have been attributed to the space programme, some of it overplayed, but arguably the greatest benefit for the broadest use in the lives of ordinary people is in this area alone. Computer science, software development and hardware manufacturing and design tipped the balance between government-funded research and development and commercial products for the retail market. From the 1980s, private industry picked up the pace and, along with the Pentagon, NASA and the aviation industry became just another customer for a range of products funded and manufactured for domestic and export consumer markets.

But not everyone was happy. Astronaut John Young was critical of the way the computers had seemingly been configured. "What we have in the shuttle is a disaster. We are not making computers do what we want," he said. This view was shared by flight trainer Frank Hughes who believed: "We end up working for the computer, rather than the computer working for us!" A view perhaps shared by users today trying wrestle the deterministic demands of a laptop or a smartphone!

LEFT • The forward bulkhead in the nose of the Orbiter where most of the computer and avionics equipment was contained, behind panes accessible by the crew. (NASA)

FAR LEFT • Subject to significant evolution over time as the technology progressed, the first all-glass cockpit was fitted to Orbiter Atlantis. (NASA)

LEFT • In this view of the aft end of Space Shuttle Discovery, the three main engines are visible with the two smaller orbital manoeuvring rocket motors either side. (NASA)

THE THREE AGES OF SHUTTLE

In 135 flights, the Space Shuttle carried many different satellites to space and was the core launch system for building the International Space Station until replaced by commercial successors

RIGHT • *Here working the simulator at controls in the aft flight deck, veteran astronaut John Young (foreground) and Bob Crippen piloted the Space Shuttle on its first historic launch. (NASA)*

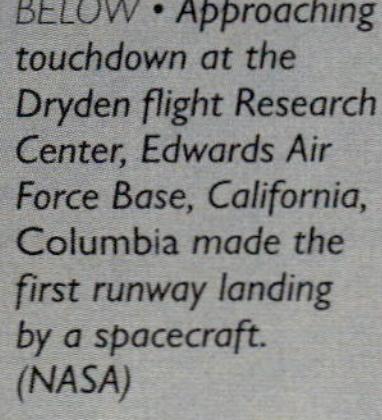

BELOW • *Approaching touchdown at the Dryden flight Research Center, Edwards Air Force Base, California, Columbia made the first runway landing by a spacecraft. (NASA)*

nitial hopes that the Space Shuttle could be turned around within two weeks were impossible to fulfil and the expectation that it would replace all expendable launch vehicles began to look increasingly difficult to achieve long before the first flight in 1981. Neither was the shuttle a cheap route to putting payloads in space and technical challenges, many of them unanticipated, were hard to overcome. Thermal protection tiles were difficult to retain in place during launch and re-entry and subject to minor damage from small pieces of debris.

That was a major problem during the preparation of *Columbia* and did much to contribute to the near two-year delay in getting it off the pad. But there were major successes too, in overcoming design and test difficulties as NASA worked its way toward a very different future, defined by routine trucking operations to space and the development of a diverse range of satellites and spacecraft, together with evolving operational challenges.

Retrospectively, the 135 Space Shuttle flights over a period of more than 30 years completely transformed NASA and provided opportunity for a wider range of diversified missions. In that time, spacecraft were launched to the planets, observatories were put in orbit, a few defence payloads were flown and numerous science missions were completed. Uniquely, the shuttle became a unifying influence forging international co-operation – it reinvigorated a liaison with Russia and brought the former Soviet Union into the partnership established through what would become the International Space Station.

Not so clear initially, in retrospect there are three very distinct phases to the way the shuttle was used and adapted for very different functions. And that is probably its greatest achievement. Whereas previous manned programmes – Mercury, Gemini and Apollo – were defined by very narrow requirements and objectives, the shuttle provided a broader capability for adapting to an evolving spectrum of roles responding to opportunities and changed needs.

The first 25 flights ran from 1981 to 1986, during which an attempt was made to increase the flight rate at any cost

and carry as many government and commercial satellites as possible. That period ended with the tragic loss of *Challenger* and its seven crew members. The next 67 flights flown between 1988 and 1998 restricted payloads to non-commercial, government needs and to docking with the Russian Mir space station on co-operative ventures. The last 43 flights between 1998 and 2011 were largely dedicated to assembling elements of the International Space Station, a period during which *Columbia* was destroyed in 2003 with the loss of a further seven astronauts, a crucial event in the decision to retire the three surviving Orbiters.

The end of the Space Shuttle programme tipped NASA into several years of uncertainty as it continued to operate the space station while seeking a more robust incentive for human exploration, returning to deep-space flight, but with an undecided goal including proposals for missions to the asteroid, a return to the surface of the Moon or on to the surface of Mars. It is within the gamut of those expectations that the overview of Space Shuttle operations is best told, as it explains the future the agency is now seeking to achieve through an international gathering of nations under its Artemis programme. Therefore, the Space Shuttle years are crucial to understanding how that plan is unfolding.

Phase 1 1981-1986

The first four flights of the Space Shuttle were for development operations, beginning with STS-1 on April 12, 1981 piloted by John Young and Robert Crippen, the former a veteran of two Gemini and two Apollo flights, one of which involved an extended mission on the Moon with a roving vehicle. Crippen had been selected for a military space station that was never built, but he had lengthy experience with space systems. STS-1 lasted two days six hours 20 minutes before returning to Earth as the world's first reusable, winged spaceplane.

Landing at the Dryden Flight Research Center (FRC) adjacent to Edwards Air Force Base, California, it was a

LEFT • The launch of *Columbia* on April 12, 1981, ushered in a new era for space activity, one focused on launching commercial satellites and building a space station. (NASA)

triumphant return with not a few surprises when cameras showed several tiles missing. After a lot of data had been analysed and some changes made resulting from initial flight results, STS-2 was launched on November 12, 1981 piloted by Joe Engle and Richard Truly for a mission planned for five days, but shortened to two days when one of the three fuel cell electrical production units failed.

Columbia's third flight got off the pad on March 22, 1982, when STS-3 carried Jack Lousma and Gordon Fullerton to a shakedown mission lasting eight days four minutes during which the crew tested the remote manipulator arm, crucial

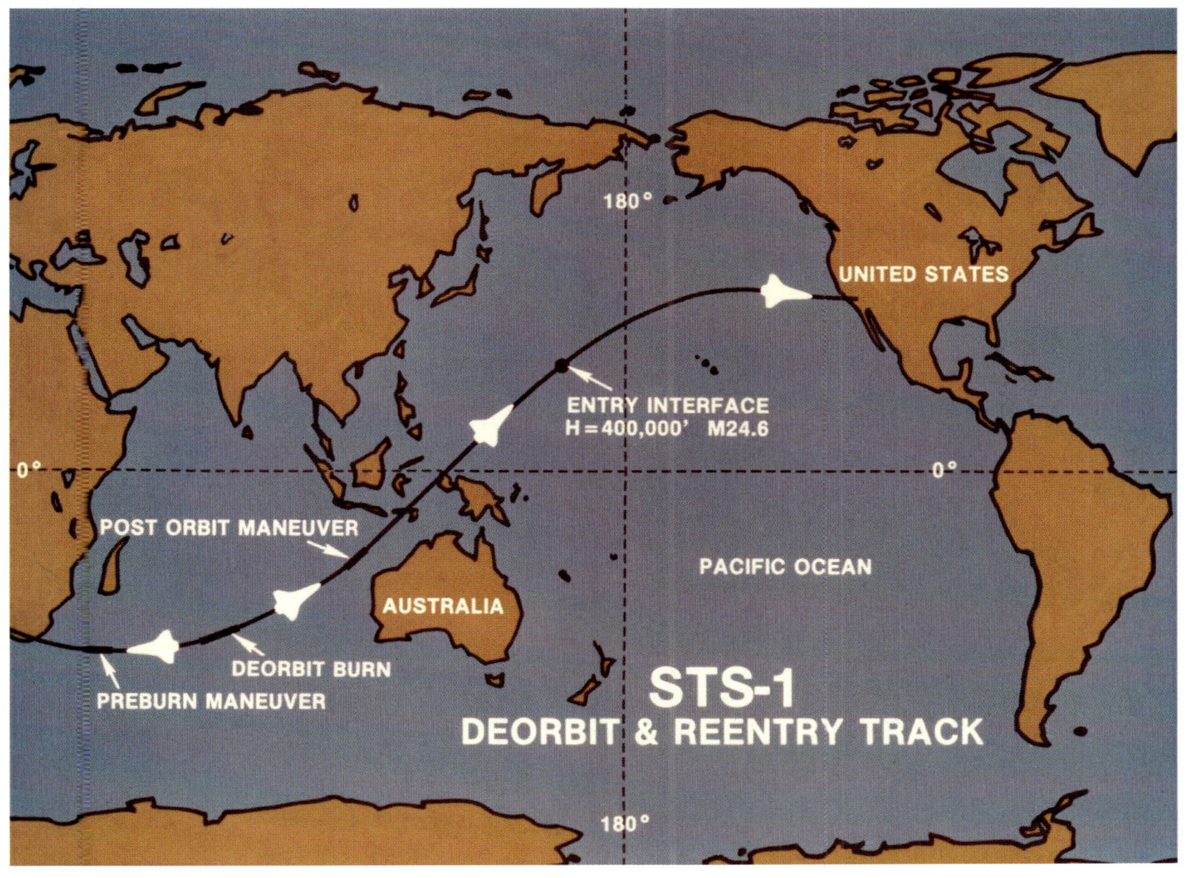

LEFT • The re-entry path for the first shuttle flight, which began its descent through the atmosphere over the central Pacific Ocean. (NASA)

ABOVE • German astronaut Ulf Merbold (right) working inside Spacelab on Columbia's ten-day mission in November 1983, during which scientists worked on research tasks. (NASA)

to future operations. The fourth and last Orbital Flight Test (OFT) mission with Ken Mattingly and Henry Hartsfield was launched on June 27, 1982, returning to land at Dryden FRC on July 4, 1982, welcomed by President Ronald Reagan, who declared the Space Shuttle operational from this point.

Nobody associated with the shuttle believed it was ever 'operational' in the accepted sense, each flight being unique from which more was learned that could be fed through into subsequent flights. But it did open the shuttle to carrying commercial payloads, marking a significant step in the plan to replace all expendable rockets except the very smallest. But it had some urgency too, as nations gathered together to enter the Space Age and wanted a ride into space.

The late 1970s and early 1980s saw a surge in space communications with TV companies in the US and abroad using satellites to expand coverage and cut costs, each of which had to get to space on a rocket produced in the United States, or on Europe's Ariane, because no one else was offering that service. The government contractor for Thor and Delta rockets, McDonnell Douglas now sought custom from these businesses, but NASA was determined to draw them to low-cost flight on the shuttle to increase traffic and reduce prices.

On the first of those launched in November 1982, STS-5 with its four-man crew carried a communications satellite for Canada and another for a commercial telecommunications company in the US. Five months later, the second Orbiter named OV-099 *Challenger* made its first flight on STS-6 and launched a tracking and data relay satellite (TDRS) to geosynchronous orbit, first in what would become a series of such orbital platforms. Instead of relying on ground stations over which it flew, the TDRS would provide continuous communications between Earth and the Space Shuttle and connect to stations on the ground an increasing number of unmanned satellites and spacecraft as more were launched into orbit.

The next two flights, STS-7 and STS-8, were also launched by *Challenger* carrying another satellite for Canada to connect its remote communities, one for Indonesia and a multi-purpose satellite for India providing communications and remote-sensing for land use management and environmental analysis. Launched in June 1983, STS-7 put five people into space including the first American woman, Sally Ride, and STS-8 carried the first African-American astronaut, Guion Bluford, performing the first night landing on September 5, 1983.

Launched as STS-9 on November 28, 1983, after a year-long hiatus, *Columbia* again took to the skies with a six-man crew including the German astronaut Ulf Merbold. It would remain in space for ten days 12 hours 47 minutes conducting a range of scientific experiments, the first of many to use the pressurised Spacelab research module funded by the European Space Agency and assembled at Bremen in Germany. It had been ten years reaching this point.

As noted earlier, the ability for foreign countries to build structural elements of the Space Shuttle Orbiter had been denied by the US Air Force, but non-US organisations could participate in payloads carried inside the shuttle. As early as 1971, NASA had conducted studies for a so-called Research and Applications Module (RAM), later called a Sortie Can, a pressurised structure for scientific research in space conducted by astronauts specially

Table 4: Space Shuttle Mission Statistics

Orbiter	Name	First flight	Last flight	Launches
OV-102	Columbia	Apr 12, 1981	Jan 16, 2003	28
OV-099	Challenger	Apr 4, 1983	Jan 26, 1986	10
OV-103	Discovery	Aug 30, 1984	Feb 24, 2011	39
OV-104	Atlantis	Oct 3, 1985	Jul 8, 2011	33
OV-105	Endeavour	May 7, 1992	May 16, 2011	25

discipline related to research activity on board. Commanded by John Young, STS-9 marked a level of maturity in the programme that NASA hoped would serve as a benchmark for an expanding flight manifest between the launch of satellites and spacecraft and in tial forays into the esoteric world of space research and orbital experiments, preparatory work for when it could afford a fully independent space station.

Repair and Retrieval

More Spacelab flights followed, along with the launch of satellites for government and commercial operators and in February 1984 astronaut Bruce McCandless made an untethered spacewalk (dubbing him 'Bruce McCordless'), his movements controlled through a backpack equipped with thrusters. Posing for some of the most iconic images of the decade, he floated freely some distance away from the Orbiter *Challenger* in February 1984 on a mission that saw the first Space Shuttle landing back at Kennedy Space Center.

The untethered flight had proved that an astronaut could move independently to satellites in need of repair and that was conducted on the Solar Maximum Mission (SMM) spacecraft, which had been sent into space in February 1980. Now suffering an attitude control problem that required a simple repair job, *Challenger* was launched in April 1984 to rendezvous with the tumbling SMM and place it in the payload bay where astronauts James van Hoften and George Nelson could repair it and release it back into orbit. This was possible because NASA had supported a range of so-called Multimission Modular Spacecraft (MMS) built by Fairchild of which this satellite had been one equipped with grapple fixtures and replaceable modular subsystems.

On August 30, 1984, *Columbia* and *Challenger* were joined by OV-103 *Discovery*, which was to play a seminal role in showing what the Space Shuttle was capable of. Two communications sate.lites, Palapa B2 for Indonesia and Westar 6 for Western Union, had been stranded in orbit after their solid rocket boost motors failed to push them to geostationary orbit 22,000 miles (35,340km) above Earth, where they would appear to remain stationary in the sky and serve their customers with TV and telecommunications. On only its second flight, *Discovery* was launched on November 8, 1984, during which both satellites were

selected for particular skills. Realising they could not build both a shuttle and a permanently manned space station simultaneously, the RAM/Sortie Can concept would give the agency a head start on basic research to follow Skylab.

But even this was too much for the pared-down budget, so NASA approached Europe, which was already deeply committed to an expanding space programme through the European Space Research Organisation (ESRO). It proposed that European industry build such a module at its own expense and recoup funds when the US bought four additional modules to pay back the initial cost. Europe would gain by being involved in cutting-edge space technology and NASA would get a research module without paying for it, only reimbursing ESRO after the peak funding years for shuttle development.

An agreement was signed on September 24, 1973, between NASA and ESRO that would eventually result in an order for two modules and a series of pallets carrying experiments that could be exposed to the vacuum of space. Combinations of pressurised and unpressurised elements would be assigned missions according to the range and type of experiments selected. Called Spacelab, modules and pallets would be carried up and down in the Space Shuttle, astronauts moving inside from the mid-deck of the crew compartment for sustained periods of scientific research.

Encouraged by this deal, the European Space Agency (ESA) was formed in 1975 around two flagship programmes: the expendable Ariane launch vehicle to compete against US expendables; and Spacelab. When signed, the agreement anticipated the first Spacelab flights in 1979 after the shuttle had completed initial tests, but those dates shifted — it was not until 1983 that the first Spacelab was launched on STS-9 on a highly successful mission demonstrating a variety of experiments and deploying a full range of crew assignments.

In addition to the two astronaut pilots, assignments included the category of mission specialist engaged in general support of the flight, and payload specialist consisting of astronauts skilled in a particular science or engineering

retrieved and brought back to Earth, where new boost motors were fitted for re-launch.

On October 3, 1985, OV-104 *Atlantis* completed the Space Shuttle fleet. NASA had hoped for five Orbiters, but the constrained budget prevented that and *Challenger* had been rebuilt for space operations after initially being assembled as a structural test article, never intended for space operations. With a full fleet, by late 1985 the pressure was on to increase the flight rate and attract more satellite payloads from commercial customers in the US and around the world. Europe's expendable Ariane launch vehicle had been flying since 1979 and was itself attracting customers who were drawn to compete with the shuttle.

Shuttle missions were being scheduled with uncompromising urgency, and NASA facilities were under intense pressure to support increased flight rates. But there were problems, with greater demand on simulators, crew preparation time, mission support operations at the Johnson Space Center and general training for a variety of payload requirements and infrastructure support. There was more to shuttle operations than getting them to the launch pads.

After just two flights in 1981, three the following year, four in 1983, five in 1984 and nine flights in 1985, plans envisaged a rapid acceleration in the schedule. Long gone were expectations of 60 flights a year, but there were still baseline projections for more than 24 flights annually. *Columbia* was launched on January 12, 1986, from the storied LC-39A launch pad while preparations were under way on LC-39B for the flight of *Challenger*, which would be carrying another TDRS communications relay satellite for geostationary orbit.

Commanded by Robert Gibson, *Columbia* carried a seven-man crew including Congressman Bill Nelson for a six-day flight, with astronaut Charles F Bolden who would fly three more missions, the last of which he commanded in 1994. In 2009, Bolden became Administrator of NASA, in post for eight years, and Nelson would serve in that capacity from May 2021. This flight was unique in that no other future NASA boss had flown in space and from this one mission, two would reach that exalted position.

The first phase of the shuttle programme ended on January 28, 1986, when, after launching in freezing temperatures, the O-rings ostensibly protecting the SRB's tang and clevis joints from leaking hot gases between segments failed. The ensuing blast of hot gas severed an aft SRB restraining strut causing the booster to pivot and break open the external tank, igniting the cryogenic propellants it contained and separating *Challenger* and the two SRBs in the ensuing blast, breaking it apart.

The catastrophe occurred 73 seconds after lift-off, in full view of crew families, VIPs, guests and NASA personnel at the Kennedy Space Center. Among the seven crew was teacher Christa McAuliffe and the launch was beamed to school audiences across the country in preparation for live lessons she was to have conducted from orbit. The event brought a state of national grief and an awakening of just how dangerous and fraught with risk the business of manned space flight was. But it changed the orientation of the programme forever.

Phase 2 (1988-1998)

The loss of *Challenger* and its crew was a profound shock inside and outside NASA. The launch occurred at 11.38am local time and within two minutes the White House communications director Pat Buchanan brushed aside aides and burst into the Oval Office where President Reagan was holding a briefing, to pronounce the grim news: "The Space Shuttle just blew up." For several seconds the room fell silent and nobody spoke until Reagan asked the question to which everyone knew the answer: "Isn't that the one with the teacher on it?"

The President had been scheduled to deliver his State of the Union address later that evening. It was deferred to February 4 and instead of addressing Congress he spoke to the nation in a televised address at 5pm in which he reminded viewers: "On this day 390 years ago, the great explorer Sir Francis Drake died aboard ship off the coast of Panama. In his lifetime the great frontiers were the oceans, and an historian later said, 'He lived by the sea, died on it, and was buried in it'. Well, today we can say of the *Challenger* crew: Their dedication was, like Drake's, complete."

The shuttle was grounded for 32 months while a presidential commission investigated many aspects of the entire programme. The reason was all too self-evident. It should never have been launched at those low temperatures, given the vulnerability of the SRB O-rings and other temperature-sensitive parts of the shuttle. Frantic efforts by engineers at SRB manufacturer Morton Thiokol to halt the countdown had been disregarded by senior NASA managers who insisted on launching that day. They were single-mindedly focused on pushing forward and in denial of the critical danger evident from previous flights, where near complete burn-through of O-rigs had been observed in retrieved boosters after launches in cold temperatures, but never as low as those on the morning that *Challenger* flew for the last time.

Plans to fly from a new air force shuttle facility at Vandenberg Air Force Base on the West Coast for defence-related missions were abandoned, as was the entire concept of flying commercial and foreign, non-government satellites. Inherently reluctant to place all its payloads on the shuttle, the air force had already reinvigorated the flagging expendable launch vehicle market, which also saw a return to production for the launch of commercial satellites no longer assigned to the shuttle.

Back into full-scale production went the Delta launchers the shuttle had been expected to replace. Atlas and Titan had

a more assured future due to the air force maintaining those as back-up to the shuttle programme and many procedures and processes were put in place to ensure greater safety margins. There was now none of the 'launch on time, every time' mentality that had pushed the entire programme to dangerous levels with inadequate resources to cope with unachievable goals demanded by the drive to increase flight rates.

Technical changes too were made in the design of the SRB segment joints, with greater protection from failure. Ice-teams would be sent out before each flight to alert launch control to potential threats from cold temperatures. There had been plans to launch planetary spacecraft by carrying them attached to a cryogenic Centaur stage inside the payload bay. This had potential risk and the idea was dropped, replaced for those missions by a solid propellant alternative, the two-stage IUS.

The consequences of *Challenger* lasted many years after Space Shuttle flights resumed, as science experiments, satellites and payloads queued to get a ride on an expendable launcher. The air force did have payloads that could only fly on the shuttle and those were added to the manifest over time; eventually they would fly in Orbiters. Meanwhile, Congress voted for funds to build a replacement Orbiter. Named OV-105 *Endeavour* after Captain Cook's ship, it would make its first flight on May 7, 1992.

The second phase of shuttle operations began with the return-to-flight on September 29, 1988, and lasted until 1998, during which time a range of government payloads, satellites, astronomical observatories and Earth resource payloads were carried into space. Delayed by the restoration of flight operations and the funds required to build a replacement for *Challenger*, plans for a space station had already been set in motion in 1984 when NASA Administrator Jim Beggs received approval to sign up international partners from Europe, Japan and Canada.

Initially called Freedom, the station would be assembled by the shuttle, with modules contributed by ESA and Japan and the robotics provided by Canada, which had already provided remote manipulators for the Orbiters. Gone were the days when NASA wanted to launch a fully equipped station on a Saturn V rocket, capable of supporting 12 people. Instead, a modular space station would be put together in orbit and for that the shuttle was the perfect truck. After assembly, it would support the station through crew exchanges and the provision of food and general

ABOVE • The SMM solar research satellite is repaired by van Hoften and Nelson inside the spacious payload bay of Challenger. (NASA)

LEFT • On January 28, 1986, the crew of Challenger died when the Space Shuttle was destroyed shortly after launch. Seated from left: Mike Smith, Dick Scobee and Ron McNair. Standing from left: Ellison Onizuka, Christa McAuliffe, Greg Jarvis and Judith Resnik. (NASA)

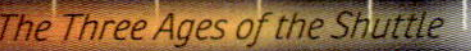

ABOVE • The initial configuration of the Freedom station was a dual-keel design to which the shuttle would dock and provide additional modules. Note the servicing hangar for the Hubble Space Telescope. (Boeing)

logistics as well as carrying experiments up and down and adding additional elements as required.

The early 1990s saw the collapse of the Soviet Union and the emergence of Russia with associated territories as federated states. Since the 1970s, the Russians had pursued development of their own space stations, called Salyut and Mir, together with manned Soyuz crew capsules and their

RIGHT • NASA Administrator Jim Beggs persuaded the Reagan administration to develop a space station called Freedom with Japan, the European Space Agency and Canada as partners. (NASA)

derivative, the unmanned Progress logistics vehicle. The Russians had chosen this path after four failures in four attempts with their Moon-booster called N-1, ending funded plans for putting cosmonauts on the lunar surface.

However, since it was first proposed by the White House in 1984, for nearly a decade NASA had not received from Congress the money it needed to start building Freedom. Each year, Congress came close to cancelling the project and when Bill Clinton became President in January 1993 he ordered a full review. For their part the Russians had scant resources to build on previous successes and begin work assembling their own, Mir-2, station.

Seeing an opportunity to share resources and expand the potential, on September 2, 1993, both sides signed a partnership agreement for what was now to be called the International Space Station (ISS), joining ESA, Japan and Canada. It would be a difficult relationship at first. Where once the Europeans had been the strongest partner with the United States, now its former adversary replaced ESA, which could not provide manned vehicles to ply back and forth there, nor logistics modules for supplying the ISS with cargo.

For the US politicians previously opposed to the Freedom station and for the White House it was an opportunity to keep the Russians very close, as there was widespread suspicion regarding motives. Moreover, it was a chance for cost-sharing a very expensive project over which there had been much concern by the bean-counters. And there was another view. Would NASA become so committed financially that there would never be any other money for resuming the human exploration of the solar system?

There was much the Americans learned from the Russians, who received support for what was potentially an unsustainable programme of national expenditure at a time when the country faced economic pressure from its newly-found democracy. And for NASA, there was a more favourable hearing in Congress with Russia providing two major core modules for assembling the ISS. Slowly, confidence began to build back in what was deemed the biggest international engineering venture of all time.

All this gave the Space Shuttle renewed purpose, but before assembly of the first elements could begin, in February 1995 NASA flew a rendezvous mission to Russia's Mir station followed by nine docking flights between June 1995 and June 1998. On those missions, cosmonauts and astronauts learned to live and work together and develop co-operative practices as a prelude to building the ISS.

This relationship would last for several decades, but as far as the shuttle was concerned it finally provided the very reason it had been proposed, back in the late 1960s. The wheel had come full circle: the shuttle would end its days being a taxi to and from the ISS as had been envisaged, when George Mueller addressed the British Interplanetary Society in London on August 10, 1968, before the first manned Apollo flight and a time when the Moon landing goal was still some way off.

Phase 3 (1998-2011)

It was always understood that the International Space Station would be a colossal undertaking that would stress the new-found relationship with Russia close to breaking point. With understandable pride in their existing achievements, the Russian engineers felt cheated from their plausible goal of reaching the Moon by inept leadership, insufficient funds and a lack of physical and human resources. However, their space stations in the Salyut, Almaz and Mir programmes had been a staggering success.

While NASA developed the shuttle and drew in partners to provide Spacelab, the Russians ran a complex programme of orbital research, Mir being their supreme achievement. Now they were being asked to give up its successor Mir-2 to become a partner of their ideological adversary. For some Americans, it was a shamefaced way to cosy up to a former communist state that had worked long and hard to outpace US technological superiority; after all, had they not lost the Moon race?

Fortunately, conflicting views were suppressed in pursuit of the grander goal, to forge an enduring relationship and build a 400-ton laboratory consisting of modular clusters made in many different countries and brought together for the first time in space. This final phase in shuttle operations would be primarily committed to lifting elements of the ISS into orbit, but also to launching major observatories such as the Hubble Space Telescope, the Chandra X-ray Observatory and the Gamma Ray Observatory. Two flights were also dedicated to flying the Space Radar Laboratory for detailed surveys of special sites on Earth.

The observatories programme for astronomical research was a major initiative in development and deployment, Hubble itself originating in the late 1960s when it was known as the Large Space Observatory. Apollo had dominated NASA activity from very early in its formation to the mid-1970s and much science and many projects were put on hold until that goal had been achieved and the orientation of the space programme given greater diversity. In every essential element, the shuttle enabled that shift and gave wider meaning to space activity and, through the ISS, a broader engagement with space-faring nations around the world.

During the development and uplift phase of assembling the ISS, different Orbiters were assigned particular roles. Considerable improvement to equipment and upgrades to ageing elements were introduced and *Endeavour* benefitted from a major weight-saving programme, based on lessons learned from the other four Orbiters. Along with *Discovery* and *Atlantis* it was assigned to the ISS. Operations involving the shuttle were integrated with launches of Russian modules from Baikonur and Japanese elements from the Tanegashima launch facility. ESA used the Space Shuttle for launching its own habitation and experiment modules to the ISS.

Assembly of the ISS began on November 20, 1998, with the launch of Russia's Zarya module on a Proton rocket, followed on December 4 by *Endeavour* carrying NASA's Unity module. Other elements followed and the permanent occupation of the ISS began when NASA astronaut Bill Shepard and cosmonauts Yuri Gidzenko and Sergei Krikalev were launched on a Soyuz spacecraft on October 31, 2000 from Baikonur, boarding the still incomplete station two days later. There has never been a day since when the station has not been crewed, a building site at first and growing inexorably over time. The first US pressurised module *Destiny* arrived on February 7, 2001, with a plan to install modules from Europe and Japan.

In support of some experiments of a specific nature, a long-duration shuttle mission saw *Columbia* lift off on January 16, 2003, carrying seven crew on an independent

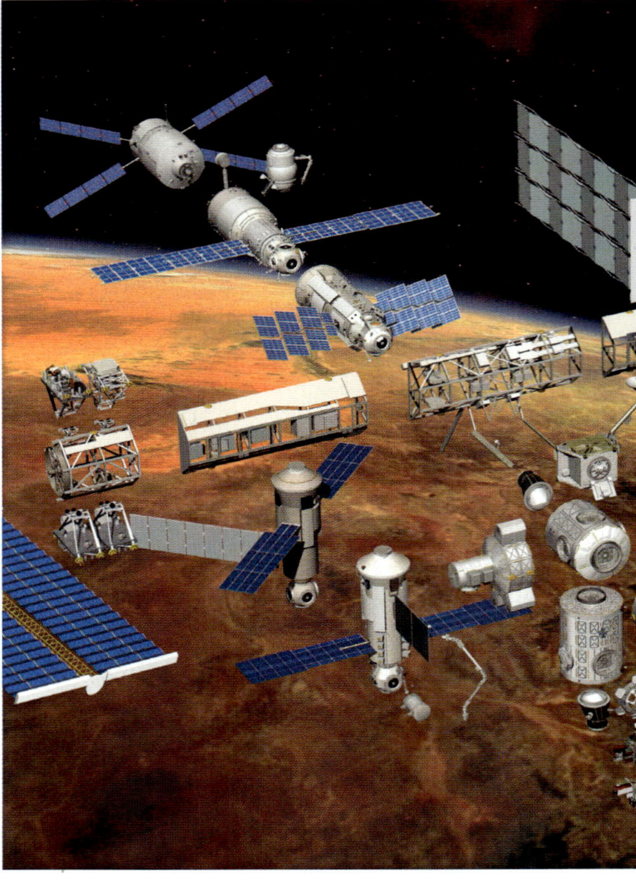

flight lasting almost 16 days, which was about the limit for an Orbiter equipped with additional packs of life-support consumables. From shortly after launch it had been suspected that insulation falling away from the external tank had struck the leading edge of *Columbia's* wing, damaging the RCC thermal protection. When *Columbia* re-entered the Earth's atmosphere during February 1 on its

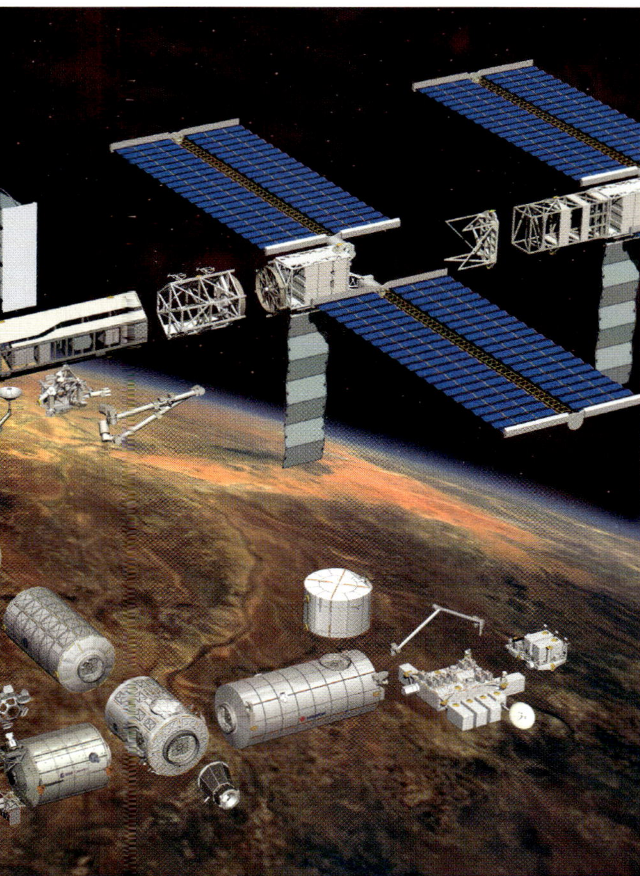

Table 5: Shuttle Dockings with Space Stations

Orbiter	Completed orbits	MIR dockings	ISS dockings
Discovery	5,830	1	13
Atlantis	4,848	7	12
Discovery	4,677	1	12

Note: MIR is the Russian station, ISS in the International Space Station. No station dockings were made by Columbia or Challenger. In total, Shuttle Orbiters made 46 dockings, more than one third of all 135 Shuttle missions.

ABOVE • *SpaceX has been flying crew members to the International Space Station since May 2020 at approximately six-month intervals. (SpaceX)*

way to a landing at Kennedy Space Center, heat entered the wing's interior and the vehicle was destroyed as it crossed the United States.

There was no question of building a replacement; *Endeavour* had been assembled after the loss of *Challenger* largely from spares and additional structural parts held aside from assembly of the other three Orbiters and the cost would be too great. Shortly thereafter it was decided to retire the shuttle after assembly of the ISS had been completed. Flights did not resume for 30 months, when *Discovery* resumed its role of lifting structures to the ISS, on July 26, 2005. In the interim, the Russians launched all station crew members with their Soyuz spacecraft. Europe's *Columbus* module was launched by *Atlantis* on February 7, 2008 and Japan's *Kibo* pressurised module by *Discovery* on May 31, 2008.

The last Space Shuttle mission was launched with a four-man crew on July 8, 2011, *Atlantis* carrying a full logistics module and a cargo pallet, returning to land at the Kennedy Space Center just before dawn on July 21. It would be almost nine years before another American manned spacecraft would take off from US soil carrying astronauts. In question was whether to put meagre funds into modifying and extending the life of the three remaining Orbiters, or to invest in a partnership with private industry to send astronauts into space. The obvious answer was to do the latter, while Russia, as a full partner in the ISS, charged NASA to use Soyuz rockets to send non-Russians to the station.

The long-term solution to delivering cargo to keep the ISS operating evolved from a government-industry partnership in 2008, with contracts to SpaceX for Dragon capsules and to Orbital Sciences for their Cygnus module. Dragon would be launched on the SpaceX Falcon 9 rocket and those flights began with the first delivery of cargo on

May 25, 2012, followed by the first Cygnus on an Antares rocket arriving at the ISS on September 29, 2013. As precursor to a future manned variant of Dragon, the SpaceX cargo-lifter would return safely to Earth and a splashdown from where downloaded equipment from the station could be recovered. The Cygnus module was only good for a one-way trip and burned up in the atmosphere.

To carry astronauts to the ISS, NASA began a similar government-industry partnership in 2011 and three years later awarded fixed-price contracts to SpaceX for Crew Dragon and Boeing for its Starliner spacecraft. Crew Dragon began carrying astronauts to the ISS with the launch of the second demonstration flight on May 30, 2020, several years later than anticipated due to unexpected technical delays, and a docking at the ISS the following day.

After many delays to the programme and to the first crewed flight attempt, Boeing's Starliner conducted two preliminary test flights in 2019 and 2022 before delivering its first crew to the ISS with a launch on June 5, 2024 and a docking next day. The crew consisted of Barry Wilmore and Sunita Williams and after entering the ISS, an assessment of Starliner's performance indicated doubts about its safety for returning the crew to Earth after a planned eight days in space.

Leaving the crew aboard the ISS, Starliner returned to Earth on September 7 at the White Sands Space Harbor after several additional issues causing concern for its suitability as a crew-carrying vehicle until further tests, and probably another uncrewed space test, which is unlikely to happen until late 2025. The SpaceX Crew Dragon has already delivered 17 crew teams to the ISS and privately funded space flights and is at the core of NASA's human space flight support for the International Space Station. But while all this space activity was going on, the agency never forgot the first 'A' in NASA – Aeronautics.

HIGH SPEED AND HIGH FLIGHT

From supersonic flight to winged spaceplanes and from new forms of propulsion to safety for commercial flights, NASA provides the aviation industry with research and support

RIGHT • Out of several contenders, North American Aviation built the X-15 powered by the first throttleable rocket motor designed for use in a manned vehicle. (North American Aviation)

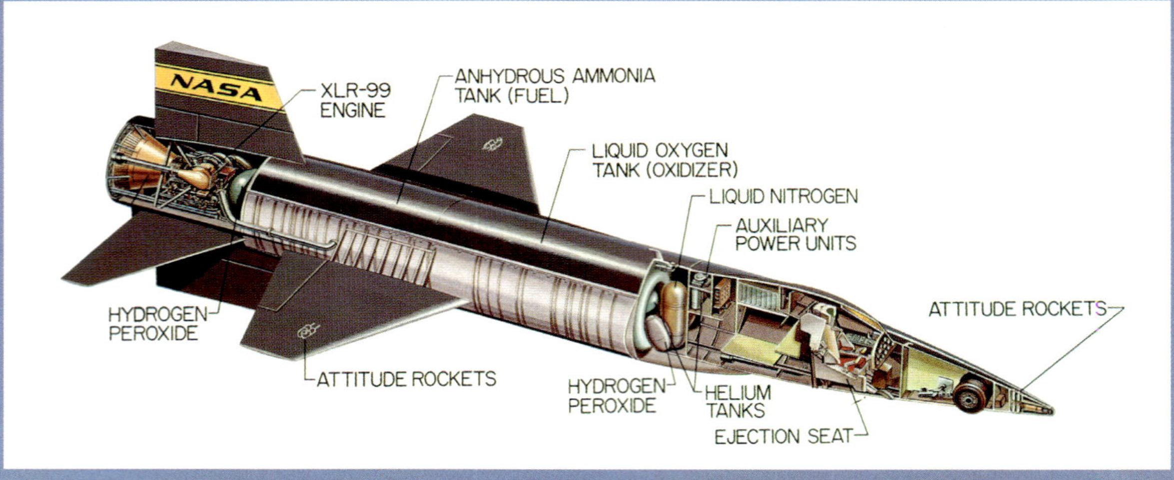

BELOW • Initial flights with the X-15 were made with two packs of XLR-11 rocket motors, as seen here. (NASA)

The aviation pioneer Wilbur Wright said: "It is possible to fly without motors, but not without knowledge and skill." When it opened for business on October 1, 1958, NASA inherited vital assets it had acquired since formation of the National Advisory Committee for Aeronautics (NACA) in 1915, from which it emerged. Nudged into setting up a government-funded research establishment for aeronautics, aero-engines and aircraft design by similar organisations in Britain, Congress set up the NACA as a short-term measure, but it became the bedrock on which aircraft engineering design flourished.

Since World War Two, the NACA had been increasingly involved in fundamental research for combat aircraft, but was denied the design and flight testing of experimental aircraft, which became largely the concern of the US Air Force and Navy. It was with aircraft designed and built for the armed services that supersonic flight research had been funded, until the need arose for hypersonic, trans-atmospheric vehicles to test the outer regions of speed and altitude exceeded the requirements of the military, which then lost interest.

The NACA had been studying the possibility of hypersonic flight since the early 1940s, but the limitations imposed by the available propulsion systems delayed serious analysis of how that might be accomplished. Theoretical study of the physics of flight at Mach 5 and beyond provided abundant evidence that it was more a thermal barrier that could only be addressed through the development of advanced materials capable of withstanding very high temperatures. That, and the lack of a plausible engine remained the real barrier to hypersonic flight. But when it was built, the X-15 was in a class of its own.

The first real indication of a desire on the part of the NACA to develop a hypersonic research vehicle came during a meeting of the aerodynamics committee held on October 4, 1951 proposed by Robert J Woods from Bell Aircraft, a respected engineer who worked with Walter Dornberger. The proposal stimulated further discussion at several more meetings and on June 24, 1952, a formal motion was passed to develop a programme for flight at Mach 4-10 and altitudes of 12-50 miles (19-80km). The full executive committee of the NACA ratified this in July and a study group chaired by Clinton E Brown was set up at the Langley Aeronautical Laboratory on September 8, 1952.

The goal was impressive. Scott Crossfield had still to push the Skyrocket through Mach 2 and he would only achieve that in November 1953, while Mach 3 would await the fateful X-2 when it was destroyed accomplishing that in September 1956. Much had still to be learned about the design and handling of aircraft in the supersonic regime and at high altitude. When the hypersonic project was approved, the NACA was effectively sanctioning development of an aircraft capable of three times the speed and altitude of any other research aircraft. For many, research into hypersonic flight was aligned more to the concept of a spaceplane than to an aircraft.

The Air Force Air Research & Development Command received formal evaluation of the NACA proposal on August 13, 1954, and it was forwarded to Air Force HQ exactly one month later with a technical endorsement. On October 5, the NACA Committee on Aerodynamics met at the High Speed Flight Station (known as the High Speed Flight Research Station prior to 1954) where Walter Williams, the powerful and influential director of the centre at Edwards Air Force Base, pressed home the timely need for what would become Project 1226. There was some opposition from manufacturers and design leaders, including Clarence 'Kelly' Johnson, the man behind the U-2 and so many other Lockheed successes, on the basis that industry was doing it already and would soon be flying hypersonic aircraft of its own. It was not and did not.

The definitive contract to build the X-15 was signed with North American Aviation on June 11, 1956 for three flight vehicles because experience with the X-series showed that it was possible to carry out a meaningful research programme with two but a third aircraft provided a quicker response to evolving requirements. Embedded within the X-15 programme from the outset was a deep need to provide a research tool that could fly an expanded research effort based on knowledge gained during initial flight activity, rather than having to develop another air vehicle for further research work. There was also the prudent hedge against the loss of a single aircraft bringing the entire programme to a halt.

The X-15 programme would grow in capabilities, accomplishments, expansion and cost. It would absorb more than two million man-hours, logging 4,000 hours of tests in 15 different wind tunnels and it would reveal unimagined problems to which solutions were found only as the programme evolved. It was essential that the NACA and the air force keep close contact with the development of the programme and for that a series of conferences would be held to monitor progress and air problems.

Over the next two years an intensive effort worked on materials and detailed design as structural elements of the aircraft began to take shape. The single-chamber XLR-99-RM-1 rocket motor was selected to deliver a maximum thrust of 50,000lb (222.4kN) at sea level and 57,850lb (257.32kN) at 100,000ft (30,480m), to be throttleable between 30% and 100% of rated thrust and to have a maximum burn duration of 90 seconds at full power. Engine testing began in the latter half of 1958 with eight flight-worthy motors produced for the development programme.

Because the XLR-99-RM-1 would not be ready by the time the X-15 was available for powered flight tests, an interim solution adopted the XLR-11, mainstay of earlier

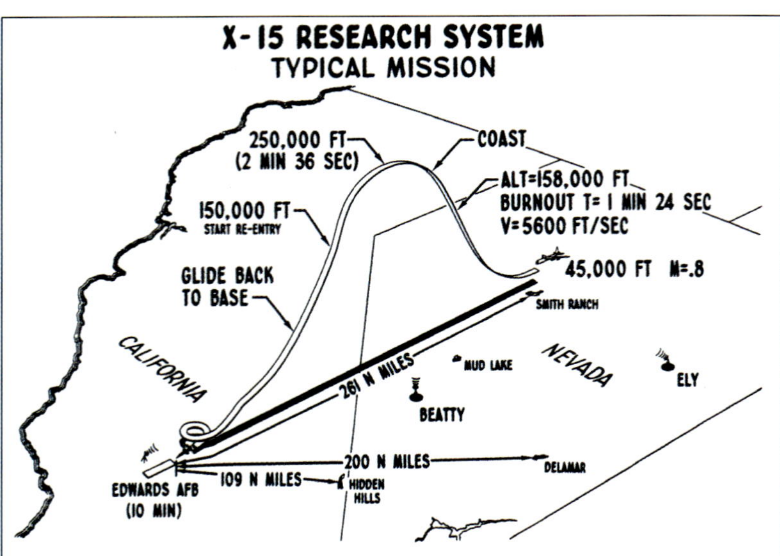

ABOVE • The simplified flight profile for a high-altitude research flight from release over Nevada to a landing at Edwards Air Force Base. (NASA)

FAR RIGHT • Following a redevelopment into the X-15A-2, the second aircraft of this type shows off its external drop tanks on rollout from the factory in Inglewood, California. (North American Aviation)

BELOW • Showing ice over the skin panels under the liquid oxygen tank, X-15-2 shortly before release for a powered flight. (NASA)

X-series research aircraft and several other types at Edwards Air Force Base. It would serve well and it was a relatively simple task to build it in to the aft fuselage.

The first two X-15s would be powered initially by the XLR-11, each aircraft having two quad-units stacked one above the other within the structural cradle designed for the XLR-99. As built, the frame for the more powerful motor was bolted straight on to the rear fuselage and the only interface changes necessary were to attach the two XLR-11s to the frame. Some ballast was also required, but in all other respects the substitution was a relatively easy task. Each new quartet of combustion chambers had a combined thrust of 5,900lb (26.24kN), together producing a maximum thrust of 11,800lb (52.48kN), approximately 20% of the XLR-99.

Building it for Space

The general appearance of the aircraft was of a conventional mid-wing monoplane with low aspect-ratio wings, large wedge-shaped dorsal and ventral tails, with a circular cross section fuselage to which were grafted full length, side-wall tunnel chines. Rarely for the aircraft industry, though, the real difference lay in the materials employed – they were selected on the basis of strength, temperature regime, resistance to corrosion and their processing requirements.

Chief structures engineer Dr R L Schleicher calculated that most of the surface would experience temperatures of 800-1,200°F (427-649°C) and that the high strength

required could only be met by titanium and nickel-based alloys. None of the exotic structural material from rare elements had yet been developed, limiting to some extent the flight envelope aircraft of this type could fly.

The only solution for the hottest areas was to employ Inconel-X and due to its stability it was selected for the entire exterior surface. Under thermal stress, Inconel forms a passivating oxide layer that protects the surface and arrests degradation. In the 1950s, it was the ultimate high-technology material. Over time, Inconel would have a very wide range of applications from rocket motor chambers to 3D printers.

The fuselage employed a mix of monocoque and semi-monocoque structures based around frames and bulkheads for load distribution with Inconel-X for the outer skin stabilised by bulkheads using J-section frames with longitudinal stiffeners in selected areas. The structure was a stiff unit dangerously capable of overload due to the relatively unknown environment in which it was to operate, with an engine delivering a considerably higher thrust/weight ratio (1:0.75) affording a wide range of research possibilities.

The fuselage centre section was a monocoque consisting of two main propellant tanks with circular cross section. The LOX tank had a total volume of 1,038 US gallons (4,088 litres) with a propellant mass of 10,400lb (4,717kg). The liquid ammonia fuel tank had a capacity for 1,445 US gallons (5,469 lit) with a fuel weight of 8,400lb (3,810kg). A spherical, 854lb (387kg), 10ft³ (0.283cm³) hydrogen peroxide tank was located aft of the ammonia tank and had a capacity of 77.5 US gallons (293.3 lit) to pressurise the LOX system at 48psi (331kPa).

The wing for the X-15 was of trapezoidal shape, a modified NACA aerofoil with no dihedral but with a 5%

thickness/chord section and a 2.5:1 aspect ratio. The leading edge of the wing had a 25° sweep at quarter-chord and was thin but not sharp, while the blunt trailing edge was 2in (5.1cm) thick at the root and 0.375in (0.95cm) at the tip. The wing was clean, without control surfaces except for a small, hydraulically actuated flap at the inboard trailing edge. Attitude control within the sensible atmosphere was maintained through the control surfaces in the horizontal and vertical tail assemblies.

In several respects the wing was of standard construction, being of multispar box beam design. Reinforced Inconel-X skins were the material of choice, withstanding creep and providing strength to the calculated maximum temperature of 1,200°F (649°C). The skin varied in thickness, from 0.09in (0.28cm) at the root to 0.40in (1cm) at the tip of the upper surface, and 0.065in (0.165cm) to 0.40in (1cm) at the tip of the lower surface.

First-generation rocket planes adopted a tricycle undercarriage and were nose-sitters. The X-15 had a nose leg and wheel arrangement with two skids deployed from the rear of the fuselage. The nose leg was housed in a conventional wheel well with two boat-shaped skids stowed externally within the aft chines. The legs were rigid, but some degree of outward play was possible through an air/oil shock absorber attached to the upper end while the skids were located to the far aft of the fuselage.

Hydraulic and electrical power to the X-15 was provided by two 40hp (29.8kw) auxiliary power units (APUs) operating on decomposed hydrogen peroxide driving a hydraulic pump and electrical generator. Each APU was turned on or off using a switch in the cockpit, the start-up process activating a solenoid valve that released a flow of monopropellant through the gear case for cooling before it was routed to the unit itself.

In flight, the X-15 could cover a ground range of approximately 345 miles (555km), operating in excess of Mach 6 and at altitudes of 350,000ft (106,700m). Monitoring the flight required use of the NASA High Range, three radar ground stations with the flight research facilities at Edwards as the prime control station. The Edwards control room received real-time velocity and altitude data from the three radar stations with altitude and ground track displayed on large plot boards and velocity indicated on a meter for the use of the ground controller.

The X-15 had a specially designed ejection seat with a new type of restraint harness together with small stabilisers so it would operate like a shuttlecock when taken by the slipstream and prevent it tumbling or oscillating. The seat ejection rocket motor had a thrust of 3,000lb (13.34kN) to propel the seat well clear of the fuselage. The detailed design of the seat required it to be operable up to Mach 4 or to a maximum altitude of 120,000ft (36,576m), which was the zone where the X-15 was most likely to encounter an emergency situation.

The design loaded weight of the X-15 was 34,000lb (15,420kg) and the only suitable carrier-airplane was the B-52 equipped with a shoe under the inboard starboard wing. Debate surrounded the inevitable consequence of hanging the X-15 out on a pylon – the pilot would have to ingress the cockpit before flight and remain there until the aircraft was back on the ground. This had never been necessary on previous rocket plane programmes and North American Aviation gave particular attention

to the physiological stresses of being in the X-15 for the 1.5 hours it would take to climb out and reach altitude before the drop.

Trials and Achievements

The first of its type to arrive, X-15-1 was delivered to Edwards by truck from Inglewood, California on October 17, 1958, for a series of contractor flights to prepare the aircraft for hand-over to the customer and a demanding series of experimental flights made by NACA, air force and navy pilots. Preparations for the first flight went well and beyond the expectations of personnel schooled in the art of patience. With some 400 people now at the Flight Research Station, NASA was in its infancy, formed less than three weeks earlier out of the NACA.

The first captive flight occurred on March 10, 1959, with test pilot Scott Crossfield in the X-15 and lasted one hour eight minutes and the first glide flight occurred on June 8 followed by the first powered flight on September 17 made with X-15-2 equipped with two XLR-11 engine packs standing in for the XLR-99. The first powered flight with X-15-1 took place on January 23, 1960. The US Air Force had 'accepted' X-15-1 on February 3, 1960, and on March 25 Joe Walker achieved Mach 2, exceeded by Robert White reaching Mach 3 on May 12.

A ground accident on June 8 blew the forward fuselage off X-15-3 when an engine exploded, necessitating a rebuild. Progress was rapid, Crossfield making the first powered flight with the XLR-99 in X-15-2 on November 15 when he reached Mach 2.97. On March 7, 1961, Robert White reached Mach 4.43 and on June 23 exceeded Mach 5. On October 11, 1961, X-15-2 achieved almost the design altitude when White reached a height of 217,000ft (66,142m), 41miles (66km) above the surface of the Earth. On November 9 he took the same aircraft to a new record of Mach 6.04.

On July 17, 1962, White flew X-15-3 to a new record height of 314,750ft (95,936m), or 59 miles (95km), which comfortably exceeded the 50 miles (80km) altitude set by the air force as the qualifying height for the Astronaut Wings award. A day later, President Kennedy presented the Robert J Collier Trophy to the X-15 programme, received by Scott Crossfield, Joe Walker, Robert White and Forrest Petersen. In time, eight pilots would make 13 flights also qualifying for Astronaut Wings.

On November 9, 1962, pilot Jack McKay flew X-15-2 on what should have been a heating research flight to Mach 5.55 and 125,000ft (38,100m). Commanding the throttle open to 100%, McKay realised that it was stuck at 35% and shut the engine down at 70.5sec into the 90sec burn. Jettisoning most of the remaining propellant he turned back to conduct an emergency landing at Mud Lake, a well-rehearsed procedure. As he came in, the flaps stuck and he touched down at 295mph (474km/h), but the left skid strut dug in and turned the aircraft sideways, flipping it over. As it rolled McKay jettisoned the canopy, but his head struck the ground, compressing his spine, crushing several vertebrae and reducing his height by an inch (2.54cm).

NASA took advantage of rebuilding the X-15-2 with a 28in (71cm) increase in the length of the fuselage and provision for two auxiliary propellant tanks to increase the burn time of the rocket motor, with an ablative coating for thermal protection in an attempt to push the speed to Mach 7. Returned to flight on June 25, 1964, as the X-15A-2, it achieved its fastest speed of Mach 6.7, or 4,520mph (7,272km/h), piloted by William 'Pete' Knight on August 3, 1967. The highest altitude logged by the X-15 was 354,200ft (107,960m), achieved when Robert Rushworth piloted X-15-2 on September 29, 1964, crossing the line internationally recognised as the height where space begins.

BELOW • Milt Thompson boards the M2-F2 lifting-body air vehicle suspended under the starboard wing of the NB-52B carrier-airplane. (NASA)

Table 5: X-15 Specifications

Parameter	X-15-1, -2, -3	X-15A-2
Length	50.25ft (15.32m)	52.42ft (15.86m)
Span	22.36ft (6.82m)	22.36ft (6.82m)
Height	11.62ft (3.54m)	11.62ft (3.54m)
Weight empty	11,374lb (5,159kg)	18,340lb (8,319kg)
Weight loaded	31,275lb (14,186kg)	56,130lb (25,460kg)
Flights	177	22

As the X-15 programme began to wind down there was still a lot it had yet to achieve but flight research is a balance between the cost and the results that money could buy through other programmes. On November 15, 1967, Michael Adams was killed in X-15-3 when it went out of control and crashed, its complex control characteristics coupled with pilot disorientation and a lack of awareness about the aircraft's true pointing angle mixing a lethal cocktail from which Adams was unable to recover, high g-forces preventing him from regaining control.

The last X-15 flight took place on December 12, 1968, completing 199 flights in nine years with only one fatality. Its achievements had been great, this unique aircraft providing a wealth of data as the only winged flying machine built to fly in both space and Earth's atmosphere. In all, 12 pilots had flown it, including Neil Armstrong who would walk on the Moon, and Joe Engle, denied a lunar landing but commander of two Space Shuttle missions.

A successor had been considered in the late 1950s just before the X-15 began to fly, a vehicle for research in the region of Mach 10-18, the most intense environment for aerothermal challenges. But by the time NASA opened for business that concept had been adopted by the US Air Force Air Research and Development Command (ARDC) in response to Sputnik and it became the Dyna-Soar boost-glide vehicle, launched by a rocket and returned through the atmosphere to a controlled landing. It was cancelled in December 1963.

NASA meanwhile had studied the idea of a delta-wing variant of the X-15 for improved lift-drag ratio equipped with a small hypersonic ramjet engine for research purposes. The

BELOW • Numerous proposals for different applications saw one idea for the X-15 launched off the top of a Mach 3 XB-70 Valkyrie to achieve higher speeds. (NASA)

ABOVE • *The M2-F2, one of several lifting-body air vehicles flown during the 1960s to evaluate their aerodynamic characteristics. (NASA)*

BELOW • *Test Pilot Bill Dana beside the HL-10 as he watches the NB-52B fly overhead. (NASA)*

tremendous value for space flight because it eliminates the slender protuberance of a wing that heats up on re-entry and in the absence of which the challenges of providing thermal protection are significantly reduced.

NASA wanted to conduct research with different lifting-body configurations and began a programme at its Flight Research Center, co-located with the military at Edwards Air Force Base in California. Development began with the M2-F1, a small unpowered precursor first flown in August 1963 and followed three years later by the larger M2-F2 and the HL-10. Both were built by Northrop and powered by the XLR-11 rocket engine that had been fitted to the Bell X-1 on its transonic and supersonic flights from 1947 and for initial flight trials with the X-15.

Carried under the wing of a B-52, the M2-F2 had a chequered history from its first flight on July 12, 1966, to the last of 16 unpowered glide flights on May 10, 1967, when it crash-landed and overturned six times, trapping pilot Bruce Peterson who incurred severe injuries. Insensitively, film of the event was used in the opening sequences of the TV series *The Six Million Dollar Man*. The M2-F2 was rebuilt into the M2-F3, which made the first of 27 flights on June 2, 1970, completing a credible record of test flights to Mach 1.6 and an altitude of 71,500ft (20,790m) before it was retired on December 20, 1972.

The HL-10 took to the skies on December 22, 1966, and conducted 37 drops from the B-52 carrier-airplane, including the fastest lifting-body speed of Mach 1.8 on February 18, 1970, shortly before its last flight on July 17. Compared with the M2 series, the HL-10 had a convex lower body profile, the opposite of the M2 lifting bodies and which provided a valuable comparator with regard to aerodynamics and for pilot handling characteristics. Both M2-F3 and HL-10 made significant contributions to the Space Shuttle programme.

The third lifting-body concept, the X-24 was a joint venture with the air force and consisted of a short, teardrop shape with vertical fins and also powered by the XLR-11. It made

idea had merit, but was too costly at a time when the agency was suffering from a declining budget, and with no future application it was abandoned —as had been an earlier proposal to stack an X-15 on a conventional rocket and send it into orbit, an idea fraught with technical difficulties, not least of which would have been finding an applicable heat shield. There was a parallel idea to use the X-15 as a satellite launcher, but that had more merit for keeping the manufacturer in work than anything else, and came to nothing.

Lifting Body Flight

In parallel with the development and flight phase of the hypersonic X-15, and prior to its commitment to a reusable Space Shuttle, NASA developed a lifting-body research programme, which owed its origin to theoretical studies just after World War Two. A lifting-body is a wingless vehicle that flies in the atmosphere in a controllable manner due to lift generated by the shape of the fuselage — or 'body'. It has

Table 7: Lifting Body specifications and performance

Parameter	M2-F1	M2-F2	M2-F3	HL-10	X-24A	X-24B
Length	20.6ft (6.1m)	22.16ft (6.76m)	22.16ft (6.76m)	21.16ft (6.76m)	24.5ft (7.47m)	37.5ft (11.43m)
Width	14.16ft (4.3m)	9.66ft (2.95m)	9.66ft (2.95m)	13.58ft (4.15m)	13.64ft (4.16m)	19.16ft (5.84m)
Height	9.5ft (2.9m)	9.5ft (2.9m)	9.5ft (2.9m)	9.58ft (2.92m)	10.3ft (3.15m)	10.3ft (3.15m)
Weight empty	1,000lb (454kg)	4,620lb (2,096kg)	5,071lb (2,300kg)	5,285lb (2,397kg)	5,978lb (2,712kg)	7,800ft (3,538kg)
Weight loaded	1,182lb (536kg)	6,000lb (2,722kg)	6,000lb (2,722kg)	6,000lb (2,722kg)	11,446lb (5,192kg)	1,800lb (6,260kg)
Flights	77	16	27	37	28	36
Max speed	149mph (240km/hr)	410mph (661km/hr	1,063mph (1,714km/hr	1,228mph (1,976km/hr)	1,036mph (1,667km/hr	1,164mph (1,873km/hr
Max altitude	11,975ft (3,650m)	45,000ft (13,716m)	71,500ft (21,800m)	37,688ft (26,726m)	71,400ft (21,760m)	74,130ft (22,590m)

its first glide flight from the B-52 carrier-airplane on April 17, 1965, followed by the first powered flight on March 19, 1970. The X-24 made 28 flights and achieved a top speed of 1,036mph (1,667km/h). Seeking a research vehicle for a very different design, the X-24 was returned to its manufacturer, the Martin Aircraft Company, and rebuilt to have a slender double-delta planform and a pointed nose. Re-designated X-24B, it made a preliminary glide flight on August 1, 1973, followed by a powered flight on November 15. It was retired after completing the last of 36 flights on November 26, 1975.

There had been a successor proposed by NASA and the US Air Force, the Lockheed L-301, which was an evolved variant of the X-24B, proposed as a Mach 8+ research vehicle for which two were proposed, each conducting 100 flights in the atmosphere. There was no requirement for such a project and, once again, NASA's declining budget had no margin for such exotic possibilities and it was abandoned in 1977, just as air-launched test flights were being conducted by the Space Shuttle Orbiter *Enterprise*.

The contribution made by the lifting-body programme across 222 flights was important and helped build confidence in NASA that it could return a vehicle from orbit and use energy-management to effect a safe landing on a conventional runway. It provided a wide range of different technical challenges to test scientists and engineers in the design and development of digital control systems and computer-assisted flight management through which pilots could perform high-altitude, high-speed flight profiles. That was the essence of shuttle descent and landing requirements.

Aeronautical research at NASA embraced a wide variety of activities, including applications using WB-57 weather aircraft to conduct data-gathering and measurements in the atmosphere. It conducted long-term investigations into quiet engine technology and is leading an industry-wide effort to get aviation to net-zero emissions by 2050 through tests and engineering projects looking to use hydrogen fuel and other ways of significantly reducing reliance on hydrocarbons in the commercial sector. It is also deeply involved in working with other government agencies to improve airline safety and to develop technologies for greater reliability and by reducing risk in the air and on the ground.

A significant effort is under way to develop and test new materials, coatings, lubricants and hybrid engine systems together with developing enhanced rotary-winged aircraft for other applications within NASA and for industry in the commercial sector. Software development and improved electronic and digital flight control systems have come

naturally to NASA due to the amount of effort it commits to uncrewed vehicles for use in its own programmes of planetary exploration and for applications throughout the aviation industry.

Much of this work comes directly from its predecessor the NACA and the commitment that organisation made to aviation in general. It continues to study wing shapes, variable wing geometry, differential wing forms that are changeable in flight and in the way new technologies can be made available to the aeronautical industry with the emerging material base it is assembling from its own research facilities. At the core of everything is the theoretical research through its wind tunnels and the flight test programmes it manages.

Today, the Aeronautics Research Mission Directorate (ARMD) has responsibility for a range of aviation-related programmes working with other government bodies such as the Federal Aviation Administration (FAA). Formed at NASA in 2004, the ARMD receives a small budget, in 2023 the amount allocated for aeronautical research being almost $900million or about 3.5% of NASA's total budget that year of $25.4billion, which itself was a meagre 0.4% of US government spending.

NASA Dryden Flight Research Center Photo Collection
http://www.dfrc.nasa.gov/gallery/photo/index.html
NASA Photo: EC75-4643   Date: 1975   Photo by: NASA

X-24B in Flight above Lakebed

BACK TO THE MOON

With the Space Shuttle retired and a commercial programme flying cargo and people to the International Space Station, NASA sought a return to exploration of the Moon

After *Columbia* fell apart over the United States on February 1, 2003 as it re-entered the atmosphere on its way to a landing at the Kennedy Space Center, NASA conducted an in-depth analysis of just how vulnerable to catastrophic accidents the Shuttle was. It was on the basis of its age, vulnerability to another disaster and the need to plan for the future that its fate was decided, bringing an end to the programme in 2011.

Assessing the potential for disaster, much had changed over time. From an agency conducting cutting-edge missions and placing men on the Moon, to supporting long-duration flights aboard the Skylab space station, risk had been a constant companion. The loss of both *Challenger* and *Columbia* together with 14 lives in the first 113 missions introduced a rethink about risk assessment and how the agency viewed safety.

The belief that the Space Shuttle was capable of surviving failures that would normally have destroyed a conventional rocket and spacecraft pervaded early thinking on vehicle safety, and this influenced judgements about survivability of the crew and the vehicle itself. After the Space Shuttle programme was retired, a deeper analysis was possible, which brought startling conclusions.

During the development of the Shuttle and prior to the first launch, NASA had thrown around figures projecting a loss rate of one in a thousand flights, but two had been lost in 113. Further engineering analysis from the Safety and Mission Assurance Office at the Johnson Space Center in 2011 indicated that there was a one-in-nine probability of loss of vehicle and crew and only a 6% likelihood of completing the first 25 flights — one in which *Challenger* was destroyed.

There had been significant improvements to the equipment and the procedures for mission operations, which raised the probability of loss to one-in-90 by the end of the programme, but that figure applied only to the final few flights. Beneath the public façade of pervasive self-confidence, these conclusions shocked engineers and managers and a new culture took seed in which failure analysis and risk mitigation became a primary concern throughout the agency. A caution many would attribute to a lack of 'go-culture' in which derring-do was the order of the day, as it had been so often throughout the agency's remarkable history.

Rebirth

As noted earlier, the shift from government-owned spacecraft for supporting space station operations with cargo and crew delivery to a deal whereby private operators built the hardware and NASA contracted out the supply services from them, boosted the emerging entrepreneurial industry and undoubtedly saved money. By the time SpaceX was routinely flying crew members to the International Space Station, Russia was charging NASA almost $100million a seat and the cost of flying on Crew Dragon was substantially less. The government's inspector-general estimates that cost is now around $55million per seat and falling.

Of course NASA provided seed-money to help SpaceX get to this position, but the long-term logic of contracting out is paying off and during the last decade that process has been adopted for other programmes. Buying-in services is the

BELOW • Commercial operators like SpaceX with its reusable rockets such as Falcon 9 shown here support logistics and crew delivery to the International Space Station and will perform that role around the Moon. (SpaceX)

allows NASA to do more with less, to have a portfolio of projects and programmes that would cost the government far more if it had to do business the way it had 40 years ago on a model practised during the Space Shuttle years.

With the retirement of the shuttle and a new approach to sourcing and funding programmes, several managers and top NASA executives left the agency and went to work for the emerging generation of New Space companies, as they were known, sloughing off the ways of Old Space with its rigid adherence to archaic practices and conservative ways of developing programmes. None of which were conducive to fast-tracking the decision process between government and the agency, where the rapid-response approach in private industry was somewhat mired by the slow and ponderous process within federal government that made decisions appear sluggish and implacably welded to outdated processes.

Just as the Apollo programme and the Space Shuttle decision had been made in the White House from a menu

preferred way NASA now has for future programmes so that the net worth of all its activities exceeds the cost it would have to find if it was all funded out of the federal budget. How can this be so? Why is it cheaper for private companies to achieve more with less money?

The secret lies in what industrialists call vertical-profiling in which an independent company either makes all it needs or buys the company delivering what it wants. By keeping everything under one roof it can fast-track deliveries because it is routinely talking to subcontractors it already owns, making decisions quicker because it has closer connections to all the participants and achieving more with less money it would otherwise have to spend buying in services nationwide.

At one time, NASA had to show politicians that it put money in worker's pay packets in numerous companies and contractors all across America. Now, it buys what it wants from a few companies where there is only one profit-tag rather than each supplier adding its own mark-up. That

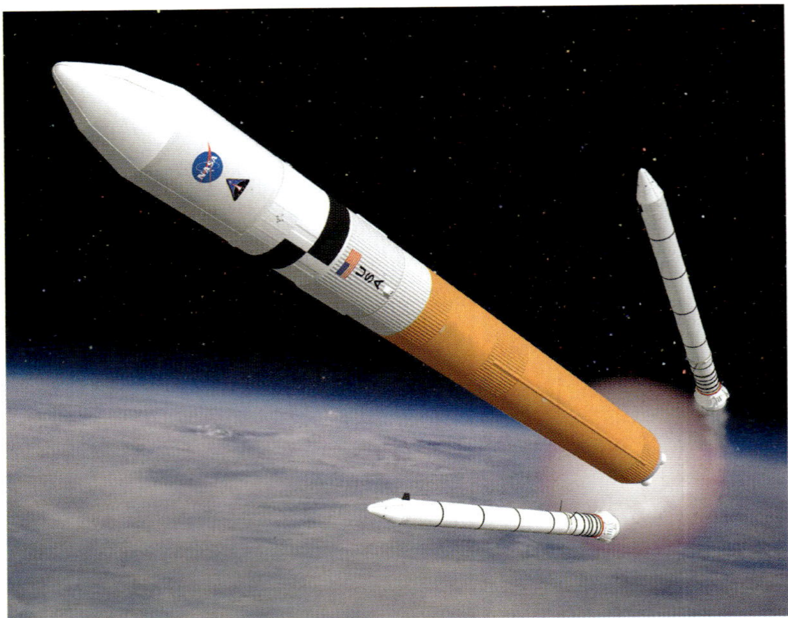

ABOVE • *The Ares V launch vehicle depicted here would be the heavy-lifter that Congress was unwilling to abandon and it was reconfigured into the Space Launch System. (NASA)*

of possibilities offered up by the engineers, scientists and managers at NASA, so too would the post-shuttle decisions emerge from a political edict. Only this time, it was Congress and not the White House that called the shots, running counter to government preferences and contrary to the choices of many at NASA itself. It was a fight for the future of the American space programme and what exists today began with a bitter struggle.

George W Bush was President when the decision was made in 2003 to retire the Space Shuttle by 2010 and in a new 'Vision for Space Exploration', he outlined future objectives: fund the space station until 2010 before abandoning it to the international partners or to commercial operators; use money saved to fund development of a return to the Moon under the Constellation programme; plan for the manned exploration of Mars at some date in the future.

Constellation would take elements of the Space Shuttle programme and repurpose them through development of two new launch vehicles – a manned space vehicle called Orion, hailed as the Crew Exploration Vehicle (CEV), and a new lunar lander known as Altair. The smaller launch vehicle, Ares I, would be a single solid rocket booster from the shuttle programme with an upper stage lifting Orion into Earth orbit where it could deliver crew to the International Space Station. The much larger Ares V would use six shuttle engines from the Orbiter attached to a first stage developed from the shuttle's external tank and an upper stage to lift cargo or the Altair lander. Launched by Ares I, Orion would dock with Altair in Earth orbit and use the upper stage of Ares V to head for the Moon. It all looked a lot like Apollo on steroids.

The sheer scale of Constellation worried many and despite repeated requests from Congress, NASA was unable to come up with a definitive budget estimate. There were significant technical challenges, especially with the Ares V rocket, which would have greatly exceeded that of the Saturn V due to the size and weight of the Altair lander. Predicted at around 101,000lb (45,810kg), that was approximately three times the weight of the Apollo Lunar Module, the price to pay for a more sustained lunar basing requirement. It was also challenging for engineering capabilities in that some Shuttle-derivative technology would not be compatible with each other when scaled up.

RIGHT • *The Space Launch System utilised the Space Shuttle Orbiter main engines in the core stage and extended-length solid rocket boosters. (NASA-KSC)*

A critic of Constellation, when Barack Obama became President in January 2009 he ordered an extensive review by a committee of experts chaired by Norman Augustine, a highly respected aerospace engineer and senior industry executive. His report was damning, of the technology choices, the overall cost and the fast-track schedule it was on citing haste as the parent of failure while recommending a range of alternative, affordable options that would provide the nation with the semblance of a deep-space objective.

But there was a problem. By this date, NASA was well under way with development of the Orion spacecraft, Lockheed Martin having been contracted to build it in 2006, and detailed design and testing for the two Ares launchers were also progressing. In July 2009, Obama appointed Charles Bolden as NASA Administrator, the first astronaut and the first black man to hold that office. Bolden fought hard to maintain a forward-thinking strategy, but his deputy, Lori Garver, was committed to the Obama desire to get NASA out of the manned spaceflight business to leave it to commercial companies and she had great influence with the President.

On February 1, 2010, the US government released its proposed budget for the following financial year to begin on October 1, deleting all funds for Constellation and redirecting NASA to work with commercial companies to contribute toward future high-ticket programmes such as manned vehicles. The first that NASA personnel and the senior leadership heard about this was when the White House issued the press release that day announcing the budget proposals. The mood was one of shock, gloom and despondency by some, disbelief by a few and opposition to the blunt dagger by many.

Some in Congress had been sympathetic of the attempts by Administrator Bolden to represent NASA in the exalted

Capitol where, during hearings and grilling by committees and subcommittees, he had appeared less the politician and more the astronaut than previously. Nationwide, there was universal criticism of Obama's decision and on April 15 he convened a space conference at which he declared the focus to be on commercial support beyond the crew cargo contracts to SpaceX and the then Orbital Sciences, now part of Northrop Grumman.

The Orion contract was redefined as the Multi-Purpose Crew Vehicle (MPCV) on May 24, 2011, providing assured access to the space station that NASA was no longer retiring from. The MPCV was also back-up to the commercial crew programme expected to begin flying astronauts from 2017. Orion consisted of two elements: the crew module and the service module, much like Apollo decades previously.

It quickly became apparent that the contract price quoted by Lockheed Martin was unaffordable and, in late 2012, NASA signed a deal for the European Space Agency to build the Orion service module in return for which its astronauts would get to fly on that spacecraft. At this date it was not quite apparent just what the long-term objective was to be for Orion, but for the first time in its storied history, the future of US manned spaceflight would rely on a group of foreign countries. The die was cast.

An Embarrassment of Riches

In political time, events moved rapidly from the varied and fast-changing set of missions to which the Orion spacecraft could be applied to the present direction, which puts NASA firmly on track to establish bases on the Moon, plans based on the development of the Space Launch System (SLS). Within weeks of President Obama's cancellation of Constellation,

reeling from the unilateral dismissal of that programme, in 2011 Congress insisted on replacing the Ares V heavy-lifter with a new and less technologically challenging rocket, the SLS.

With a first stage powered by four shuttle motors and assisted off the pad by two solid rocket boosters longer than those used by the shuttle, the Block 1 SLS would carry an upper stage derived from that for the Delta IV expendable launcher while a subsequent variant would fly with a more powerful upper stage. Like Ares V before it, the SLS would use the Launch Complex-39 pad facilities at the Kennedy Space Center, but the more powerful SRBs would not be reusable.

In 2011, there was no specific mission for which the SLS was designed, its configuration being the biggest rocket that could be put together with the greatest assurance of matching technology to affordability. SpaceX was a force for

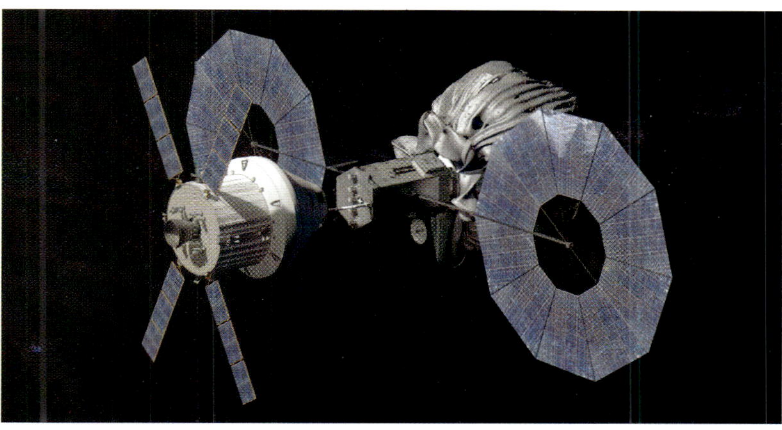

ABOVE • *Seeking a mission role for Orion, capturing an asteroid was a clearly defined goal that could be accomplished without the cost of a lander. (NASA)*

the future and at the time the commitment was made it was the only game in town for that class of rocket. In insisting that it was a national asset, Congress had been adamant that NASA was to have a heavy-lift launcher against the day it was appropriate to once again send astronauts into deep space.

For almost six years, various mission options were discussed and proclaimed by NASA, none of which were relevant to sustainable goals, all of which embraced deep-space destinations without the unaffordable lander that made Constellation too expensive. Appealing to public concerns from a minority aware of the consequences from Earth-impacting asteroids, NASA turned to exploring these bodies, returning to Earth with chunks of asteroid, even towing them to the vicinity of the Moon for better access and sustained scientific study. It was the classic case of a capability looking for an application.

Recognising the difficulties in continued funding for both the station and development of the Orion spacecraft, NASA sought further ways of releasing strain on the budget by leaning more heavily on the part played by commercial organisations. SpaceX began lifting cargo to the International Space Station in May 2012 and with astronauts by Crew Dragon from 2020. That company had made tremendous progress with its Falcon 9 rocket as a launch provider for customers in the United States and around the world and was delivering on its promises to NASA.

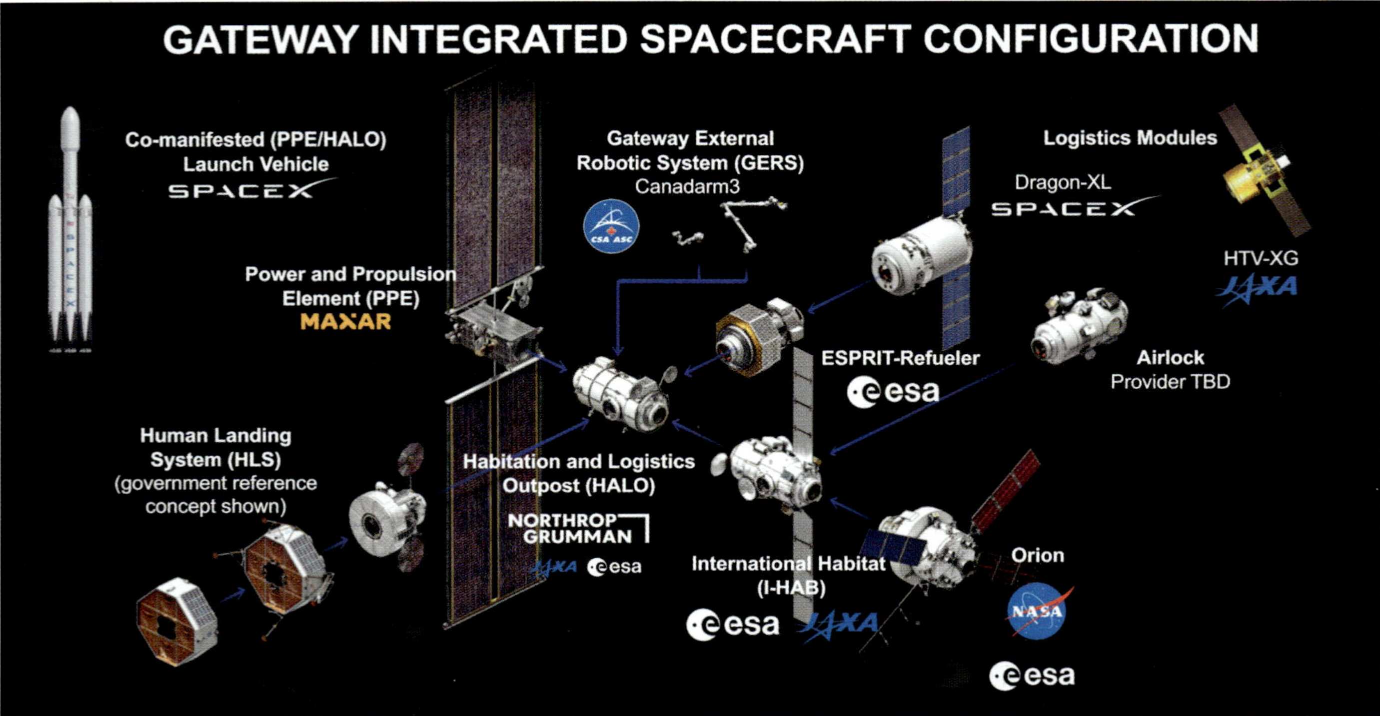

Frustrated at the languid pace of NASA's efforts to recharge the agency's mission and nearing a full year after achieving office, on December 11, 2017, President Donald Trump issued Space Policy Directive-1 in which he charged the agency to "lead the return of humans to the Moon for long term exploration and utilization, followed by human missions to Mars and other destinations". There was appetite for this both at NASA and in Congress where it was believed the shift to full commercialisation for human space flight had gone too far.

On March 26, 2019, Vice-President Mike Pence, chairing the newly reconstituted National Space Council, advanced the date of the Moon landing to 2024 and on May 14, 2019, NASA Administrator Jim Bridenstine named the new programme Artemis, in Greek mythology the twin sister of Apollo. But that still left the question of a lander, an added cost invoking the same problem that had doomed Constellation. However, now there were credible commercial contenders for the job of building a human landing system (HLS) and NASA turned again to New Space for a way to get its astronauts back on the lunar surface.

In 2018, NASA produced a reference design that it took to industry as a guide to the kind of vehicle it required, one which would be launched on a commercial launcher and not on the SLS. Required to support four astronauts for up to two weeks on the Moon, NASA proposed a three-stage configuration and a full review of all potential possibilities was examined at a meeting of the Lunar Exploration Analysis Group on November 14, 2018, involving a waystation in Moon orbit eventually named the Lunar Gateway.

Studies of a waystation had begun several years earlier, situated in an elliptical path around the Moon known as a Near Rectilinear Halo Orbit (NRHO) taking about 6.5 days to make one revolution in which it passes quite close to the surface before looping far out and back again. This orbit is stable and requires very few thruster burns to stay in place ideally situated for spacecraft from Earth to meet up and descend to the lunar surface. It was found to be necessary because the main propulsion motors on the Orion spacecraft had insufficient thrust to get to the correct path to support a landing in many regions.

The Gateway would allow access to all areas of the Moon rather than within a belt at relatively low latitudes as had been the case with Apollo and it would require the least amount of energy for rendezvous and docking. It would be a vital element within the Artemis programme, a mini-space station periodically occupied by astronauts but mostly controlled from Earth or operating autonomously. It would be critical as a receiving platform for goods and crew from Earth transitioning into a lander.

Development of the HLS got under way in December 2018 when NASA asked industry to come up with proposed designs before SpaceX was chosen on April 21, 2021, for a version of its massive Starship as the lander. Starship would be launched by a SpaceX Super Heavy Booster and critics worried that delays to getting commercial cargo and crew services up and running were not a good precedent, a portent of disaster.

To support each lunar landing, a Starship propellant depot would remain in Earth orbit until fuelled by ten-15 Starship tankers, each launched by a Super Heavy rocket. The Starship lander would lift off to dock and refuel at the depot before setting off for the Moon where it would rendezvous with an Orion spacecraft or dock at the Gateway. Initially, the Starship lander would enter the HALO path passing 930 miles (1,500km) over the Moon's North Pole and 43,000 miles (70,000km) over its South Pole. Once connected to Orion, two of the four occupants would transfer into Starship and it would make its descent to the surface.

Starship and Super Heavy had been proposed by SpaceX in 2012 when it was known first as the Mars Colonial Transporter and then the Interplanetary Transport System. With a fuelled weight of more than 5,000tons and a

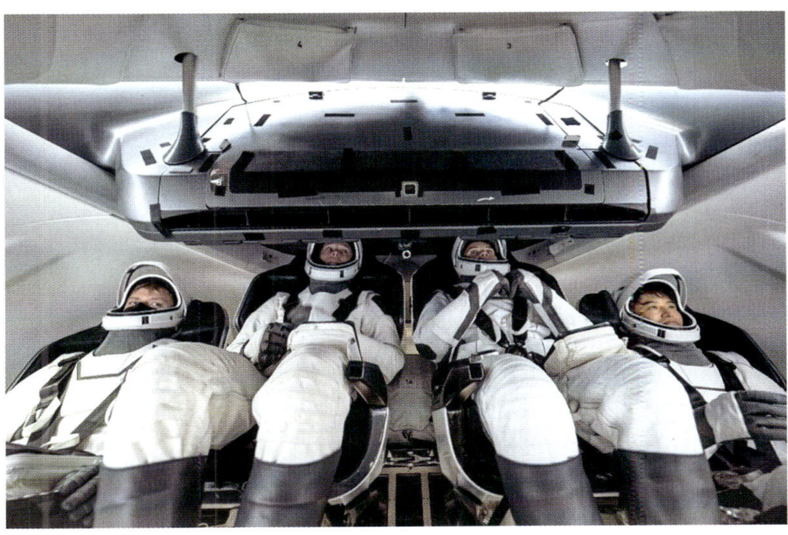

ABOVE • *The Artemis I launch on November 16, 2022, sent the unmanned Orion spacecraft around the Moon and back for the first time on an SLS (Space Launch System) rocket from the Kennedy Space Center. (NASA)*

thrust of 16.7million lb (74,282kN), it is more than twice as powerful as the Saturn V. The Starship second stage has a thrust of 2.9million lb (12,899kN) and both stages are designed to be reusable, but not for the Starship HLS variant, which would remain in space.

Launch and Test

The first flight of this massive rocket took place on April 17, 2023, but three of the 33 rocket motors failed followed by numerous technical problems, and three minutes after launch it began tumbling and broke up in a massive explosion. After substantial redevelopment at the pad and several changes to the rocket, the second flight was launched on November 18 when all 33 Raptor engines operated as planned before Super Heavy separated and was destroyed, followed by destruction of the Starship second stage eight minutes after lift-off. The third flight on March 14, 2024 was a partial success followed by a fourth flight on June 6, which accomplished all its objectives, Starship surviving re-entry despite burn-through of heat tiles.

The fifth flight test of the Heavy Booster/Starship rocket took place on October 13, 2024, when the first stage was recovered back at the Boca Chica, Texas, launch site, but several more steps have to be completed before Space X puts the system though an unmanned lunar landing and demonstrates that it has a safe and reliable method for putting astronauts on the surface. Only after those are accomplished will astronauts have the chance to get back on the Moon for the first time since 1972.

Concerned at the slow pace of SpaceX in flight testing the Heavy Booster/Starship rocket, on May 19, 2023, NASA selected Jeff Bezos' Blue Origin to build a second vehicle known as the Blue Moon lander, capable of supporting four astronauts on the lunar surface for up to 30 days as part of what NASA terms its "sustainable lunar program". With an

RIGHT • *The SpaceX Human Landing System, a variant of Starship, which will take astronauts from Orion in lunar orbit down to the surface of the Moon and back in Artemis 3. (NASA)*

unmanned test demonstration in 2027 it will be followed by the first crewed Blue Moon landing in 2029. Like initial proposals for further use of the Apollo lunar module, Blue Origin offers cargo versions for supporting bases on the surface with a one-way delivery of 66,000lb (29,937kg).

As for NASA itself, the first flight of the Orion spacecraft had been accomplished on December 5, 2014, when a Delta IV Heavy rocket began a mission to test the heat shield. The Artemis I launch took place on November 16, 2022, the first SLS sending an unmanned Orion spacecraft around the Moon and back to a safe splashdown. Artemis II is scheduled for September 2025 when American astronauts Reid Wiseman, Victor Glover and Christina Koch will be accompanied by Canadian astronaut Jeremy Hansen on a flight around the Moon and back, qualifying Orion for the first landing on Artemis III with Starship HLS in September 2026, a date very few believe can be met.

Under current schedules, the SLS Artemis IV mission would fly in September 2028 to build up the Gateway the first elements of which, comprising propulsion and habitation modules, will have been delivered to a HALO path around the Moon by a single Falcon Heavy rocket in 2027. The Gateway will apply experience from the International Space Station (ISS) to lunar orbit, a very different environment in that astronauts will be living and working beyond the protective radiation shield of Van Allen belts and the Earth's magnetosphere. The last few years of this decade will see a greater transformation since the end of the Shuttle era as operations shift from a close orbit around Earth to lunar-based activities.

Currently, the plan to end the ISS begins in early 2029 when a Deorbit Vehicle, or DV, is launched by SpaceX to dock with the station and go through a verification phase before the last crew return around mid-2030, leaving it under remote control from Houston. Later that year the DV, a variant of Crew Dragon, will fire its thrusters to slow the station, allowing Earth's gravity to pull it inexorably

back down through the atmosphere by early 2031. Precise tracking will allow flight controllers to target its re-entry to a remote location, such as the South Pacific Ocean perhaps, but a lot of it will survive and plummet into the water.

In the five years remaining this decade, NASA wants to transfer government-led activities in Earth orbit to commercial space stations, picking up where the ISS leaves off, developing new technologies and efficient research platforms where the microgravity work that has proven so productive over the past 25 years for science can continue. Under the Artemis accords, at the time of writing 47 countries have already signed up to a non-binding agreement led by NASA and the US State Department, which pledges the peaceful and co-operative use of Space, the Moon and Mars.

In establishing a cislunar and Moon-based infrastructure, NASA hopes to develop the tools, the spacecraft and the rocket capabilities to reach out and begin the exploration of Mars, embracing commercial providers under government programmes supported by international partners. And if all that sounds a bit too ideological, perhaps it is. Within the last few years, China has made great strides with highly successful space flights to the Moon and Mars and within its manned flight activities involving the Tiangong space station. When coupled to its political stance over China, the United States views this as a challenge to US leadership.

The National Aeronautics and Space Act of 1958 that established NASA put American leadership in space as a priority goal, but many today question whether that is once again using politics to establish policy over a measured and affordable programme — to be doing things ahead of other nations. China has declared that it intends to put its own astronauts on the Moon by 2030 and although many challenges remain for it to achieve that, it is quite possible that it can do so.

Given its political differences with China, the US has openly stated that this is unacceptable and once again NASA is plunged into a less visible, but no less transformative Space Race with a communist country. Many within NASA would like to see the international tone set by the space station embrace

all space-faring nations irrespective of their cultural and political affiliations, but that requires a shared commitment to which many are opposed. NASA is and forever will be a flagship for American excellence, in science, engineering, technology and exploration, both by the remote sensing of planet Earth and through the automated robotic emissaries that are now operating throughout the solar system.

At its core, the civil US space programme is best defined by its people and through individual achievements and the inspiration that flows across to others and into new generations. The agency is frequently criticised by government watchdogs for trying to do too much with too little, perhaps without accepting that it is only through reaching beyond pre-set limits that the dream can truly come alive and breath-taking goals be reached. As many have said before, those who achieve great things stand on the shoulders of giants. Those giants are still around and mentor the space farers of tomorrow.

NASA WHERE IT IS AND WHAT IT DOES

NASA field centres have grown and adapted to changing requirements and different needs but they remain the cornerstone of US aerospace research

ABOVE • The recently refurbished entrance to the Glenn Research Center, a national facility for jet and rocket propulsion and related technologies. (NASA)

RIGHT • Head of NASA since May 2021, Bill Nelson is a former US Senator and flew on Space Shuttle Columbia for six days in space during January 1986. (NASA)

The pace of NASA's expansion in the first decade of its formation had been astounding, increasing the acreage of all its facilities from 5,179 (2,095ha) to 142,000 (57,465ha) by June 1968. The total invested property value at that time increased from $268million to $4.4billion then. During the first ten years, it installed capital equipment then worth $400m in 20,000 prime and subcontractor facilities. Today, it employs around 17,900 people.

Over time, NASA has acquired, or temporarily operated, several unique offices or small facilities that have long since been passed on to other users. One such opened in July 1962 as the Eastern Operations Office and was to be the site of the Electronics Research Center (ERC), formally in existence as such from September 1, 1964. Its primary function was to develop an expertise in electronics during the rapidly expanding challenge of the Apollo programme. Situated in Cambridge, Massachusetts, opposite the main MIT building, the ERC was developed to a level where NASA expected it to have a staff of 2,100, of whom 1,600 would be professional workers.

ERC is historically interesting in that it is the only NASA facility to have been closed. This despite its survival through one of the most troubled periods, when the collapse of NASA's budget saw layoffs and cutbacks at every other centre. The ERC was arguably one of the most important facilities, strongly supported by Administrator Webb, but brought down by political infighting and partisan issues. The building is now the John A Volpe National Transportation Systems Center.

Langley Research Center

When NASA began, this facility was known as the Langley Aeronautical Laboratory, the oldest and then the largest of

the National Advisory Committee for Aeronautics (NACA) facilities. Located about 150 miles (241km) south of Washington, DC, it employed 3,200 people. It conducted research into aerodynamics, aircraft structures and the operating problems of aircraft and objects travelling through the upper atmosphere and back to Earth, with about 40% of its work assigned to space research of various kinds, although in 1958 that term was rather loosely applied, much of that work being on understanding the upper atmosphere as far as it related to flight.

Engineers at Langley were responsible for several vital steps in human space flight, their technical development and in pioneering options for landing men on the Moon and the methods it would use underpinning lunar landing flights in the Apollo programme. Switching rapidly from working on development of the Mercury programme, Langley engineers decided to go all out for Moon landing studies and taught themselves the mathematics of orbital mechanics using a book written by British author Forrest R Moulton.

Langley was pivotal in getting men to the Moon and aerospace engineer John C Houbolt would pioneer the Lunar Orbit Rendezvous mode adopted in late 1962. After the formal announcement of the Moon landing goal, Langley bequeathed much of its relevant personnel to the new Manned Spacecraft Center, but it focused too on how to control a manned vehicle in the final 150ft (45.7m) down to the lunar surface.

This resulted in construction of the Lunar Landing Research Facility, a 400ft (120m) long A-frame gantry, 250ft (76.2m) tall, from which an overhead bridge crane would support a Lunar Excursion Module Simulator (LEMS) to

ABOVE • Tests at Ames on a rotating cylinder flap during aeronautical research in the 1970s into short take-off and landing concepts. (NASA)

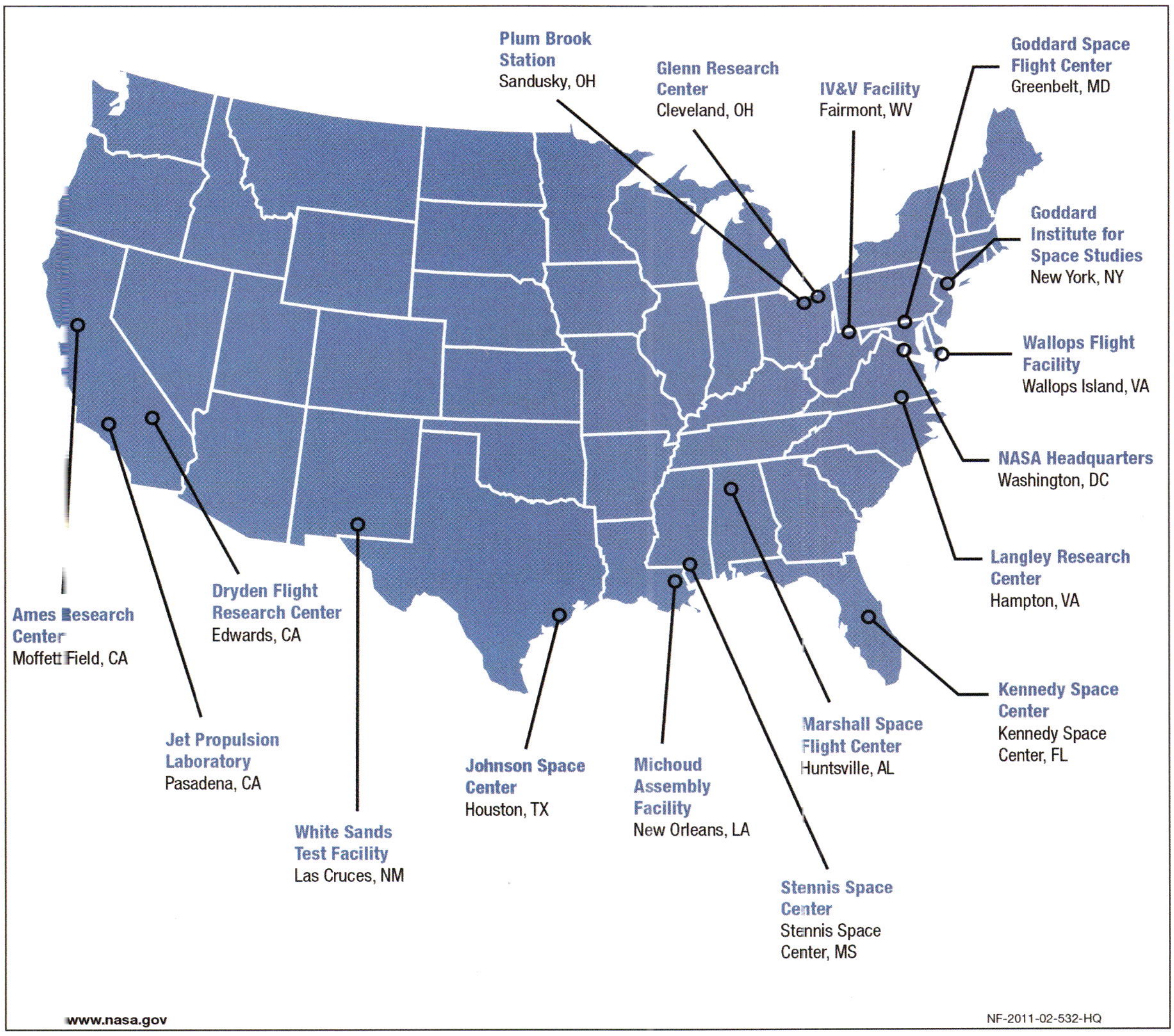

LEFT • NASA facilities are found across the continental United States, three of which were inherited from its predecessor the NACA. (NASA)

give astronauts experience with 'flying' down to the Moon. Langley made additional contributions to human space flight, including the six-degree-of-freedom Rendezvous Docking Simulator, completed in 1963 to give astronauts experience with manually docking a Gemini spacecraft to an Agena stage and later docking an Apollo spacecraft with a Lunar Module.

Under the Lunar Orbiter programme, Langley demonstrated 100% success with five missions flown in 1966 and 1967 without a single failure. The images they returned constitute some of the best available in libraries today and remain a strong source of reference.

Langley has a proud record in project management of the Viking missions to Mars launched in 1975, which successfully put two spacecraft in orbit and two landers on the surface. By the early 1980s, Langley had largely returned to its origins — conducting vital research on aerodynamics, flight and the challenges of flying new and innovative aircraft. Manned flight was very firmly in the hands of the Manned Spacecraft Center and planetary

missions were overwhelmingly in the hands of the Jet Propulsion Laboratory (JPL).

Langley has about 1,800 employees and it is in the critical areas of aeronautical research that it is now dedicated, as well as advanced materials research, electron beam freeform fabrication and the application of plastics to reformation processes.

Ames Research Center

One of the original NACA facilities, in 1958 when NASA formed it was known as the Ames Aeronautical Laboratory, employing 1,450 people and with an annual budget of around $87million. It supported a range of multifunctional facilities with a greater emphasis on high-speed aerodynamics, 29% of its work going on space activities.

Ames had been authorised by Congress on August 9, 1939 as the NACA's second laboratory, its location at Moffett Field, Mountain View, Santa Clara County, California. It was named in honour of Dr Joseph M Ames, chairman of the NACA from 1927 to 1939.

The first 7ft x 10ft (2.13m x 3.05m) wind tunnel started operations on March 13, 1941, followed by the 16ft (4.8m) tunnel. Dedication took place on June 8, 1944, when the 40ft x 80ft (12.19m x 24.38m) tunnel was completed. The mix of wind tunnels continued to grow with the Unitary Plan Wind Tunnel in 1956, the most commonly sought facility in the nation.

When the NACA became NASA, its facilities were quickly utilised in the development of the DC-8, -9 and -10, the F-111 fighter-bomber, the B-1 Lancer strategic and tactical bomber and the C-5A Galaxy heavy-lift transport aircraft.

One of the most ambitious and useful tunnels at Ames is the 80ft (24.38m) by 120ft (36.5m) tunnel, the largest in the world. Entire aircraft, up to the size of a Boeing 737 are tested there as well as a variety of space vehicles and parachute devices. Decommissioned in 2003, it is now under the management of the US Air Force Arnold Engineering Development Center.

NASA-Ames began to orientate itself toward life sciences in February 1961, its first space project being the Pioneer programme from November 1962, followed by the Biosatellite project in February 1963. While these programmes would achieve public acclaim, the real

substance of its work was sustaining active research in all forms of powered and unpowered flight.

It had been the Ames aerodynamicist H Julian Allen who, in 1952, had developed the blunt-body concept solving severe aerodynamic challenges about how to get missile warheads back from space. This work led to the study of conical lifting bodies, blunt shaped structures with a flat or highly convex under-surface equipped with or without small lifting devices for aerodynamic control.

Ames used models fired from light-gas guns to simulate high-speed atmospheric entry, making a lasting contribution to aerothermodynamics in arc-jet development, which took advantage of additional funding in 1961-62 to provide a wide range of data supporting the entry of probes into planetary atmospheres at great speed, surviving to transmit data.

Ames became the go-to facility for physical and life sciences including development of biological instruments for NASA's Viking Mars programme of the mid-1970s. Prior to this it had conducted eight successful Pioneer missions from 1965, culminating in the Pioneer 10 and 11 missions to Jupiter and Saturn.

NASA-Ames is also engaged in supercomputing and artificial intelligence (AI). These projects feed into the International Space Station, various space science missions, development of the Orion spacecraft and NASA's human factors programme. It operates Pleiades, one of the world's fastest supercomputers, which achieved ten petaflops of processing power in 2012.

The NASA Ames Exploration Center is located at the entrance gate to the facility and contains several iconic displays including a Moon rock brought back to Earth by the crew of Apollo 15, the Mercury 1A spacecraft from 1960, and an immersive theatre with a screen that has a rolling series of movies from major NASA missions.

John H Glenn Research Center

Congress authorised a new facility for flight research on June 26, 1940 and ground was broken on a 199.7acre (80.8ha) site adjacent to Cleveland-Hopkins Municipal Airport at Cleveland, Ohio. At first named the Aircraft Engine Research Laboratory, on September 28, 1948, it was renamed the Lewis Flight Propulsion Laboratory to honour Dr George W Lewis, the NACA's Director of Aeronautical Research from 1919 to 1947.

After the war, work focused on jet engines, afterburners and combustion efficiency. By the early 1950s research resulted in pioneering work on fluorine and hydrogen instead of using liquid oxygen as an oxidiser. Several studies examined the possibility of using a fluorine/hydrogen combination, but these were never realised due to the difficulties with handling this highly reactive and toxic propellant.

The formation of NASA in 1958 brought a name change to the Lewis Research Center, with 2,700 employees and an annual budget of $120 million a year, 36% of work attributed to space research. Focus switched to new ways to propel vehicles in space and this led to research on ion propulsion supported by new facilities. By 1961, Lewis had the world's first mercury bombardment ion engine.

On September 30, 1962, Lewis got management of the cryogenic Centaur stage from the Marshall Space Flight Center followed by the Agena upper stage programme from December 1962. Centaur would be the means by which Surveyor unmanned Moon probes were sent to the lunar surface.

By this date Lewis had begun to consider alternatives and NASA had already contracted several manufacturers for post-Saturn rockets known as Saturn II and considerable work was carried out on nuclear propulsion, with potential applications through the Saturn V launcher for increased payload capability to deep-space destinations. Lewis was given responsibility for the Nuclear Engine for Rocket Vehicle Applications (NERVA) programme that would base its tests at Jackass Flats, Nevada, a co-operative venture with the Atomic Energy Commission (AEC), but it fell victim to funding cuts and was cancelled in 1972.

Lewis had responsibility for the electrical power production system on the International Space Station along with industrial contractors. It developed the System Power Analysis for Capability Evolution (SPACE) computer code, used as a tool to predict the maximum power levels that could be achieved on the ISS for sustained continuity during the continual switch between the solar arrays and nickel-hydrogen rechargeable batteries providing power during

ABOVE • *JPL's high-bay test area and clean room for deep-space robotic spacecraft. (NASA)*

eclipse periods and the day/night cycle when the station was in darkness.

On March 1, 1999, Lewis got its present name, commemorating the achievements of the former test pilot and NASA's first astronaut to orbit the Earth, John Glenn. Today, the facility is a diverse and energetic centre for many

RIGHT • *Nestled in the Santa Monica hills, the Jet Propulsion Laboratory is world-famous for planetary spacecraft and robotic missions to other worlds. (NASA)*

research activities, including some unique capabilities at its Plum Brook outstation.

Sadly, the NASA Glenn Visitor Center closed in September 2009, but most of the exhibits were transferred to the Great Lakes Science Center, which merged these with new displays. In an integrated section that uses the same name, it now attracts more than 300,000 visitors a year, compared with 60,000 when it was at the NASA facility.

Jet Propulsion Laboratory

The origin of JPL dates back to 1936 when experiments began at the California Institute of Technology (Caltech) in the Guggenheim Aeronautical Laboratory, known commonly as GALCIT. Under Dr Theodore von Kármán research on jet propulsion and rocketry was encouraged, resulting in a contract from the army, awarded on June 25, 1940, for solid and liquid propellant rockets carried on aircraft, boosting take-off speed on short runways.

On June 22, 1944, GALCIT received a contract for that, which led to a focus on this class of rocket, the name Rocket Propulsion Laboratory being proposed. Given the 'Buck Rogers' association with comic-books, the title Jet Propulsion Laboratory was selected instead and became official from November 1, 1944.

JPL developed the Corporal, America's first tactical missile, and the WAC Corporal, a sounding rocket for carrying instruments to the upper atmosphere and the fringe of space that made its first flight on September 16, 1945. JPL also set up extensive tracking and data networks and pioneered radio and inertial guidance systems as well as FM-FM telemetry, technologies incorporated into rockets and missiles. JPL supported rocket scientist Wernher von Braun's bid to launch an artificial satellite for the International Geophysical Year and successfully placed the first US satellite in orbit on January 31, 1958.

The executive order moving JPL to NASA was signed on December 3, 1958, effective from the end of that month. Qualified to take on the role of planetary science, JPL struck out early with plans for sending probes to the Moon, Venus and Mars, and later into deep-space exploration of the outer solar

RIGHT • *Located in leafy Maryland, the Goddard Space Flight Center is home to Earth science satellites and studies of the planetary environment, its climate and meteorology. (NASA)*

system. It also had responsibility for development of the Deep Space Network (DSN) that would maintain communication with spacecraft out to the most distant reaches of the solar system.

With major achievements in its portfolio of successful planetary programmes, JPL became the lead centre for asteroid detection and mapping, 95% of known near-Earth objects being attributed to this facility.

An unsung achievement has been its support for getting women into the space programme, employing an all-female computer group to calculate trajectories. But support for women engineers originated back in the 1940s and when computers began to take hold in the 1950s these women were hired out to schools and universities to teach staff operating procedures. Scientist Barbara Paulson played a major role in the launch of Explorer 1, the first US satellite plotting data from a network of tracking stations.

When JPL designed its early rockets, the Friden mechanical calculators of the time could not do logarithms and Paulson used huge books of atmospheric densities compiled by the Works Progress Administration. Set up during the Great Depression and national austerity to get people working, it retrained in total almost nine million people so they would be ready to re-mobilise the nation when times changed. Paulson's female team took up those vast manuals and compilations and did their own calculations using this data taken to the next level.

Today, JPL employs almost 6,000 people with more under support services contracts or suppliers working off site. It has internships for High School students, post-doctoral and faculty students and offers job opportunities to many from those groups.

Goddard Space Flight Center

Not long after it was decided to set up NASA, a decision was made to build a dedicated space centre for research and development of science satellites, located on land surplus to the US Department of Agriculture Beltsville Agricultural Research Center. What was then named the Beltsville Space Center, formally came into existence on January 15, 1959, before being renamed the Goddard Space Flight Center on May 1, 1959, after Dr Robert H Goddard who on March 16, 1926, became the first man to fly a liquid propellant rocket.

Initially, staff levels for what was only a framework organisation before the facility was formally opened, increased from 216 to 1,117, this figure inflated initially by the transfer of the Space Task Group (STG) responsible for the Mercury project from Langley to Goddard. The STG became independent on January 3, 1961, which reduced the Goddard staff by 667 positions for a group that would form the core of the Manned Spacecraft Center.

The first weather satellites were developed at Goddard, with Tiros 1 launched in April 1960 providing the first global cloud-cover photographs, maturing into the ESSA (Environmental Science Services Administration) series from February 1966. Contemporaneously, Goddard developed the Nimbus advanced atmospheric science satellites, first launched in August 1964 for studying environmental issues covering polar ice cover, the Earth's radiation budget, the ozone layer and general weather.

Goddard was also responsible for the first Applications Technology Satellite, launched in December 1966 for communications research, but the series included some very advanced telecommunications satellites including the last, ATS-6 launched in May 1974. Placed in geosynchronous orbit, it was used to demonstrate the way satellites could be used to disseminate lessons to remote rural communities in isolated locations, in this case the Indian subcontinent.

In a UN-backed programme, ATS-6 was moved to beam directly down to India schools programmes picked up on television sets provided to several thousand villages via antenna fabricated out of chicken wire by the students themselves. Programmes included instruction on how to use school chemistry sets to conduct soil tests to determine the best crops to grow in a particular area.

From early research came a deepening interest from the commercial telecommunications satellite industry with the launch of Telstar from AT&T in July 1962, built in a multi-national agreement with NASA, the UK and France. The first international telecommunications service was offered by Early Bird in April 1965 for the Intelsat network, a global venture with signatories from the national post and telecommunications agency of countries around the globe.

Goddard managed environmental monitoring from the launch of Landsat 1 in July 1972, a pioneer in providing free access to global environmental data through a series of ground stations in participating countries, many in the developing world and which benefit from data on water

ABOVE • Familiar to visitors at the Kennedy Space Center, the wildlife refuge co-exists with powerful rockets and frequent launch activity. (NASA)

LEFT • One example of work at Goddard, the Magnetospheric Multiscale Mission satellites launched in 2015 to study the interaction of the atmosphere with the magnetosphere and likely to remain operational until 2040. (NASA)

run-off, snow levels, the condition of surrounding seas and the advance and retreat of crop infestation.

Today, the Goddard Space Flight Center employs about 10,000 people, most of whom are non-NASA contractor personnel. It still capitalises on 65 years of outstanding contribution to every essential element in space research, astrophysics, astronomy, instruments for planetary exploration — more of which have been contributed by Goddard than by any other centre.

It is the depository of a permanent archive at its National Space Science Data Center, first set up in 1966, and has a modest visitor information space with a small rocket garden around the back, pride of place going to a full scale model of a Delta launch vehicle, a rocket that has carried so many Goddard creations into space.

John F Kennedy Space Center

Next to the Johnson Space Center, the Kennedy Space Center (KSC) is one of the most publicly reported places in America. Site of so many NASA launches, it was built to support the manned lunar landing programme. Today, it sits on 219 square miles (567 square kilometres) of Merritt Island, northwest of Port Canaveral and not surprisingly is the most visited NASA facility of them all. Boasting a Visitor Complex and a rocket garden, it also contains the Shuttle orbiter Atlantis in an impressive display inside its own special building and a separate site for the Saturn V.

The Kennedy Space Center is located on Merritt Island between the Indian River and the Banana River, with Cape

BELOW • *Sent to Jupiter from KSC on October 14, 2024, the powerful SpaceX Falcon Heavy launched NASA's Europa Clipper on a six-year flight to Jupiter. (NASA)*

Canaveral Space and Air Force Station located on the spit running down between the Banana River and the Atlantic Ocean. The KSC Industrial Area is accessed across the Indian River via the NASA Parkway.

NASA took over responsibility for the Saturn I space vehicle in 1959, selecting a launch site, LC-34, on June 3, 1959. The overall design of the complex was based on the principle of vertical assembly of stages and elements on the pad itself. LC-37, a second Saturn I launch complex, was completed on August 7, 1963. Only five months before the flight of the first Saturn I, in May 1961 NASA was tasked with putting men on the Moon. The design of the Saturn V complex was in support of two pads, LC-39A and LC-39B. They would be part of a complex involving some of the biggest building projects of their time, creating a region known as Moonport USA.

The US Air Force, NASA and the Department of Defense signed an agreement on August 24, 1961, for 80,000 acres (32,373ha), located north and west of the Cape Canaveral Missile Test Annex where NASA would build its assembly buildings, launch control facilities, launch pads and infrastructure, becoming a NASA field installation effective July 1, 1962, as the Launch Operations Center (LOC).

A week after President Kennedy was assassinated, on November 19, 1963 President Lyndon Johnson, who had done so much to create NASA and then persuaded Kennedy to commit to the Moon goal, renamed Cape Canaveral as Cape Kennedy and the Launch Operations Center as the John F Kennedy Space Center (KSC). Later, citizens would lobby for the name Cape Kennedy to be revoked and it was so, leaving KSC as NASA's launch facility.

Nearly eight years separated the launch of the last Saturn V and the first flight of the Space Shuttle and almost six years separated the flight of the last shuttle and the next use of LC-39A. Companies such as SpaceX bargained a lease on LC-39A, from where today Elon Musk has been launching his Falcon 9 and Falcon Heavy rockets since February 19, 2017, a total of nearly 200 having been launched to date.

Lyncon B Johnson Space Center

Arguably the most famous and certainly most quoted NASA facility anywhere, the Johnson Space Center, named as such on 19 February 1973 in honour of President Johnson, started out as the Manned Spacecraft Center, which, since 1965 during the two-man Gemini programme, has been responsible for operating all the agency's human space flight activities. But its origin began long before then. Today it employs around 3,200 personnel.

As early as 1960, NASA had been concerned about the lack of a single dedicated facility for supporting manned operations. At the time, and for the immediate future, NASA's Space Task Group (set up by Administrator Keith Glennan in November 1958), a component of the Langley Research Center, was the field element responsible for carrying out management and direction of operations leading up to the first US manned space flight when Alan Shepard made a ballistic flight on May 5, 1961. That gave the green light for President Kennedy to announce, exactly 20 days later, that America was heading for the Moon.

To give the manned flight programme a proper home, Glennan had considered converting the Ames Research Center into NASA's manned flight facility and when James Webb succeeded him in 1961 he asked for money to build a new centre located near Houston, Texas. Construction of the new facility started in April 1962. Officially, the Manned Spacecraft Center opened for business in September 1963, but the first operational use of the facility to support a space flight was the Gemini IV mission launched on June 3, 1965.

The 1,620acre (655ha) site is about 25 miles (40km) southeast of Houston alongside Clear Lake on land donated by Rice University. It consists of around a hundred buildings from the nine-storey project management offices to tiny traffic booths at each entrance! A lot of buildings contain office space, but others are dedicated to specific tasks and activities. Mission control operations would move to the new Manned Spacecraft Center that would have two Mission Operations Control Room (MOCR, pronounced 'moker') facilities — one to conduct flight operations, the other to prepare for the next mission. It was first tested during the Gemini 2 flight of January 1965.

Probably the most famous building at the Manned Space Center is the originally named Integrated Mission Control Center (IMCC), or MCC officially on site as Building 30. Known since April 14, 2011, as the Christopher C Kraft Jr Mission Control Center in recognition of the outstanding work carried out by its first flight director, 30-M (for Main building) is the historic core of the Mission Control Center, the heart of mission operations.

In support of spacecraft development and engineering, Building 32 houses the Space Environment Simulation Laboratory (SESL), two vacuum chambers, one 120ft (36.5m) high and 65ft (19.8m) in diameter, the second 43ft (13.1m) in height by 35ft (10.7m) in diameter. Here, spacecraft or elements of a vehicle can be subject to vacuum conditions and temperatures between -250°F (-157°C) to +250°F (121°C). Contrastingly, Building 14 houses an Anechoic Chamber Test Facility where foam-covered walls, floor and ceiling soak up stray signals during spacecraft communication tests.

Public access to the Johnson Space Center is via the Space Center Houston, a non-profit organisation that opened in 1992 and contains a variety of exhibits and themed displays as well as a movie theatre screening a selection of space films showing the achievements of the NASA facility. An open-air tram tour takes in Mission Control, a restored Saturn V lying on its side and to various locations, access to which is dependent on centre activity. But a special Level 9 tour limited to 12 people at a time lasts more than four hours and provides access to many facilities, to Mission Control and to some of the engineering test areas that would not normally be accessible to the general public.

THE TIMELINE OF
NASA HISTORY

October 1, 1958	NASA opens for business in response to the launch of Sputnik 1 on October 4, 1957
May 5, 1961	Alan Shepard becomes the first American in space
May 25, 1961	President Kennedy directs astronauts to land on the Moon before the end of the decade
February 20, 1962	John Glenn becomes the first American astronaut to orbit the Earth
December 14, 1962	Mariner 2 flies by Venus for the first time
March 23, 1965	John Young and Gus Grissom fly the first of ten manned Gemini spacecraft
June 3, 1965	Ed White performs the first American spacewalk
July 14, 1965	Mariner 4 speeds by Mars and sends 21 pictures back to Earth
June 2, 1966	First of five successful unmanned Surveyor Moon landings
January 27, 1967	Astronauts Gus Grissom, Ed White and Roger Chaffee lose their lives in a pad fire
November 9, 1967	Apollo 4 launches the first Saturn V
October 11, 1968	Apollo 7 is launched with Wally Schirra, Donn Eisele and Walter Cunningham on a ten-day Earth orbit test
December 24, 1968	Frank Borman, Jim Lovell and Bill Anders orbit the Moon aboard Apollo 8
July 20, 1969	Apollo 11 astronauts Neil Armstrong and Buzz Aldrin land on the Moon
April 17, 1970	Apollo 13 astronauts splash down after a failure on the way to the Moon
July 31, 1971	Dave Scott drives the first electric 'car' on the Moon
July 23, 1972	First of many remote sensing satellites, Landsat 1 is launched
December 14, 1972	Apollo astronauts leave the Moon's surface for the last time
December 3, 1973	Pioneer 10 becomes the first man-made object to fly by Jupiter
May 14, 1973	Skylab space station launched prior to occupation by three teams of astronauts
March 29, 1974	Mariner 10 conducts first of three flybys of Mercury
19 July, 1975	Apollo docks with a Russian Soyuz in space
July 20, 1976	Viking 1 lands on Mars followed by Viking 2 on September 9
August 20, 1977	The first of two Voyager spacecraft is launched for flybys of Jupiter, Saturn, Uranus and Neptune
April 12, 1981	John Young and Bob Crippen fly the first Space Shuttle into orbit
January 28, 1986	Seven astronauts lose their lives when Space Shuttle *Challenger* is destroyed
April 24, 1990	Hubble Space Telescope is launched
July 4, 1997	Mars Pathfinder lands on Mars and releases its tiny rover Sojourner
November 2, 2000	Permanent occupation of the International Space Station begins
February 1, 2003	Seven astronauts lose their lives when *Columbia* is destroyed
July 21, 2011	The last Space Shuttle lands at Kennedy Space Center
November 26, 2011	The size of an SUV, the rover *Curiosity* lands on Mars by way of a sky-crane
May 25, 2012	First SpaceX Dragon cargo delivery to International Space Station
July 14, 2015	New Horizons passes the Dwarf Planet Pluto and its moon Charon
May 30, 2020	First astronauts to International Space Station riding SpaceX Crew Dragon
December 25, 2021	James Webb Space Telescope is launched
November 16, 2022	Artemis I sends an unmanned Orion spacecraft around the Moon

RIGHT • Satellites close to the Earth communicate with a wide range of ground stations round the world. (NASA)